Envious and Deceived:

How Classical Education and Psychoanalysis Could Have Saved Us

J. J. Penniman

Envious and Deceived:

How Classical Education and Psychoanalysis Could Have Saved Us

J. J. Penniman

Academica Press
Washington

Contents

Thersites yells at Agamemnon:

“Son of Atreus (Agamemnon), now what’s wrong? You want even more? Your huts are full of bronze and women, spoils we picked out for you, first among all, whenever we captured a citadel. Or maybe you’re thirsting for gold, lucre that a horse-taming Trojan would bring you from Ilium to ransom his son, whom I or some other Achaean has bound and led away? Or maybe you want to fornicate with another girl, whom you’ll keep for yourself?” (*Iliad*, II, 227-233, translation mine)

Preface: A Guide to the Reader

We're in this mess together, wrecking our habitat, marking time, and not asking: Why did we do this to ourselves?

But I do answer. I use old ideas refreshed by a new paradigm. It's a framework carefully assembled, after much trial and error, from the conceptual trusses and joists of remote domains and disciplines: Biophysics, ecology, Greek *paideia* and psychoanalysis.

So, to read this book, you'll need to think like the old Greek sages and psychoanalysts. You'll need abstractions and symbols to recognize the unfamiliar patterns that emerge in this book. Then you'll see why, and how, we doomed ourselves.

Introduction

In 1986, during a long psychoanalysis, I taught myself ancient Greek and Latin. My motives for submerging myself in the classics were deep, and not entirely clear to me. I do know that, with middle age approaching, I had seen on my mental horizon the specter of an old, uneducated man. I was haunted by Dr. Johnson's reminder that "there is the same difference between one learned and unlearned, as between the living and the dead."[1]

I resolved to make myself more like him and others I admired, people like Darwin, Einstein, and Freud. All these men had learned Latin and Greek. So, I devoured the same intellectual aliment, devoting myself to the study of these languages, the foundations of humanist education and the liberal arts.

Day and night I toiled, memorizing Greek vocabulary as I drove to work, rehearsing declensions while sitting in dull professional lectures, conjugating verbs as I fell asleep. I chanted a growing repertoire of Homeric lines within earshot of my poor family. I ate, slept, and breathed Homer until, two years later, I could read *The Iliad* aloud in its ancient lyric beauty. Next, I drew a bead on Latin. I groped, then slowly marched, through the luxuriant verses of Virgil.

I felt changes in my mind. Memorization improved my memory; and exercising my memory sharpened my thinking. Sharper thinking became more pleasurable thinking, and pleasure and confidence together emboldened me to tackle advanced calculus and competitive bridge. My study also proved to be a capital investment in my craft as a psychoanalyst.

As I psychoanalyze, I try to remember that the mind always works metaphorically, on several levels, each level reinterpreting the subject's here-and-now experience in its own terms. Consciousness is irradiated with unconscious meaning. A cigar has never been just a cigar. Reality, while perceived as social, is simultaneously interpreted personally. The criminal justice system, for example, is a public reality. But it also represents a private superego for each of us. When the twirling blue light appears in our rear-view mirror, we not only fear arrest, but cringe with guilt and shame.

---

[1] Dr. Johnson, quoting Aristotle (Boswell, 1894, p. 531).

The study of Latin and Greek filled my mind with the layered, hierarchized meanings of words and syntax. This helped me better understand the encrypted communications of patients. It enriched my psychoanalytic understanding of the flow of English words I heard every day, deepening and expanding their resonances.

For example: Before Greek, when a peevish patient, impossible to please, said "I'm such an idiot," I might have thought that his offhand comment was diverting us from a more disturbing self-observation. Maybe he was expressing remorse or keeping himself from calling *me* an idiot.

But now, "idiot" resounds with the Greek ἰδιώτης (idiotes: Someone perversely private), a word with two long, drawn-out vowels (ω and η), implying by both sound and sense an obstinate remoteness. So, I can supplement my pre-Greek speculations with, "Has he sensed that I'm disgusted by his emotional distance, and being the target of his unfeeling spitefulness, and am ready to retaliate? Maybe he's postponing *my* attack by attacking himself." This is one of a thousand ways Greek has made my world fuller and deeper.

Laden with such treasures, treasures undreamt of in my youth, I wanted my daughter, Abby, to have them, too. Nearly nine, Abby was leaving behind the easy language-learning phase of childhood. So, on her ninth birthday, I announced that one of my gifts to her might not thrill her right away, but in time she would appreciate it as the best gift anyone could have ever given her. I was going to teach her Greek.

Abby knew I'd been learning this funny-sounding, funny-looking language. Several years earlier, she'd watched me recite Homer for her first-grade class. Two years before that, perhaps imitating me, perhaps suing for love, perhaps punishing me for my preoccupation, she vandalized our living room, scrawling a big theta (Θ) on our new wallpaper in crayon. As her mother erased it, she cried that she'd never ever remember which letter she'd drawn.

So, she knew what I was proposing and screamed:

"NOOO!"

I was prepared for this. "People say that Greek is where knowledge begins," I began. My wife and I had already explained college to her so I cunningly added, "In a few years, it'll be a ticket to the college of your choice."

By her twelfth birthday, Abby and I were doing public recitations of *The Iliad*.

But self-deception waylays even our best laid plans. The college application process wasn't only an opportunity to launch our daughter into the life of the mind and open doors of professional opportunity; it was also my way to redress disappointments of my own.

Even at the time, I knew that college was not what it once was. I knew that college professors, administrators, and trustees no longer shaped public opinion but were being shaped by it. But I ignored all the evidence and clung to the belief that colleges still embodied the values of a humanist education; the values of *paideia*—an ancient Greek education. I had convinced myself that the old academy was merely in a state of suspended animation, ready to be instantly quickened, could it only once again hear the sweet strains of Homer and Virgil in all the beauty of their native music.

How badly I was deceived.

Worse than that, I'd led my daughter into the snare. When Abby had finished her junior year of high school, we sat with her, contemplating a list of colleges. "Choose a school." I said, "Make its day."

Eight years after the Great Birthday Prophesy, Abby's chosen schools shattered my starry-eyed vision. They ignored Abby's ability to read, recite and teach the Ἰλιάς—they showed no interest in their own foundations. How had I hoodwinked myself? I traced my illusion about the university to my old sense of exclusion and thirst to belong. What, after all, had really pushed me to pursue classical learning? Why did I need the colleges' love? After the rejections, I realized: It was *envy*.

I am richly endowed with envy, one of the most destructive human emotions. Studies have abundantly demonstrated envy's powerful influence on interpersonal attitudes and behavior (e.g., Feather, 1989, 1991; Parrott & Smith, 1993; Salovey & Rodin, 1984).

Envy is, brutally put, deadliness; the death-drive turned outward, toward others. It's implanted in humans, certainly in some other animals, by the great entropic, destructive principle of Nature. I am not proud of it, but must admit to my own envy. Still, I have a saving grace: I can choose to recognize and restrain my envy.

We all can.

But we haven't. And that leads to the heart of the book:

Envious and Deceived uncovers our implicit social contract. This pact renounces the rigor of self-awareness. It rejects the discipline of recognizing and managing envy and other life-tensions. Under its sway, we didn't seek the clarity to confront our envy, endure our tensions, and seize our chances to improve ourselves.

Admittedly, that would have been hard to do. Envy is indomitable, destructive, and treacherously disguised. And it's relentless; one peculiar, and permanent aspect of life ceaselessly provokes this ugly emotion: *Exclusion provokes envy.* And of all the tensions in human life, the abhorrence of exclusion is perhaps the most despotic. To humans, exclusion is almost death; inclusion, life. Why are these experiences so powerful and hard to manage? They derive, of course, from our social primate heritage, from the phylogenetic imperative to huddle up for survival. But the desperation to belong has another source: It's what psychoanalysis calls "the primal scene."

Freud discovered the primal scene. But before I explain the concept, I should address the skepticism which surrounds psychoanalysis: Its reputation, and Freud's, fell on hard times long ago. So hard were they, that society came to arraign psychoanalysis as pseudoscience, and Freud as a fraud and anti-feminist. So, I will say here that some of the charges are true; most are not. Chapter 7 will describe, for example, Freud's advocacy for women. It will also describe scientific support for some fundamental psychoanalytic concepts. In any case, you needn't accept all of Freud's theories to gain something from psychoanalysis or this book.

Though experiments have not yet verified the primal scene, clinical and observational settings attest its universal significance.[2] The scene seems to inhabit every baby's fantasy life—and sometimes living awareness—of parental copulation. The baby interprets this obscenity, the theory argues, as mutual sexual feeding and, strange as it seems, locates the conjugal act inside the mother's body—a kind of Eden before the Fall, that is, before birth.[3] The mother's post-natal interior has become a forbidden parental enclave. The infant imagines the parents selfishly, even maliciously excluding it, hoarding their attention, milk, pleasure, and love for themselves.

Why or how do babies imagine such things? The answer lies in an inborn knowledge of our copulatory origins. Precognition may seem a dubious idea, but science has shown it to be common throughout the biological kingdom.

---

[2] But see Hoyt, M. F. (1979).

[3] Or—when distorted by the infant's rage—sadistic brutalization, rape.

A baby monkey, never having seen snakes, nor having been taught about them by older monkeys, can, on being shown photographs of flowers, quickly recognize, with a full adrenalin rush, snakes camouflaged amongst the plants.[4] Humans too know something about extrauterine reality before leaving the uterus. Newborns distinguish female from male voices, smells, and skin textures. They are born with a propensity for complex language, the detection of patterns and meanings in sequences of events, and recognition of the shapes and functions of certain body parts. The psychoanalyst Wilfrid Bion called such inborn knowledge *preconceptions. Preconceptions* may be considered psychobiological expectancies or set points. *Set points* are physicochemical conditions, default states, normal and settled states. When disturbed, set points pull the unquiet organism back toward homeostasis, a relatively stable balance among the organism's components. Set points make the organism operate properly. In the same way, preconceptions serve the mind.

So human infants seek their preconceptions. And when they meet a corresponding real object, like the nipple, the preconception becomes a *conception*, a thought. The baby first represents this in images, and later with words. Both become ideational building blocks that the child fashions into larger and larger cognitive structures.

Among the basic preconceptions are *containers,* like bodies and minds, and their *contents*, like the milk, penises, breasts or even other infants the baby's imagination has stockpiled in the mother. Often too, the baby expels, or projects its anxieties into her. Ideally, the mother soothes or detoxifies the pain with reassurance and understanding.

Other basic preconceptions are *links* between the container and the resource-seeking subject. The most vital links are the bodily organs that facilitate nutrition, excretion, and reproduction. The infant uses its preconception of the mouth containing the nipple, to initiate and facilitate nursing. An innate gender distinction helps the neonatal mind associate the mouth-nipple preconception with another: The mouth-like vagina containing the nipple-like penis. The infant also preconceives two parents, male and female. The mother contains the *father*, having incorporated him through her mouth or mouth-like inlets, and the two constantly conjoin in mutual sexual feeding.

---

[4] *J. Compar. Psychol.*, Vol. 123, no. 2: Lab-reared baby macaques, never before having seen snakes, identified them in pictures of flowers among which the snakes were hidden.

These and other preconceptions form the background to the *primal scene*: Parental coitus traumatizes the baby because it excludes the infant and shatters its fantasy of monopolizing the mother. That consoling fantasy had eased the anguished transition from womb to world. This disillusionment, Mother of all Exclusions, mobilizes envy. Envy spawns a fantasy of attack (*on* the parents) and vengeful counter-attack (*by* the parents).

The primal scene preoccupies children in their fantasies. It haunts the nightmares of three-to-five-year-olds, often as monsters that symbolize coition (viz. Shakespeare's "beast with two backs").

Babies' preconceived bodily links facilitate sucking and condition their latent sexuality So, physical intercourse in all its modes engrosses the infant. Inborn copulatory concepts rule infants' interpretations of all their experiences—whether internal or external.

Here is the central point: Coital preoccupation prejudices infants' interpretation of *thoughts*. Babies notice their own mental activity, not as vividly as the colorful mobile spinning above them, but vividly enough to make them wonder what thoughts are and where they come from. Under the coital regime, babies analogize their own mental activity, their linking activity, as oral and genital linking between the parents. This conceit doesn't die in childhood. Infantile fantasy permanently sways our adult minds. And this infantile equation between thinking and parental copulation, has enormously influenced humanity's attitude toward thought, foresight, reflection, and education.

So, the baby, to evade the pain of exclusion, ejects the primal scene from consciousness. This is one of the earliest evasions of tensions provoked by exclusion and envy. Evasion may obscure babies' awareness of envy, but deprives them of a confrontation with reality. It sacrifices to tension-evasion the precious gift I will broadly call "mental growth." What's worse, evasion fails; it does not extinguish envy and aggression, but only redirects it. We psychoanalytic theorists argue that evasion and suppression further inflame the baby's wish to plunder the mother's intima and to attack, separate, and destroy the selfish parents. Above all, it produces the deathless desire to infiltrate every group, every circle: To get "inside" all human relations. Goldilocks (bears' home), Red Riding Hood (deep woods off the path), Hansel and Gretel (gingerbread house), all represent the child's thirst to penetrate forbidden spaces. Their triumphs reassure young audiences against the terror of the imagined punishments: Being eaten, dismembered, or worse.

The desire for knowledge itself is a kind of a penetration into the unknown—a desire that derives from, and is sometimes cowed by this primal response to envy.

Each maturational stage imposes the primal scene anew. Each new exclusion from family or public life—parental whispers; a circle of other children; neighborhood gangs; high-school cliques; chat rooms—makes us smolder with envy and burn for inclusion. As we approach adulthood, we dread exclusion from the partnered world. Later we long to infiltrate the ultimate in-crowd: That of parents.

Parenthood entails sex, though sex without parenthood was difficult, especially for women, until the birth control pill liberated copulation from pregnancy. There are, to be sure, reasons for sex and babies beyond evasion of exclusion and envy: We are driven to reproduce our genes, mitigate loneliness, disperse the tensions of a two-person household, and exchange mutual pleasure.

Here, however, I will focus on the most obscure and destructive motive for sex: The urge to rid oneself of the sense of exclusion, hatred and *helplessness* provoked by the primal scene. We want to avenge that exclusion and to foist our pain upon our neighbor. Every sexual act, linked to a fantasy of being watched and envied, temporarily relieves that tension. We could say that every sexual act evokes an image of triumphalist revenge.

I believe revenge and dread of retribution, that is, paranoid anxiety, grew more savage with population growth. Crowding exacerbated envy. Crowding forced the paranoid anxiety associated with envy up toward consciousness. Paranoid anxiety, in turn, prevented global birth control.

Prehistorically, resource scarcity prompted foragers to practice birth control, sometimes by abortion and infanticide. But crowding tightened our interdependency and increased our closeness in status and lifeways. This condition, which cultural anthropology calls *social propinquity*, made infanticide repugnant, abortion disturbing, and even birth control audacious, a defiance of natural law, a profane exclusion of unconceived beings. Psychoanalytic experience suggests that a dim awareness of this deepest, most disturbing association burdens birth control with a dread of retribution. The pro-life movement expresses this dread. So, by the modern era, even the least invasive, most voluntary methods triggered overt or covert social resistance. This resistance, rooted in paranoia, postponed depopulation, our only salvation.

The central idea bears repeating: Paranoid dread arises from an envy-motivated fantasy of raping the mother and attacking the babies sheltered inside her, provoking a terrible vengeance from both parents. This terror of vengeance, usually unconscious, I call *envy-fear*. It's a paranoid fear originating in envy, energized by envy, and suffused with envy. Anthropologists, sociologists, primatologists, even 16th century philosopher Francis Bacon have described this phenomenon, under various names. Psychoanalysts see it in people who can't stand being in positions of advantage, of those who choke when they're winning, or those "wrecked by success." Uneasy, Shakespeare wrote, lies the head that wears the crown. Later, I will show how society's successes, real and imagined, and its overgrowth heightened the species' envy-fear.

Overgrowth also fed *omnipotence*. The omnipotence of thoughts is a universal feature of infantile human thinking. Omnipotence is the magical belief that we "have done" what we "want to do": Infants believe that they *really have* pillaged mother's body: They have succeeded. And they believe that this success has provoked a horrendous revenge. At the same time, omnipotence implies invincibility.

For two reasons, then, omnipotence is overwhelmingly seductive: Rising envy-fear makes the infant desperate for invincibility. The *helplessness of envy*, too, makes omnipotence irresistible.

Omnipotence eventually consumed humanity. Overgrowth and collective learning conduced to scientific and technological success. Success bred triumphalism and a global gossip of invincibility—a cultural conceit highly attractive to frightened beings. Humanity's triumphalism reawakened the infantile belief that it could perpetrate and—by the law of omnipotent wish-fulfilment—*had* perpetrated, its most horrible wishes. As the crime grew more plausible, so did punishment. In response, anxiety mounted.

To defend against growing anxiety, a threat to the social order, the culture used *reaction formation*. This is an exchange of opposites, like cleanliness for dirtiness or love for hate. Reaction formation denies badness by overcompensating with goodness. Crowding inflamed the impulse to kill one's neighbors, one's communal siblings. Our fellows had become, after all, swarming competitors for resources, space, and sexual partners. So, humans overcompensated for the cruel impulse: They denied their hatred of crowding and exalted the cults of parenthood, maternal love, universal benevolence and, above all, unconditional inclusion. On a global level, reaction formation sanctified prosperity, because it promised universal inclusion. Accordingly, the world sanctioned runaway growth, the engine of prosperity.

All these unacknowledged strategies calmed envy-fear, fear of the envy—real or illusory—we imagine igniting in those we are tempted to exclude. It reassured us against retaliatory exclusion by those we might enrage.

Note that these strategies constitute a gigantic evasion, rather than collective management, of tensions.

And so, the specter of revenge drove us on and on to the most compelling escape from exclusion: Parenting. It even forced us into foster parenting: Immigration. Parenting of both kinds confers—and acquires, through the child or immigrant's real or imaginary love—inclusion. Parental love and charity defang the envy of their supposed suppliants. So, despite the ecological and social dangers of crowding, overcompensation made us open our borders to immigrants.

Open borders are self-defeating, and self-defeat is another propitiation of envy. The charitable indulgence of over-immigration aggravates the strain of crowding, increases homelessness, raises housing costs, and accelerates resource depletion in the host country. Globally, reaction formation toward immigration expands humanity's carbon footprint, as immigrants adopt the higher consumption habits of their—temporarily wealthier host. Overall, unrestrained reproduction and immigration, here and globally, together with ever longer lives, led to the catastrophic overpopulation of the planet. This may be history's most ambitious appeasement of envy.

Long before psychoanalysis explained the primal scene, Classical thinkers had contemplated envy. They described the private and public challenges and benefits of tolerating envy and other human tensions. Imagine an education which joined the intellectual rigors of reading the ancient languages to the richness of classical philosophic, psychological, and political wisdom. Then, by adding psychoanalysis, we could have had an educational combination that might have restrained the worst human drives. As I will show below, a true humanist education teaches restraint and tension-tolerance. And a psychoanalytic education offers the key to managing tensions such as envy and envy-fear: Self-knowledge.

Self-knowledge: At the high point of my investigation into these questions, I realized this was the heart of Greek education, the essential teaching of the ancient world, and the cultural purpose of psychoanalysis.

During my Greek and Latin studies, I rediscovered the legendary warning, one that gratified my psychoanalytic sympathies: Know Yourself.

I was aware, even in high school, of Delphi and its famous inscription. And doubtless I'd heard about the Greek call to self-knowledge, but I didn't take it too seriously; it even annoyed me. I thought it superficial. In college, dazzled as I already was by Freud's achievement, I dismissed the Greeks' insight. A quarter-century later, when I recognized the direction society was taking, I understood their prescience.

At least two thousand years ago, the Hellenes warned the world to be more self-aware. The philosophers and poets of Hellenic Greece and early Rome searched the causes of human misery and repeatedly shined their lamps on self-oblivion. In particular, they focused on self-deception. Their solution to the ubiquity of self-deception was *paideia*: An education that teaches us to recognize error and tolerate the tensions truth causes, rather than flee them through self-deception.

As to the tension of envying virtue in another, Plato and Aristotle urge emulation, not malice. We all can, with effort, sublimate envy into emulousness. This frees us to admire and protect, rather than tear down, the educational ideal of mental growth and cultures that extol it.

Paideia confronts its students with specific values that generate specific tensions. One value is awareness of others' thoughts and feelings and openness to novel mindsets; this entails repudiating egocentricity and rigid, deep-rooted character defenses. For example, *isolation,* an unconscious defense we'll examine later, makes people tone-deaf to one's own and others' experience. Indeed, Plato's dialogical style, as in *The Symposium's* sequential speeches on love, exemplifies the airing of different perspectives. The Greek Chorus, too, contravenes the views and values expressed by the actors in tragedies. The chorus in *Oedipus Rex* commands the mulish king to abandon his inquiry, exemplifying the perspectivism at the roots of Greek cultural life.

A second value is critical reflection on contemporary social beliefs and a third is freedom of public expression. Both these values constrain us to tolerate fears of retaliation, seclusion, exclusion and shame. A fourth, visible even in Homer, is scientific and synthetic. This value holds that definite and comprehensible laws govern the world. It involves submission to those laws, and renunciation of omnipotence. To renounce omnipotence exposes our helplessness.

The highest Hellenic value was the fulfillment of human intellectual and ethical (character) potential through the ardors of compulsory education. Here we arrive at the true meaning of education:[5] Education is the lifelong, progressive knowledge of *both* the outer and inner worlds: The "mental growth" referenced above. Education not only serves both the individual's and the community's mental growth, it links individuals to their community. So, education embodies the purpose of all human effort. Yet this value entailed an endless strain on society, a strain accepted and borne because only this value could sustain individual, national, or global dignity.

Only by tolerating the tension of education, the tension of mental growth, will we find comfort in our existence. To urge this truth is central to this book. This exclusively human comfort is what moved fourth-century Athenian dramatist Menander to write:

Λιμὴν πέφυκε πᾶσι παιδεία βροτοῖς
(*Paideia* is the haven for all mortals).

Whether or not Sigmund Freud knew this line, he knew its lesson. Hundreds of citations from Greek literature, philosophy and science inform, illustrate, and adorn Freud's 23 volumes of work, and will convince any reader of his immersion in Hellenic culture. Oedipus's tragedy, and the disturbing relationship between Chronos and Uranus, for example, informed the analytic concepts of, respectively, the oedipal complex and castration anxiety. Allusions to Apuleius, Archimedes, Aristotle, Democritus, Euripides, Homer, Ovid, Pythagoras and Virgil, and other luminaries from the Greco-Roman world, clarify and enrich Freud's speculative meditations, from his earliest writings in the late 1880's to his death in 1939. By thinking in Greek fashion—using analogy, empiricism and speculation—to formulate his theories, Freud made advances unachievable by those uneducated in classical Humanism.

His immersion in Classical culture helped Freud identify the chief challenge to the human mind: To respect inner and outer reality.

Plato identified a part of the mind that reconciles reality, drives, and conscience. Partly upon this suggestion, Freud postulated an ego function he

---

[5] "education" derives from the Latin first conjugation verb *educo/educare* and its supine form *educatum,* meaning to grow, or to nourish. Others believe it derives from the third conjugation verb *educo/educere,* supine *eductum*, to lead out of.

called *reality-testing*, a function that requires tension-tolerance.[6] Like many of Freud's concepts, this one evolved over time, and was never finalized. Fundamentally, though, reality-testing distinguishes stimuli originating in the outside world from those originating in the inner world. Reality-testing is critical, because it forestalls confusion between perception and imagination, a confusion at the root of hallucination. Although adults seldom hallucinate, their unconscious strategies of self-deception, their wishful or fearful fantasies, and their cultural fictions similarly deceive them.

In this sense, the Greeks revolutionized reality-testing. They designed a method, albeit incomplete, to validate perceptions of the inner and outer worlds. This was the Socratic, or maieutic method. American scholar Thomas Cahill describes the Socratic method as defining abstractions and exposing ignorance and error through dialectical inquiry. This marked the completion of a cultural transition from an impressionistic or even superstitious conception of reality to a systematic examination of the world using rational deliberation, conscious choice and precision.

Greek works, beginning with *The Iliad*, also attacked the human temptation to omnipotence, the great saboteur of reality-testing. They perpetually present life as limited and disappointing E. C. Kopff (2001). writes: "A vision of life that insists that there are rules and limits—and that they apply to you—informs most ancient literature." The Greek student sees the warnings everywhere: In Prometheus, who dared to give divine fire to mortals and for his daring was disemboweled daily by an eagle; and Arachne, who touted her weaving as better than the gods' and was turned into a spider.

Socrates made it his life's work to expose the limitations of human knowledge. His was an educational mission to persuade people to "care for their souls" by knowing themselves. The late fifth-and early fourth-century BCE Greeks understood that the hatred of disappointment leads to the mindless morbid greed they called πλεονεξία (pleonexia). They detected a dangerous group denial of that hatred, a denial that allowed over-reaching to flourish. It was not the over-reaching, but the obliviousness to it, that they judged the gravest danger.

To care for the soul seems to have been the goal of Athenian state-sponsored contests in tragedy, the theatrical representation of life under the shadow of death and disaster. Aeschylus, Sophocles, Euripides and others

[6] Please see Glossary. This term is used throughout the book.

portrayed heroes with whom the audience could identify; heroes entangled in an inescapable web of intolerable circumstances. These heroes represented humanity itself. Ignorance, arrogance, or obligation trapped them within certain life limits; and from these limits no greatness could save them. Omnipotence was impossible. This was the *tragic vision of life*, a vision the Greeks regularly confronted, reminding themselves that contempt for limits could ruin their blessings.

Athenians loved their comic playwrights, but revered their tragic poets. They were the spiritual leaders, the civic guides of the city. They bore a responsibility heavier than the constitutional authority of her political leaders. Aeschylus, Sophocles, and Euripides, no doubt also lost Greek tragedians, bore this responsibility: To remorselessly warn citizens and state against their hatred of limits, and the elusiveness of this hatred in shape-shifting arrogance. Arrogance is protean; it takes many shapes—impudence, complacency, greed, promiscuity, contempt, idealization, magical thinking, and many others. No matter its shape, arrogance baffles and overwhelms the community's capacity to restrain it, and the tragedians recognized this fact of political science.

ὕβρις (hubris) is the Greek word. "Arrogance" is perhaps, after "hubris," our closest English equivalent. Hubris is defined as wanton violence arising from pride of strength or passion; sometimes as insolence, lust, lewdness; sometimes as the outrage, violation or rape of a person. We should also think of ὕβρις as the presumption of any kind of limitless power, knowledge, or cleverness.

Here we think of the catastrophes stemming from Oedipus's obstinate and sacrilegious investigation into his father's death. We see the tragic condition emerging even in Homer, two hundred years before the first Athenian play, when Odysseus's complacency and greed lead to six of his men being cannibalized by the Cyclops.

Tragedy is not reserved for the evil man. Tragedy discovers hubris in the best of us. Sophocles, in both *Antigone* and *Oedipus Rex*, presents good men with good intentions, falling helplessly to their pride, bringing ruin on themselves and their people. In his zeal for answers (omniscience) and overweening confidence (omnipotence), Sophocles' Oedipus illustrates how easily arrogance, even when subtle, even for the peoples' welfare, can plunge a man or woman, and their community, into wretchedness.

Creon, in *Antigone*, ruthlessly pursues what he thinks is right. In so doing, he ruins the House of Oedipus, himself, his own wife, son, their love for him, and Antigone, the one most dedicated to the Right, the most pious, the most loyal.

Humans can outsource their own hubris. Euripides' Jason (of Argonaut fame) hubristically appropriated limitless power by conjugating with a sorceress, Medea. The results were, again, educational: Both Medea's brother and Jason's uncle Pelias dismembered, Creon and his daughter poisoned and burned, and Jason's and Medea's children murdered by their own mother.

The tragic hero horrifies us by showing how easily we relax self-scrutiny and forget that omnipotence is not for human beings. We forget too easily that we hate limits and helplessness. We become cat's paws of ὕβϱις, guilelessly slipping into delusions of invulnerability, dreams of self-sufficiency. We ruin ours and others' lives.

The poet makes the audience tremble as the mythical hero—deceived and misled by overweening pride—stumbles into disaster. The audience pities the hero as he tries, but fails, to heed great Solon's warning: Abundance leads to hubris, and hubris leads to ruin. Today's descent into plutocracy and autocracy, confronted in Chapter Two, is bitter proof of Solon's wisdom.

When we forget that omnipotence is not given to humans, we commit a profound injustice, an assault on the natural order. Seventeen hundred years after the decline of Athens, as southern Europe was recovering Greek wisdom, Dante was repeating this monition, using Christian mythology, in the *Inferno's* Canto III, in the dire inscription on Hell's Gate: "Abandon all hope, ye who enter here." Superficially, Dante meant that there was no exit from the realm of death. More deeply, he meant: Abandon your omnipotent fantasy of self-sufficiency, of being able to thrive without God's help.

The Greeks understood that humans hated limits, were mad for omnipotence, fell repeatedly under its spell, and ignored its unattainability. Plato himself made a misbegotten, albeit reluctant voyage to Sicily, thinking to make an educational experiment on the tyrant Dionysus II. In this, he denied the limits of his talent and educational regimen.

I think the Hellenes' literary consistency in presenting the perils of hubris shows us indisputably that they recognized the deep hatred of limits and tendency to deny that hatred.

Tragedy, then, had great importance. When you don't yet know that humanity is doomed, you will naturally try to restrain destructiveness the best you can with what you have. If you have tragedy—the communal warning against omnipotence, magical thinking, and denial—you are wise to use it.

But I would, of course, be hubristic to teach others about hubris, self-deception, and envy, had I never struggled to manage my own.

And when Greek—the Greek over which Abby had drudged—failed to open the arms of the academy, I came face to face with my own hubristic self-deception. And then what happened to me?

I was outraged. That is, I turned my rage outward, away from myself, toward the school and the culture which supported it. Worse, envy of the chosen ones burned inside me. This occasioned a regression, making me more childlike, lost in identity-confusion. I forgot that I was a middle-aged, socioeconomically-secure professional man. I over-identified with my daughter, as though I were the young, unestablished, insecure applicant. I almost felt not smart enough, well placed enough or cool enough to get chosen by a selective institution.

In my regression, I reexperienced an old exclusion. My father was the excluder, though not deliberately so. He was a gentle, loveable, courtly and handsome man, attractive to children and adults alike. As a boy, he'd been a star athlete, and was distinguished, even as a teenager, by his civilized constraint and quiet dignity. He became a twenty-year-old Navy hero.[7]

When returned from the South China Sea to his wife and newborn son (my older brother), memories of the mayhem he'd endured had hardened his native reserve into a shield against mental shocks, both great and small. A child's impulsiveness or pleas for play could only have irritated or repelled him. This may partly explain why, after expending his modest discretionary mental capital on his first son, he economized on his second.

Fathers' enthusiasm for their toddler sons soothes the wounds of the primal scene. Unfortunately, that wasn't my patrimony. So, I resolved to earn his love, or failing that, coerce his admiration. When I was eight, I realized my athletic efforts weren't really winning his attention. And when, as a teenager, I learned my father venerated educated people, I pursued the life of the mind.

This strategy succeeded, but only modestly. Vengefully, I turned my heart to stone against him.

To fill the void, I substituted the academy for my father, and idealized college as a toddler idealizes his dad. By winning academic acceptance,

---

[7] His story, among others, is told in Roy Andersen's *Three Minutes Off Okinawa*. Worcester, Mass.: Jana Press, 2007.

maybe even glory, I might nullify the Great Exclusion. A wild idealist even then, I inflated college into a magical enclave in which a dedicated professorship, by trials of talent and self-discipline, would transform ignorant boys into educated young men. It would elect a worthy few for places of honor in the collective paternal/academic heart. Though I never truly found it in my own college experience, this ideal of mine never died.

Until Abby applied to college. When her top schools shrugged off our efforts to satisfy what I believed were their deepest values, they shattered my hopes. They reawakened my envy and I eyed with malice all those who, less deservedly than Abby, had won paternal approbation.

I realized too late that what I had sought from the university through my daughter was my father's pride and gratitude. I had deceived myself. What did it mean?

I studied the envious roots of my naiveté and the seemingly innocent idealization of the academy which reality had so instructively punished. My inward inquiry, by outward comparisons, led to a discovery of social importance. Long reflection on my private envy, my fear of exclusion and helplessness (punishments for my envy), my attempt to evade these tensions with idealization and an academic glory grab, revealed a broader and more momentous phenomenon: The world had given itself up to tension-avoidance.

The world more and more, I realized, was evading tensions, and particularly those of envy and envy-fear. I began to see that envy and fear of envy had undermined the university itself.[8] My own crisis uncovered what I believe to be the deepest roots of the historical crisis of humanist education.

On one hand, my envy of the highly educated led me to idealize the university as a place of the highest academic rigor. And in fairness to myself, it had been that from time to time. But public envy of the educated, cloaked in the creed of social justice and of universal inclusion, intimidated the university, and made it change its values. Humanist education, the tradition of education that unified ancient Greece and Rome with both medieval Europe and the premodern world, disappeared. Greek and Latin, Homer and Plato have been abandoned almost everywhere in favor of STEM programs, trade schools, and, in a growing number of cases, remedial English. And when colleges teach the ancient greats, they tar them as racists, misogynists, and

---

[8] This and all other speculations in this book, it is understood, are susceptible to the *psychologist's fallacy*, that is, the unwitting attribution to the [public] mind under examination what is actually true of the psychologist's (author's) own mind.

classists. Or they squeeze Plato and Aeschylus under the microscope of Critical Theory/Deconstruction/Marxist/Anti-colonial Analysis. In this book I restrict my focus on earlier (pre-1950) attacks on *paideia*, but it hasn't escaped me that the Envy-Fear Theory helps explain the origins and durability of Critical ideology. In any case, the education we've lost is far more important than any gains in social equality. What was society really trying to do?

We can answer this only if we make society psychologically intelligible. Depth psychology makes this possible. I studied the antagonism toward humanist education guided by what might be called prelapsarian psychoanalysis, the discipline before its political correction and ostracism. To understand the fall of the humanist university I had to go beyond the assumptions of social justice. I needed to know not only what provoked such bloody-minded indignation in the masses, but also, more puzzlingly, why the university allowed itself to be undone by mass resentment.

In my own college days, back in the 1960's, the study of ancient Greek and Latin and the outworn ideal of Classical Humanism still haunted campuses like an unquiet spirit. After its enshrinement in the schools of ancient Greece, the humanistic ethos inhabited the academy for twenty-four centuries. By 1920, however, the world's universities had turned away from Greek and Latin scholarship. Then, starved by academic and public apathy, the humanist curriculum shriveled into a faint memory.

How could this have been allowed to happen? After all, the humanist university, the classical tradition, *paideia*, whatever one calls the foundations of western education, was a social necessity. The rigors of its languages, philosophies and values, as well as the beauty of its literature, promoted mental growth. Mental growth, I will argue, is key to withstanding destructive envy and all the other tensions of life.

In its beginnings, higher education was dedicated to mental growth, which I define, again, as the progressive knowledge of both the inner and outer worlds. *Paideia* was a social contract, framed to protect civilization by strengthening the collective mind and deepening its interest in both worlds.

The modern university, however, rejected this covenant. I saw the abandonment of compulsory Greek and Latin in the late 19th century as higher education's self-inflicted death-blow. If this is correct, the university's reidentification as a school of utility was a deathbed conversion, an appeal for forgiveness, a propitiation of cultural envy. The university devalued the interior life and consigned its students' minds to the great, growing, grinding global economic machine. The university, swamped by envy-fear, jettisoned its duty and burden of teaching self-understanding, tension-regulation, and envy-management.

We ought not dismissively retort that the academy has simply become more socially responsible, that the principles of humanistic education have merely changed. No, we've buried them, and draped a flag of Humanism over their gravestone. Gone is the formation of the mind with Greek and Latin languages and literature. Gone is the compulsory confrontation with the interior world. Gone are the remorseless reminders to remember the costs of human exceptionalism, reminders like haughty Prometheus, disemboweled daily, forever, by the vulture.

As I sought the causes of the humanist university's demise, I tried to draw insight from its consequences. For millennia, the linguistic training, the exhortations to self-examination, the warnings against human arrogance and pleonexia, had helped society sustain at least a small measure of mental growth. But society made a fateful decision to flee the tensions and discomforts of human life, rather than confront and manage them. After this decision, it regressed. Society's regression dragged down the modern university, which devalued the mental growth it once valorized. The academy shape-shifted into an acolyte of technology and the marketplace, the churches of omnipotent growth. All this accelerated cultural death. The collective will for mental growth withered away. So, our destruction of an elite academy may seem to have alleviated divisive cultural envy. But dumping the institution for mental growth called upon our heads apocalyptic consequences.

Before I name these consequences, one thing must be acknowledged: To deal with tension-evasion, humanist education was only a half-measure. Psychoanalysis was the more targeted, systematic, rigorous and thoroughgoing method. Only psychoanalysis systematically investigates unconscious strategies of self-deception.

Nonetheless, by encouraging free inquiry, expression, and self-reflection, and by the examination and praise of these activities, classical education anticipated the basic aims of psychoanalysis. But society rejected both.

Then, standing disarmed and naked against our destructiveness, we raced headlong to monocide, or anthrocide, or whatever we call universal suicide. For I contend that we see the ultimate failure of humanist education, surprisingly, in overpopulation, a failure to restrain ourselves, but more fundamentally, a failure to manage envy of inclusion and its sister, envy-fear. If we had preserved our schools of tension management and self-knowledge, we might have saved ourselves. Instead, we let envy of inclusion overwhelm and destroy us. Absent a cultural bulwark to prevent its 20th century explosion, uncontrolled reproduction and immigration left a dying habitat for posterity, our true and most neglected underclass.

This book is my own interpretation of the marginalization of classical and psychoanalytic wisdom, and the costs of this cultural decision. Some will argue that other factors contributed to our fall, or even—against copious counter-evidence—that the university is doing fine. Few, however, I think, will say that psychoanalysis has flourished.

Others may agree with me that the rejection of classical learning and psychoanalysis were harmful, but disagree that these misfortunes caused over-population and the ruin of civilization. But I'll try to convince them that intolerance of exclusion and envy-fear undermined the two institutions of mental growth; that their decline weakened our minds further; and that, in our weakness, we couldn't resist ruining our habitat and civilization.

I should put my argument in a different way: When we do not grow mentally, we wither. Accordingly, we feel, and have, less reason to live. Humanist education sprang from the principle that the talented as well as the ordinary can improve their native mental endowments, enrich their knowledge of the inner and outer worlds, and deepen the experience of our short lives. So long as this gleaming goal, this educational ideal, lighted our way, society stood a fighting chance to elude the pitfall of collective self-deception. When that moral polestar went dark, civilization slipped into a delusion of tensionless lives. To have discarded a principle so humane, so consoling, and so necessary to a sustainable society appears to have been humanity's fallacious solution to all tensions.

This was not a straightforward research project. As I confronted the fascinating task of psychoanalyzing social life, I soon found myself plunged into an intellectual labyrinth. To find my way out, I had to navigate the sinuosities of basic "complexity science," the study of highly-organized systems like whirlpools, bacteria, human beings, their societies and ecosystems. Complexity science then entangled me in biophysics, the science that studies the relationship between energy and life.

How did I end up there? The broad subject of my study was tension-avoidance as the enemy of mental growth, and as I followed this phenomenon to its roots, I found myself pushed beyond psychoanalysis. I eventually discovered the force driving our envious destruction of humanistic ideas. This force appeared at the point of synthesis between the psychical and the physical.

I discovered that the humanist university opposed the most elemental forces in existence. I understood it this way: The natural disposition of any organized system is to maintain its complexity by resisting the tensions that will inevitably tear it apart. Human beings, however, alone among complexities, can recognize these fundamental tensions. Rather than evade them, they can embrace and incorporate them through humanist education, courage, and other virtues of character—thereby neutralizing their destructive work.

But how could we really know whether we were truly embracing and assimilating tension? After all, humans are thoroughly self-deceptive. So, we needed a method to expose unconscious strategies of self-deception.

As of the late 19th century, there was no such method. Self-deceivers had only the expedient of dialogue, developed by the Greeks, to correct their errors. But after correction, self-deceivers, as a rule, would fall back into their habits, and delude themselves with yet more subtlety. Humans needed a systematic strategy to permanently modify their private penchants for self-deception.

Psychoanalysis, as I defined it above, was that strategy, the second key tool in managing tensions.

In human psychology, the impulse to evade tension expresses itself as denial, disavowal, repression, or other unconscious defenses. These defenses often impair our minds. Psychoanalysis, the culmination of humanist education, teaches true, rather than imaginary, freedom of thought. It builds up the capacity to recognize and confront, rather than flee, the strains of life.

But we fled them; and today we see the results more clearly than ever.

Overshoot Day, conceived in 2006 by Andrew Simms of the UK think tank New Economics Foundation, is the day of a given year by which humanity has consumed all of Earth's annually-renewable resources.[9] Global population growth has dragged Earth's Overshoot Day—December 23 in 1970, when we were less than half our current size—all the way back to July

---

[9] Our mere existence eats up 80%; our excessive consumption habits, 20% (Rees, 2023).

24 in 2025. To see our predicament in a different way: Excessive births, relative to deaths, have swollen our species into a population that needs 1.75 Earths to sustain it.

Casualties of the population explosion are mounting: U.S. beekeepers have lost 30% of their stock since 2006. Humans have destroyed proportionally as many birds, having eliminated 30% of all breeding bird pairs (3 billion birds) in the last half-century.[10] We are wiping out butterflies across the Western U.S.[11] 40% of all insect species are declining around the world, every year disappearing at a rate of 1-2%.[12] Even seven years ago, the UN Convention on Biodiversity reported that, each day, 150 more species are lost, and biodiversity might be disappearing at 10% every decade.

ScienceDaily predicts a worldwide water shortage by 2040, and *Time Out* says that nine cities—including New Orleans, Bangkok, Amsterdam, and Savannah—could be underwater in less than seven years.[13]

Although the public rails—rightly—against climate change, it ignores its root cause, overpopulation. Deep psychological forces, I believe, drive this fatal selective inattention to overpopulation.

We associate depopulation with attacks on the unborn. These imaginary attacks, still alive in the unconscious, represent perhaps the most profoundly inhumane, the most revolting human impulse.[14] By even contemplating depopulation we convict ourselves of this fundamental Badness, an expression of our innate destructiveness. And we invite, accordingly, a punishment worse, perhaps, than death: An irreversible rejection by our own consciences, and by society. This was the mythical Bellerophon's punishment. He'd tried to spy on the gods, making a symbolic intrusion on the primal scene. For this crime, Zeus condemned him to blindness, lameness and utter isolation from society, to wander the deserted plain, "eating his heart out."

---

[10] Rosenberg, KV et al. Decline of the North American avifauna. *Science*, Sept. 2019

[11] Betz, Eric. Western Butterfly Populations are Plummeting Thanks to Climate Change *Discover*, 4/19/21.

[12] Benjamin Jones. An apocalypse worth worrying about. *Vox*, 3/6/22.

[13] Winnie Axelson, 7/29/14. Ed Cunningham, *Time Out*, 11/10/21, available at 9 Cities That Could Be Underwater By 2030 (timeout.com). 10/11/21.

[14] Fetal abductions—the forcible excision and theft, from a screaming woman, of her fetus—bring this impulse close to real life. During the Manson murders, the killers debated taking Sharon Tate's fetus. Perhaps envy-fear deters even homicidal psychotics.

We blinded ourselves. So, envy-fear stole in, unnoticed, among us. It made us abort every policy of depopulation even as we, in self-preservation, conceived it.

Amazement at my own blindness gave birth to my long investigation.

As I pursued it, my sympathy grew for humanity's despair over its innate destructiveness. And I finished in sorrow for our species' lost opportunity to savor, indefinitely, the inexpressible joy of expanding awareness. We seem to be the eyes and ears of inner and outer reality, enjoying the most exquisite sensorium in the known universe. Yet, owing to our hatred of tensions, we appeared, and will soon disappear, in the blink of a geological eye.

****

The Republic of Mental Growth

Before I fill out my story about how the human race doomed itself by fleeing tensions and chasing omnipotence, I invite you to imagine an alternative history. Imagine a culture following the Greeks and Greek-inspired Romans in their respect for self-knowledge and mental growth. Imagine society learning about the unconscious strategies of self-deception from psychoanalysis. Imagine our college students studying the perfidy of envy, as did humanists like Montaigne, Dr. Johnson and psychoanalyst Melanie Klein. Maybe then society could have faced reality and made the hard decisions that would have forestalled catastrophe.

I'll play out this fanciful vision, then explore why human nature and the forces of entropy, envy, and the death drive made it impossible. This visionary "Republic" might shock contemporary sensibilities; so I ask it be considered a utopian fiction that, like Plato's *Republic*, is meant to stimulate dialogue, inquiry, and reflection on the gains and losses inseparably attached to social and personal choices.

The stakes attached to our choices have risen over time. In 2013, Ilan Safit, philosophy professor at Pace University, published "The Ethics of Survival." He argued that now, in the 21st century, we have finally arrived at the profound ethical obligation to adapt human practices to historian Thomas Berry's (2000, p. 92) "ecological law of limits." Safit concludes that such an obligation, "a community-based ethic .... would pose restrictions on the liberties of individuals [and] .... even demand .... *sacrifices that are currently regarded oppressive and immoral*" (p. 78) (my emphases).

My visionary society, a Republic of Mental Growth (RMG), would demand such sacrifices.

In both my visionary and actual society, we are not born equal; are not uniformly intelligent, beautiful, clever, alert, fast, tall, strong or self-disciplined; and were never equally mindsighted, that is, psychologically-minded.[1] So, we are condemned to inequality and inequity of *outcome*, as both Confucius and Plato understood. We might nonetheless have framed a social model which offered equality of *opportunity*. This model would offer incentives and strategies for tension-tolerance and mental growth to everyone, to the benefit of all.

I have imagined a society which venerated its abler members and duly appointed them to high places in government, education, mental health care, medicine, and law; a society which regretted, but endured, the exclusion of the less able, the less disciplined, and the less mindsighted from its offices, though *not from its care*. This imaginary, exclusion-tolerant society—indeed any serviceable society—would provide opportunities for mental growth even to the impecunious, intellectually barren, and mindblind.

To this end, the RMG would mandate public schooling. It would disenfranchise renegades from this mandate. It would sprinkle into all public classrooms age-appropriate Greek and Latin words, words referring to favorite games, activities, and toys, and words for some familiar psychological phenomena, like joy, sadness, fear, spite, and empathy. This would prepare their minds for self-awareness. I would also pique the children's interest in psychoanalytic concepts. These could include forgetting, slips of the tongue, hidden meanings in dreams, and self-deception (in the form, for example, of wishful thinking). Teachers would tactfully explain anxiety, libido and aggression and their familiar manifestations (for example, nail-biting, thumb-sucking, doctor games, cheating, lying and tormenting the family cat).

Schools, in my RMG, would introduce more Classical grammar, vocabulary, and psychoanalytic ideas over the next year or two, and by the end of the third grade, children who were doing well, or—this is important—*striving* to assimilate this simpler material, would be assigned more challenging work. These Elementary Schools of Mental Growth would not bar earnest children, even the faltering, from the most esteemed of all citizen's

---

[1] I use "mindsight" differently than does Dr. Daniel Seigel (Seigel, 2010). For him, mindsight is a kind of focused attention that allows us to see the internal workings of our own minds. It is a conscious, *secondary process* (see Glossary), learnable, self-help activity. For me, mindsight is access to *primary process* activity (see Glossary), respect for *unconscious* strategies of self-deception, and the psychoanalytic assistance required to achieve these factors of mental growth. Without the humility taught by psychoanalysis, Seigel's mindsighted students may easily trick themselves into believing they are self-aware at deep levels.

achievements—admission to the Elite—since late bloomers will always be among us. These sleepers should be tutored carefully, sometimes psychotherapeutically treated, in view of their exceptional endurance, perseverance and courage. All this would afford everyone multiple chances to earn inclusion, respect, dignity and, above all, a path to mental growth.

By the middle of high school, the better students will have distinguished themselves, and those in the top third of their cohort would prepare to enter a College of Mental Growth. College would intensify classical, psychoanalytic, and mathematical educations. College would also, of course, teach the other humanities and sciences. Ecology will sit atop the sciences, and drum into students' minds the monition that science seduces us into omnipotence.

All colleges would be single sex, a nod to education over, but not in lieu of, concupiscence. The RMG would situate campuses within four miles of one another, a distance that the fleetest student-athlete, in search of amorous opportunities between classes or at mealtimes, would need at least twenty minutes to traverse. This would encourage students to identify with their particular campus, enhancing their school's *esprit de cours*. These brother and sister schools would have identical curricula, and sponsor weekly joint seminars in their various classes, on alternating campuses. When not in class, or studying, students could freely consort, so long as their activities didn't interfere with educational obligations.

The college faculty, members of the Elite, would month by month press every student to think more psychoanalytically, eventually exposing the phonies. This is the tribe that's outwardly accepting, but inwardly rejecting, of the fact and gravity of unconscious self-deception. They are glib with psychoanalytic concepts. They are prone to isolation, displacement and intellectualization, dangerous defenses described later in this book.

The colleges would require their sophomores to enter psychoanalysis. If the students and their analysts proved compatible, they would be expected to stay together, and grow together, for many years.

Any abrogation of this requirement would result in the expulsion of the analysand or the analyst from the Elite track. One may see then, that when 17-year-olds committed to their colleges, they would be promising to stay in their college's locale for a very long time. This would not be an unpleasant arrangement. Every college town would be at least 75% smaller than today's, located in areas no longer insufferably crowded, in a revived natural world. This culture would not be as agitatedly mobile as ours.

Any other education after high school would be honestly named. Such schools would be called technical or business schools, as in "Harvard Polytechnic," and these would be open to the bottom two-thirds of high school students.

This educational scheme, honestly appreciating differences in talent, would benefit everyone, even those excluded from the inner circle. That's because the less-talented, by having associated with those committed to mental growth, would have improved their minds and their lives, been challenged mentally, and learned more, and better. The whole society would thus profit, and defend its culture. It's a brave culture: It recognizes and manages, rather than denies and evades, the tensions associated with internal and external reality.

This Republic would be race-neutral but not culture-neutral. We recall my opinion that the Western culture's educational prescriptions for self-knowledge and repudiation of omnipotence—*paideia's* prescriptions—could have restrained the worst impulses of human nature, impulses that plague every culture, every nation, every age, every color. *Paideia* and psychoanalysis, practiced on a global level, might have saved first, second, and third worlds alike.

This ideal Republic would fail without depopulating the first, second and third worlds. The very idea of depopulation, of course, raises the moral horrors of eugenics and racism, fears, that is, of brutal exclusions. Although history has given us repulsive examples of both, traumatic social memory is not, as I will argue, the chief cause of depopulation-panic: It's envy-fear.

Perhaps Florence Blondell can help demolish the claim that depopulation is racist. Blondell is a Ugandan overpopulation activist. She says that wealthy anti-depopulationists (without using that word) justify their position with "excuses like 'that's racist, eugenics, etc.'" She asks, "What's racist about it? Have you been to our countries? ....Have you smelt the stinking poverty and hunger? [Have you].... found a household with .... 5 children under 5 years and another in the womb—with oldest girls married off at 13?"[2] Ms. Blondel may or may not be familiar with the concept of envy-fear, but she knows that the specter of depopulation alarms the collective mind, especially its privileged component.

---

[2] https://www.overshootday.org/florence-blondel-population/

In any case, I envision depopulation as the reduction, not of a particular group, but of human numbers. In my ideal Republic, we would have depleted our population rapidly, by attrition. We would have allowed natural deaths to outpace births and immigration, an attrition carefully randomized over all races, nationalities and ethnicities, using government-mandated birth control and hard limits on immigration.

This instantly raises a second horror: Government coercion. The RMG would not autocratically limit births and immigration, but in submission to enlightened collective self-interest. A sustainable Republic would have hammered out a global agreement to save humanity by shrinking it. This would require a maturity humans have never achieved, the flexibility to sacrifice certain cherished freedoms for human survival, and the hardiness to live under an austere Ethics of Survival.

So, whether its citizenry be white, or light brown, or black, or red, or chartreuse, the RMG would strictly maintain its polychromatic numbers at two billion. How could we do this? We could establish a reproductive lottery: A world governmental body randomly assigning each citizen of reproductive age a non-transferable number from 1-10 and allowing, say, all the 3's to have one child, if they choose. Non-3's would be obliged, on behalf of society, to endure the envy of filial love, heightened awareness of personal mortality, and other tensions of childlessness. The government would oblige them to choose between state-financed birth control or sterilization. For help in managing these or other tensions, psychoanalysis would be accessible to everyone able to comply with its rigor and discipline.

What of those who refuse contraception? This society would swiftly imprison them, and endure the tension of having excluded the recalcitrants. And if they proved intractable, the RMG would let them become envious pariahs, and endure that envy.

Under the Ethics of Survival—an Ethics shocking to a culture contemptuous of reality—a sustainable society would impose self-financed involuntary sterilization or imprisonment on recalcitrants to birth control and, in the latter case, of course, proscribe conjugal visits.

The Republic recognizes too that immigration is a fallacious escape-strategy from overcrowded misery. It is fallacious because, to every one immigrant it gives temporary relief, it guarantees perpetual misery for several hundreds of the receiving nation's posterity. Furthermore, it relieves tensions in the sending nation, and thereby, in proportion to numbers of emigrants, disinhibits reproduction there.

The Republic understands that, in the wealthier receiving nation, citizens are tempted to shield themselves from envy-anxiety with pretensions of lovingkindness, just as smokers and addicts dispel anxiety with their cigarettes or syringes. So, envy-fear drives deeper the cultural addiction to immigration advocacy. In all its policy-making, the Republic, in defiance of emotional pain, always consults both external and internal reality. So, while staring down the menaces of guilt and envy-fear, the RMG would limit immigration to a small number. This country, for example, might allow 1000 immigrants yearly. And they must either be educated or educable to mental growth in the manner described above. They must demonstrate their commitment to enhancing the mental growth of the receiving country. Even those would be excluded if their presence violated the national population's bright line, a limit informed by ecology. We might limit our country to 50 million.

Depopulation awakens, of course, a third horror: Economic disaster. And it is true, our economy would shrink with depopulation. But steady-state economists have for years advocated such shrinkage. Yes, there would be a painful phase, perhaps decades-long, of global austerity. This would be a hard necessity under the ethics of survival, and the RMG would enforce this austerity and its associated tension-tolerance.

Of course, our actual society made different choices: It abandoned education and mental growth in favor of STEM-enhanced omnipotence-training; it devalued mindsight in favor of self-deception; it refused reproductive and immigration control in favor of gross denial of overpopulation. These choices have bred collective self-loathing.

But my proposed initiative of true, rather than false, love of ourselves might have unloosed, perhaps for the first time in history, a collective joy, pride and self-respect. Such an achievement might have been possible in a culture that venerated the Greek ideal of mental growth and self-knowledge, and, on the other side, feared, pitied and, when necessary, shamed self-deception.

I must again admit that, even to imagine such a culture, a Republic of Mental Growth, a psychoanalytic society, a culture that confronted and managed hard realities, I was obliged to push aside an unwanted personal conviction: We are too envious and self-deceiving for this notion to have survived more than a breathtaking instant. Nature needed envious, self-deceived and suicidal creatures to serve her deeper purpose.

But readers still can ask themselves, privately—here is one way this grim book offers hope: Could they love a College of Mental Growth? Those who could can still, even today, autodidactically, make it come true in the heartbreakingly brief time we have left. May this book inspire a love for mental growth in the uninitiated, and comfort those who already profit, and suffer, from it.

1.

The Roots of Tension-Evasion

The impossibility of a Republic of Mental Growth was, I realized, rooted in the most basic laws of physics.

Entropy, an inviolable law of nature, is lodged even within the human mind. To fulfill its destructive mission, that indwelling entropic spirit infatuates us with dreams of limitless comfort and a tensionless existence. They are dreams of omnipotence, dreams in the pursuit of which we devised society's irreversible doom.

This book is about the fall of the two institutions of mental growth and the social decline it signaled. I began writing it to understand how and why society turned its back on humanist education. I soon realized, however, that the causes run deep; they lie in the most basic nexus of our psychological, biological, and material beings. And what unites these distinctive elements of our existence, as it seemed, is tension-management.

We don't need to understand thermodynamics to know that human well-being depends upon the handling of tensions. We manage tension at work and at home, in our relationships with others and with ourselves. What I hope to show, however, is a connection between the way we manage tensions in daily life and the deep psychological dynamics of tension regulation that unfold through history.

Will we recognize, tolerate, reflect upon and *manage* tensions, or will we *evade* them with self-deceptive maneuvers? Those who mature and thrive, tolerate tensions long enough to devise realistic solutions to them. Such solutions respect the short- and long-term realities of both the internal and external worlds. These solutions are laborious; they use more energy than tension-evasion. Those who avoid tensions with impulsive action or tension-denial, gradually damage their capacity for *reality-testing,* endangering themselves and others, such as children, or political constituents, unlucky enough to be in their care.

Tension is inclusive. It comprises physiological pressures like hunger, thirst, and sex, as well as emotional pressures like frustration, anger, depression, fear, persecution, regret, despair, envy, guilt, shame, anxiety and boredom. Tensions are the demands of existence, equivalent to what medical pioneer Hans Selye called, in his famous title, *The Stress of Life* (1956). I provisionally define tension here as any sensation or perception—including emotion, conscious or unconscious—which demands biochemical, muscular or psychological *work* in order to restore homeostasis. In amoebas, tension might arise from the perception of light. In humans, tension might be a mild gas pain (a psychosomatic reaction, perhaps, to a prior tension), shame or pity, or the terrifying approach of mental breakdown. Whatever their source, tensions push the organism to rid itself of them, obeying a *principle of least tension.* With minimal exertion, human beings, in particular, can even rid themselves of *consciousness* of tensions.

All psychological defenses are directed against mental and physical tensions, tensions felt in the present or past, or expected in the future. We endure exercise today to avoid greater discomforts, like pangs of conscience or miseries of decrepitude, tomorrow. We hate the offensive aspects of reality and try to destroy them. Often, however, we achieve this by mental trickery and even self-annihilation. When the mind cannot destroy tensions, or obliterate its perception of them, it turns its destructive hatred back upon itself, because it is a party to its own pain. The mind perceives both the offending reality and the painful tension imposed by that reality. Trying to escape itself, the mind attacks its perceptual apparatus, a component organ of reality-testing, and, if unsuccessful, repeats this attack until it ablates, or permanently impairs that organ. If our inner eyes offend us, we pluck them out. This strategy not only leads to mental errors, but to inner blindness.

The wish to conceal their own destructiveness tilts people toward self-harm. Our natural adversarial relation to tensions imposed on us by reality reinforces that inclination. Our neighbor's superiority, or our short life span, or gravity, or a professor's demand for a reasoned, well-documented argument, or any other of life's slings and arrows, frustrate us and we resent both the frustrater and our own sentience. Our own awareness, our own sensitivity, antagonizes us; this makes us, at best, ambivalent about living.

In order to minimize tensions, but stay in touch with reality, we must compromise between tolerating and evading tensions. Some compromises, for example, evade tensions with primitive defenses like *denial* or *projection,* intending to narrow and distort one's awareness; these are maladaptive. Healthy compromises tolerate tension long enough to form and execute plans to modify reality, and by that modification, reduce tensions in the future. Healthy compromises manage tension, demand courage, and create more than they destroy. They invigorate life more than deaden it and they acknowledge, rather than ignore or distort external and internal reality. To balance tension-evasion with tension-tolerance is the endless labor of human life. My work as a psychoanalyst has made this much clear to me.

Complexity, Linking, and the Second Law

The origins of tension in physical systems are assumed to lie in the early universe, in the first asymmetries in temperature, gravitation, and so on. These asymmetries generated energy flows in Nature's thermodynamic "effort" to restore symmetry, and gave birth to the organized natural systems called *complexities*. The tensions within and between the complexities took on successively different characters. At no time was this truer than at life's creation, when biophysical laws emerged from physics. Biophysics conceives of life-tensions as vital responses to the physical demand Nature makes on all complexities: To dissipate and degrade the (mainly) solar energy bathing our planet. Whether they be whirlpools or human society, all complexities on Earth are obliged to process energy, energy either radiating from our sun or seeping from our planet's core. Thermodynamic laws enforce this obligation.

In my search to understand the sources of our current cultural, political and ecological problems, I learned that all matter, notwithstanding the amazing longevity of living and some non-living organizations, also resists complexity. Or, once it has achieved complexity, matter is predestined to resimplify, to decompose, to die. This resistance, understood as entropy, is implicit in the Second Law of Thermodynamics. The theory of complex adaptive systems says that any large number of interacting agents—sand grains, for example, or ants, or people—will self-organize over time into relatively stable and coherent systems: A rippled sand dune, a busy ant colony, or a bustling community. These agents collaborate according to "principles of local interaction." The interactions those principles control we'll call *linking*. Distinctly shaped sand grains, when agitated by the winds and the rains and the washings of the waves, link together into rippled dunes. Consciousness itself, in one theory, emerges from the linking of one hundred trillion neurons snapping with electrochemical impulses.

Systems into which linking agents spontaneously self-organize take on lives of their own and, during those lives, enjoy coherence, continuity and transformability. *Complexities* are what we call such networks. But complexities, visible everywhere on Earth, most compellingly in living things, are supposed to be, in a sense, impossible. The tendency of disorganized agents to organize themselves seems to contradict nature's final intention, which is to resolve the universe, gradually but inexorably, into disorganized simplicity. The Second Law of Thermodynamics, the most robust of all physical laws, says that all the complexities of the universe, all starlings, storms and stars, must die. In the end they must disperse into their constituent parts, and those parts in turn must disintegrate until someday, in the unimaginably distant future, every last proton has died. Ashes to ashes; dust to dust.

The 2nd Law, stated another way, says that all free energy—energy that can do work—must at last degenerate into low-grade heat (*entropy*) that does little or no work. Finally, in statistical language, the 2nd Law says that whatever is improbable—as complexities are—must degenerate into the probable, into a random dispersal of matter and energy. This cosmic dissolution is sometimes called the "heat death" of the universe.

Why then do complexities exist at all?

We remember the waggish riddle: "If I am here to help others, then what are *others* here for?"

As it turns out, we're all here to help the universe die.

This melancholy law of physics resembles one of the two related fates to which Freud believed humans were consigned. We are fated, he said, to obey unconscious wishes and flee unconscious fears. But here I am referring to Freud's death drive, our destiny of ultimate repose, when the tensions we repeatedly, and tragically, try to satisfy during life are silenced forever.

Greek literature was perhaps nowhere more helpful to Freud's theoretical progress, than in constructing the theory of the twofold innate drives: One, ἔρως (eros), the unifying and creative drive, and Θάνατος (thanatos), the destructive drive. Both analysts and society resisted this latter concept. Freud himself was only willing to propose the death drive after he found confirmatory analogies in biology, physics, clinical practice, human history, and speculations of the 5th century B.C.E. philosopher Empedocles.

Empedocles believed in two basic forces, ἔρως and ἔρις (eris—strife, contention); the first is a natural propensity to unite the basic elements (air, fire, water, earth); the other, to break them apart. Freud found useful, too, the pre-Socratic philosopher Anaximander's concept of rightful requital (δίκην και τισιν [diken kai tisin]: Justice and requital). This is the principle that every creation, having appropriated—or stolen—materials from the universe for its own birth, must repay the debt, and disintegrate back into the chaos from which it emerged. All things must "pay penalty and retributionto one another for their injustice, according to the disposition of time." Such harmony among disparate sources of evidence gave Freud pleasing and reassuring support to the unwelcome concept of a death instinct.

In his meditations on the death drive, the Hellenophile Freud would not have forgotten the Greek goddess Ἀνάγκη (Ananke), mother of the three Fates, who predetermined the lives and deaths of humans. Ἀνάγκη personified necessity and inevitability, that is, limits, particularly limits to human lives and aspirations. Her birth and that of her brother Χρόνος (Chronos—Time), marked the transition of Χάος (Chaos) into Κόσμος (Cosmos—order, organization). This myth parallels the gradient-driven transformation of simplicity into complexity.

All living creatures, from bacteria to bankers, are fated to contribute to the greater cause. Many non-living complexities too, like whirlpools, hurricanes, hot air streamers and even the dust storms on Mars, all these so-called "organisms of physics," share one great destructive mission: To annihilate *gradients*. "Gradient" is shorthand for any "difference across a distance," a difference, for example, in the temperature, pressure, or chemical concentration of physical bodies or volumes in communication with one another. A gradient is any difference that generates an energy flow. The gradient most important to us is the temperature difference between the sun and cold space, a gradient that for over four and ½ billion years has bathed our planet in a perpetual shower of heat and light.

Even more abhorrent to nature than a vacuum, according to biophysicist Eric Schneider (with Dorian Sagan, 2005), is a gradient. Nature creates complexities to destroy gradients. Complexities consume, shed and degrade more energy, more gradients, than simple systems. Nature exploits her complex children to eliminate the differences that create energy flow. This is the central insight of *open system thermodynamics*.

The science of open system thermodynamics studies complexities like humans and humanity, organizations that are *open* to, and depend upon, infusions of free energy. Open system thermodynamics (also called non-equilibrium thermodynamics or NET) is Darwinian; it extends natural selection to non-living systems. Organized non-living systems, like whirlpools, were selected for their ability to persist and, eventually, reproduce. One of their progeny eventually passed the threshold of life. NET elegantly explains how free energy flow has transformed inanimate matter into biological life. It unifies the living and the dead.

Although complexities, in the statistical sense, are accidents, like throwing snake eyes ten times in a row, they're accidents that ultimately serve the 2nd Law. They help the universe more rapidly consume the heat and light of the stars; disperse concentrations of energy; and spread atomic chaos. As our universe has aged (and, in the ludic leisure of cosmic time, thrown more dice), its free energy has here and there generated progressively complex systems. More complex systems use more energy, or have higher *energy density*, and thus contrive more powerful strategies of energy-capture. Plants evolved to collect energy from sunlight; herbivores, such as deer, from plants; carnivores, such as lions, from herbivores; and omnivores, such as humans, from all the foregoing plus their primordial remains: The fossil fuels.

Schneider compares human beings to lighted candles. Both burn hydrogen-rich compounds. But the candle flame burns brightly and quickly consumes its hydrogen-rich wax. The candle can't extend its life by slowing down the combustion of its fuel. Because it doesn't burn very long or give birth to other candles, the candle doesn't use much energy; consequently, it doesn't advance the 2nd Law very far. It doesn't make much entropy.

In distinction to the candle, however, the human being, pound for pound, is the most prolific entropy maker we know. In the destruction of gradients, we put our fellow creatures to shame. And, working together with them—according to physicist Sean Carroll of the California Institute of Technology—we have *increased* the universe's entropy by four billion times the amount that life's complexity has decreased it. Life, in other words, is doing its cosmic job.

Over the vast passage of astronomical time, the energy flow mandated by these physical laws gives birth to complexities in certain cosmic neighborhoods. In our own Milky Way, gravitational energy organized a gigantic, relatively disorganized dust cloud into a galaxy, stars and solar systems. The flow of stellar and geothermal energies changed Earthly rocks, minerals and gasses into life; single-celled microbes into multicellular plants and animals; simple nervous systems into brains; brains into human minds; and human minds into civilization. The imposition of energy transformed inert substance into complex systems. At the same time, it gave those systems the ability to protract their own existences by gathering, storing and degrading progressively bigger portions of the ambient energy flow.

Sensory organs and the elaborate metabolic structures and cycles of organisms evolved to support and multiply increasingly complex life. I wondered if they had brought about, in parallel with rising complexity, more diverse tensions and progressively exquisite pain. We seem to see this progression as we climb the ladder of complexity: Hurricanes possess a crude sensor for energy differences between the warm water below and the cold air above; amoebas seem to have rudimentary sensation (irritability); porcupines and pachyderms feel pain; but only humans, the most complex of these complex systems, dread their future deaths, suffer *Weltschmerz*, or are tormented by mental illnesses.[1] Here already we can imagine gradient detection evolving into biological and even psychological pain, or tension.

Humans, as the most complex creatures, are the most versatile in detecting, collecting, and reducing gradients, both inside and outside our bodies. We make entropy like crazy. Because we burn our high-grade fuels slowly, by the process known as metabolism, we can extend our entropy-making careers. We inherited evolutionary modifications that shifted a heavy metabolic load to the central nervous system. This made us the cleverest of complexities, able to better see, access, ration and burn energy sources. Nature generously invested our brains with 100 billion neurons and those neurons with 100 trillion connections. She can arrange these connections in more ways than the number of protons in the universe. She made us the most complex of all complexities, investing us with the ingenuity to arm ourselves with the requisite technological weapons to extort from the planet an enormous proportion of its riches. We found vast quantities of free energy and dutifully contrived to burn them. Once we'd ensured our survival, we did not stop there, but expanded ourselves to incredible numbers of new gradient-destroyers. Energy usage and human numbers reinforced each other in a vertiginously accelerating upward spiral, and we spun across the face of the planet, destroying every gradient we could discover.

Thus, by the grace of thermodynamics, we had greatness thrust upon us, that we might serve its diabolic purpose. Humans are, fundamentally, small

[1] Neuroscientist and primatologist Barbara Finley (2015, pp. 28-29) observed that humans feel even certain *physical* pains (for example, labor pain) other animals do not, and in the cases of post-traumatic and post-infectious pain, agonies more intense and persistent than do other animals.

whirlpools of energy dissipation, little engines of gradient destruction. Destructiveness permeates our every cell, through no fault of our own.

Biophysical Entropy and Psychoanalysis

With this much settled, and now in dangerous possession of a little knowledge, I allowed myself to venture beyond the settled science. Is there a residue of the fundamental entropic resistance active in our minds? Might the backwards tug toward chaos (simplicity) and away from complexity have gradually evolved into what I have defined above as psychological tension?

I compared psychological tension to the resistance to re-simplification. I called this resistance "complexity-grit." Then I considered the origin of the four fundamental forces (gravity, electromagnetism, weak and strong nuclear forces). At the birth of our universe, these forces were unified, but as the universe cooled, they diverged into their distinctive natures. Perhaps in a similar way, early in our geological history, maybe before life appeared on Earth, maybe when the so-called "organisms of physics" emerged, complexity-grit budded off into a still more complex entity: *Tension*.

Tension reflects nature's greed for increasingly efficient and durable strategies of energy degradation, strategies that also oppose re-simplification. Nature needed energy-degrading tools that, on the imposition of an energy load, would not, like the candle, just flare up, burn out and dissolve into ashes or melt into lava. She needed these tools to slow and manage the conflagration, channel it into an energy-cycling process (metabolism), build themselves up, consume yet more energy and further protract the consumption for which they had been ordained. Such tools, especially plants and animals, in order to persist, had to be able to capture and hold onto free energy and, above all, recognize ensuing energy deficits.

That recognition, that *aesthesis*, the awareness of an energy deficit, is felt, for example, as hunger, thirst, or fatigue. Tension's first biological expression, one mentioned above, may have been the so-called "irritability" of single-celled organisms. Another early form may have been, as Schneider suggests, the "anticipation" of dawn by the first photosynthetic cells, suspended in the murky surface of the nocturnal ocean. Tension, whatever its form, always represents the pressure to maintain stability and resist perturbations in the system, because these disturbances represent threats to survival and, annoyingly, demands for *work* Work, after all, is the wage of survival and reproduction.

Perhaps tension also reflects the strife between the forces of growth, maintenance and reproduction, on one hand, and the forces of decay, inertia, and dissolution on the other. Tension resides between the opposing drives to live and to die.

With all this in mind, we may begin, finally, to better understand the human aversion to inner and outer reality. When tension first arose, it must have immediately provoked a rudimentary hatred, because tension imposed upon the complexity the irksome tasks of capturing and consuming energy and defying the deathless song of dissolution. Might this be the key to a connection between entropy, an invisible, alien, unfamiliar physical phenomenon, and tension, a sensation as familiar as hunger?

I was already persuaded that deep learning is a kind of self-complexification, that its neglect is a kind of regression to simple-mindedness, and that both the building up and wearing down of mental complexity have profound psychological motives. Tension could now serve as a conceptual hinge between physics and *depth psychology*. Depth psychology is any psychology that postulates unconscious, dynamic psychic activities.

I had also by now understood on at least a basic level that complexity is grounded in physics and, where it concerns living systems, biology as well. I then realized that if I wanted to explain the antipathy for humanist learning in the languages of complexity, tension-reduction, and depth psychology, I would have to unify the biophysical and psychoanalytic concepts of motivation.

Biophysics defines motivation as the impulse to do *work*; and that impulse is provoked by a *stimulus*, any detectable form of energy impinging upon an organism's *receptor* (such as a nerve ending). These concrete biophysical concepts, however, are too narrow for the abstractions of psychoanalysis. Psychoanalysis, like biophysics, studies the (human) organism's relationship to stimuli, but on a more complex level. The psychoanalytic theorist, whose objects of study are mental phenomena, needs a conceptual range and flexibility commensurate with the omnidirectional and horizonless cast of the mind. Accordingly, psychoanalysis might describe the first three phases of the biophysical process—stimulation, detection and signaling—as *tension*.

For millennia, the idea of tension was embedded in a simple theory: We flee pain and pursue pleasure to escape tensions. Even Paleolithic people must have understood this principle, and probably had language to describe human preference and aversion. The ancients did. Aristotle wrote:

Κίνησις ἐστιν ἢ φυγὴ ἢ δίωξις.
[Movement is either fleeing or seeking.]
(*Περι Ψυχης, On the Soul*, Bk. III, Ch. 9, 25)

All "movement" arises from tension and serves tension-reduction. A long line of thinkers reused this simple concept, according to their philosophical needs. For example, Thomas Hobbes (1588-1679) famously thought that the propensity to flee pain and pursue pleasure condemned early humans to lives that were "nasty, poor, solitary, brutish, and short."

Natural philosophers also exercised their minds on the mysteries of motion, the phenomena of things going toward or away from other things. Isaac Newton solved some of these mysteries in the 1680s with his laws of motion. In 1850, Rudolph Clausius, a German physicist, first described the law of *entropy,* the tendency of any closed system to become disordered, to "break down" and come to rest. Newton's first law of motion describes *inertia,* and demonstrates that all objects—like people—possess a certain resistance to influence. Inertia indicates that tension permeates nature. Eventually physicists discovered inertia at the molecular level, then the atomic, subatomic, and finally quantum levels. Similarly, the law of entropy explains Nature's fundamental clash between simplicity and organization.

These discoveries found their way into individual and group psychology.

19th century biologists applied the physical laws of inertia and entropy to living things. Life, too, expresses inertia; despite constant change, from birth, to growth, reproduction and death, life seeks stability and constancy. Eventually, entropy wins, and life breaks down. In 1849, just a year before Clausius introduced entropy, Claude Bernard formalized these biological observations with the concept of *homeostasis,* the regulation (stabilization) of the internal environment.[2] However, just as inertia and entropy entered biology, they entered psychology, and above all the deep psychology of Freudian psychoanalysis.

Born in 1856, Freud, from the ages of 12 to 18, was steeped in the German humanistic educational tradition. This tradition imposed rigorous training in the Greek and Latin languages and their literature, training which familiarized him with all the passions, desires, fears and complex motions of the soul. His education also exposed Freud to the prevailing science, a positivistic, rationalistic, deterministic and empirical approach to the human mind. So, in

[2] Not named as such until 1926, by Walter Cannon.

the 1880s, as he contemplated the structure and function of the mind, the psychoanalytic pioneer borrowed an idea from the physicist, philosopher of nature, and founder of experimental psychology, Gustav Fechner. In 1873 Fechner identified a homeostatic "principle of the tendency to stability," the tendency of living things to avoid or to shed excitations. For example, the amoeba, touching a toxic molecule, retracts its pseudopod; the rabbit flees the pursuing fox; the sexually aroused orangutan copulates. Improvising on Fechner, Freud conceived a *principle of constancy,* which became the cornerstone of his psychological theory:[3] The psychical apparatus (mind) tends to keep its quantity of excitation at as low a level—or as constant a level—as possible. He renamed this concept throughout his life, calling it the principle of neuronal inertia; pleasure principle; unpleasure principle; and Nirvana principle. Some of these variations postulate absolute reduction of excitation, while others suggest a constantly moderated level of excitation.

Freud often interpreted the biophysical need for constancy as a modification of the more fundamental tendency toward immediate and complete tension-discharge.[4] That fundamental tendency reflects the entropic drive to sustain our combustion of energy, our destructiveness. It's the drive to exceed the candle. The principle of constancy is the central force behind the more general phenomenon of *tension-evasion*.

I use "evasion" to emphatically evoke its defensive psychological purpose. By avoiding the 'work of life' we strive for biological or thermal equilibrium, a form of death. A better life, a more complex life, a life more conducive to both happiness and survival, however, comes only to those who tolerate life's tensions and embrace the work those tensions demand, especially the tensions of self-knowledge.

Tension Avoidance and Education

If we didn't expect our present efforts to save us future work or suffering, we wouldn't work much.

This simple principle regulates human behavior and all biological action. G. K. Zipf, American linguist and statistician, carefully studied our aversion

---

[3] First mentioned in a letter to his friend, Wilhelm Fliess, dated Jan. 1, 1896 (*S.E.* I, p. 389).

[4] Freud understood the constancy principle to be secondary to the inertia principle, a modification demanded by "the exigencies of life" (*S. E.*, I, 297).

to work and published his important conclusions over seventy years ago in *Human Behavior and the Principle of Least Effort* (1949). Scientists already knew Zipf for his eponymous Law, a mathematical power law (a functional relationship between two quantities) that determines proportions of word usage. He had shown that the universal tendency to communicate with the least effort determines the proportion of certain words used by a language community.

In testimony to its validity, in 1965, Benoit Mandelbrot, Polish-born French-American mathematician, complexity theorist and developer of fractals, appropriated Zipf's Power Law to make the Zipf-Mandelbrot Law, a probability relationship still used in modern complexity science. Zipf's later book on *Least Effort* generalized his Power Law, showing that people, animals, plants and even machines, in pursuing all their natural or artificial purposes, seek the path of least resistance.

That so many people work hard all their lives seems to contradict Zipf. The contradiction, however, is only apparent. No matter how hard we work, that work, as Zipf pointed out, always avoids even harder work in the present or future, work such as living hand to mouth or the work of enduring shame. This capacity of living things to anticipate, or expect, future work-demands made Zipf refine his theory into *the principle of least average rate of **expectable** effort.*

To harmonize Zipf's principle with depth psychology I will substitute for his principle, the "*principle of least* (*average rate of expectable*) *tension*," with tension defined as a demand for psychological work. The principle implies the need to reduce the most expectable tension in the shortest time. However, the human power to obliterate perception obliges us to even further refine that concept—with apologies for the ponderous phraseology—into *the principle of least average rate of expectable **perceptible** tension.*

Here we find the heart of *paideia*, the essence of the humanist university: The development of the skills needed to defy this principle, to tolerate psychological tensions through discipline, work and mental growth.

Aristotle's guiding educational principle, like Plato's, was to make not only good citizens but, nota bene, good philosophers. This creed was hard to popularize because it burdens suffering humans by obligating then to cultivate their minds. It shames those who evade tensions, who would not or could not delay certain gratifications, or acknowledge and contemplate unpleasant realities. Humanist education rooted in classical languages was once the most emphatic public endorsement of the obligation to oppose evasion and grow the mind.

The decline and fall of classical education signified to me a hidden group hatred of the higher powers of the mind, a social and historical expression of the death wish.

But isn't our aversion to work almost genetically, even entropically ordained? In one sense, I concede, the work of mental growth—education—is itself an effort to minimize or evade other tension and work. Education obeys Zipf's principle. We enrich our minds for the same reason we ignore or distort distressing realities: To lessen tensions, or at least our awareness of them. My laborious advocacy, then, seems to have miscarried—except for two considerations. The first is social: Classical education and psychoanalysis, by urging self-awareness, defend society against mental death, the "bad" equilibrium of universal tension-evasion. The second is individual: Not all evasions are equal. Some are cheap: The effort they require—the few neural depolarizations required to momentarily misdirect attention—is trivial compared to the magnitude of the tensions (such as panic or self-loathing) they instantly obliterate. Others are expensive: The effort they require—decades of solitary study and reflection—is more commensurate with the tensions (panic, perhaps, or self-loathing) these toilsome "evasions" were intended to minimize. For example, delusion is much cheaper than the modification of the painful inner or outer reality the delusion replaced with so little effort.

Cheap evasions merely dissipate tensions through easy action, or obliterate them by mental defense. Expensive evasions channel energy into *structuralization*, that is, the formation, refinement and fortification of mental *structures*. Mental structures are systems that reliably perform functions such as memory, assessment or anticipation. Humanist education, especially an education in Greek, is one of those expensive evasions.

Finally, we can make out the scope of the problem, and can begin to see why thermodynamics and complexity theory might partly explain the fall of the university. When the university discarded its compulsory classical curricula in 19th and 20th centuries, it performed, on behalf of the people, a cheap evasion. It lifted—with little administrative strain—an intellectual burden from the backs of young people. It lightened prospective students' social and vocational worries by offering job training instead. It was inexpensive to academic leaders, because society's approval negated their sense of dereliction. Job training is indeed a labor-intensive evasion, but an evasion much less strenuous than the one for which it was exchanged: The psychological responsibility that the classical academy had formerly imposed not only upon the student, but also on the faculty, administration and entire public. By forsaking that responsibility, the academy dispersed the tensions recently rising between itself and the public, and enhanced its income stream, a reliable reducer of perceptible institutional tension.

This idea implies that psychological forces build up or tear down mental growth and self-knowledge. They strengthen us to tolerate, or alternatively, weaken us to evade, tensions. If evasive forces ruined the university, perhaps they ruin other sectors of society, too, and have done so throughout history. To unveil evasion's recurring sociohistorical roles could confirm its universality.

Homer, as we'll see below, has vividly portrayed the forces that provoke evasiveness, the crucial factor in humanity's self-destruction.

2.

The Tyranny of Envy-Fear

We'll now consider envy-fear. Humanity's evasion of this complex emotion brought about our present catastrophe. We can't escape its tyranny. This chapter will demonstrate that envy-fear haunts every corner of human life, from the 8th century BCE world of the Homeric imagination, to the real world of the 21st century autocratic surge.

Let's recall, from the Introduction, that envy is the human death-drive deflected outward. Envy—as Chapter One showed—helps Nature prolong her children's lives, that they might persist in destroying gradients by burning energy.

Fear of envy is different. *Envy-fear* arises from the dim discernment of suicidal pressure, the endopsychic recognition of the raw death drive. Most, though not all infants escape this unendurable condition.

As infants, we survive the death drive in two basic ways: We turn it away from ourselves, outward, as destructive envy; or, in a paranoid strategy, we disown the drive by expelling it and harboring it in the mother. By this tactic, the baby transforms an internal threat into an external danger, that is, an infanticidal mother. Hansel's and Gretel's stepmother envies her well-loved and well-fed stepchildren. She wants to destroy them. She represents the babies' projected wickedness, and becomes a murderous predator. In self-defense, the children must destroy her. So, Gretel guiltlessly shoves the witch, the stepmother (mother) substitute, into the oven, and cooks her. Like so many other fairy tales, *Hansel and Gretel* conquers paranoid envy-fear.

This mental expedient, the projection of an internal threat into an external object, modulates what would have been perpetual panic into severe apprehension. But it fails on a social level, because envy-fear forces its subjects to appease imaginary menaces by self-abnegation. Then they envy those like the Grimm's stepmother/witch, whom they imagine to be immune to such extortion, and wish their destruction.[1] We'll observe this oscillation in

[1] That's one reason Gretel's symbolic matricide delights children. When the siblings arrive home, in triumph, they find their stepmother has (also) died.

a remarkable episode from *The Iliad.*

Bronze Age aristocracy passed away 500 years before Homer reimagined it in the 700's BCE. It seems to have been a tightly hierarchized, sclerotic, paranoid institution. It brutally proscribed envious irruptions from commoners, to whom, in any case, such outbursts were almost unthinkable. But neither envy nor the fear it evoked escaped the great poet's penetration, and he gave voice to them both. In the excerpt to follow, Homer hands the megaphone to Thersites, the ugliest, most ill-figured—presumably, the most envious—among the soldiers. Thersites' explosion recalls the poem's original conflict, Agamemnon's envy of Achilles, the greatest of the Achaean warriors.

Between a foreshortened life of rapine, conquest and man-slaying glory, or a long pastoral life of tending his orchards and herding his goats, Achilles famously chose the brief and glorious, and found himself on the battlefield in Troy. His general, Agamemnon, has just humiliated the fleet-footed hero by commandeering Achilles' "wife" Briseis, a young woman Achilles had abducted. To teach Agamemnon a lesson, Achilles refuses to fight. As the hero sulks in his hut, strumming his lyre, Greek casualties mount. Meanwhile, Thetis, Achilles' goddess mother, tearfully reproaches her father Zeus for breaking his promise to her son. Zeus detests domestic unpleasantness, so he sends a dream to Agamemnon, urging him back into battle. Zeus knows this will cause even heavier Achaean (Greek) casualties and shame Agamemnon, who still had no military victory to show for nine years of Greek blood and misery.

Deluded by the dream, Agamemnon called a general council. He expected the deliberations to provoke a blood thirst for battle.

As the council sits quietly, waiting for the leaders to speak, Θερσίτης (Thersites) begins to shout.[2] Thersites was lame in one foot, bandy-legged, and stooped. His head was deformed, sparsely covered with short hairs. His shoulders were rounded and curled around his chest. This misbegotten figure bellowed:

> "Son of Atreus [meaning Agamemnon], now what's the matter? You want even more? Your huts are full of bronze and women, spoils we picked out for you, first of all, whenever we captured a citadel. Or maybe you're thirsting for gold, lucre that one of the horse-taming Trojans

[2] Thersomai (θέρσομαι) means "I am burning."

> would bring you from Ilium as a ransom for his son, whom I or some other Achaean has bound and led away? Or do you maybe lust to fornicate with yet another girl, whom you'll keep for yourself? No, it's unseemly for a captain to bring yet more evil upon the sons of the Achaeans!
>
> (Turning to the council:) "Soft fools! Despicable things of shame! Women of Achaea, no longer Men! Let's go home with our ships and leave this fellow here in Troy to contemplate his prizes, so that he might understand whether or not we are of any use to him, this man who has dishonored Achilles, a man better far than him: For he has stolen and clings to Achilles' prize [Briseis] by his own arrogant act.
>
> (Turning back to Agamemnon:) "We can be sure there is no wrath still in Achilles' heart, or that he cares anymore, otherwise you would have worked your insolence for the last time" (*Iliad*, II, 227-242, translation mine).

Springing to Agamemnon's defense, Odysseus berates Thersites and flogs him on the shoulders and back with his gold staff, raising a bloody welt; Thersites cowers beneath the blows and cries. Everyone laughs.

This passage is well-known. Plato, Shakespeare, Hegel, Nietzsche, Marx, Simone Weil and others have cited it to make their respective philosophical, sociopsychological, or literary points. Some suggest that Thersites expresses the soldiers' unspoken opposition to this frivolous war, waged only to avenge a cuckold (Menelaus, husband of Helen); and, by drawing Thersites as ugly and degraded, the author dissociates himself from this anti-aristocratic attack.

Others call this episode an expression of the impotence of rationality (Thersites' justified complaints) in the face of power (the ruling aristocrats in Troy). A third group, with more mindsight, recognizes Thersites as the avatar of envy.

Hegel made this observation: "[Thersites'] envy… is the thorn which he has to carry in his flesh. And the undying worm that gnaws him is the tormenting consideration that his excellent views and vituperations remain absolutely without result in the world. But our satisfaction at the fate of Thersites may also have its sinister side" (*Lectures on the Philosophy of History*).

Hegel's last sentence, perhaps sinister in itself, is puzzling: Can that satisfaction have a non-sinister side? Still, Hegel has discovered the sinistrality in this passage, and we might profitably probe it. But it serves our present purpose to note the Greeks' scorn for poor Thersites, onto whose dehumanized figure they have all projected their own envy, while ridiculing his courage in speaking the unspeakable. Thersites, briefly, defied envy-fear.

Envy of Education in History

I've touched upon the general factor that vocationalized classical Humanism out of the academy: The culture's fainting tension-tolerance. Now, having begun our examination of envy-fear, I can address a more specific cause: Modern culture's intolerance of inequality. This intolerance aggravated envy and, consequently, envy-fear, arresting overall mental growth.

In the past, powerful subgroups mistreated weaker subgroups almost with impunity. This was an evil, but so was its remedy, the long crusade to exterminate envy. This seemed the natural outcome of population growth. With that, came more intensive local, then regional, and finally global interaction. These trends intensified *social propinquity*, that is, peoples' closeness in status and domestic habits. Social propinquity pushed our differences in each other's faces. This fanned the flames of social envy.

Envious resentment gradually preoccupied consciousness. Increasingly, like Nietzsche's stereotypical Christians, the commoners weaponized their "slave morality:" they shamed, guilt-tripped, and eventually intimidated the enviable. This drew the privileged into a competition for moral rectitude and prestige, obliging everyone to avoid actions, words, and even thoughts that implied superiority or exclusiveness. This contest, especially over the last 150 years, shifted political and cultural influence on previously disenfranchised groups. But not even that promising trend placated the public mind. Envy is implacable.

Until the early twentieth century it was mostly Western aristocrats who learned classical languages, literature and thought. The learning and teaching were sometimes desultory, of course. But over the centuries Greek and Latin educated many of those who were, thought themselves to be, hoped to become, or were hoped by their parents to become leaders of humankind, exemplars of honor, refinement, and wisdom. Both nobility and commoners admired these aspirations and qualities. But commoners justly feared and hated the nobility for their exclusive political, social, and economic advantages.

So, group memory still associates the Classics with aristocrats, those whose presumption of superiority insulted the common people. Education in Greek and Latin, guilty by long association, had cultivated an enemy. The adversary was at first small, weak, and disorganized, but grew stronger year by year until by the twentieth century it had become invincible. Classics' nemesis became the middle class, an outgrowth of society's thickening. As the middle class gained power, it insisted upon, and finally acquired, a right to rise.

Modern consciousness perhaps dimly remembers the hatred commoners nursed against thousands of years of aristocratic scorn and insults to their latent dignity. There was once a nobility which, on a cruel caprice, could commandeer the husbandman's property, debauch his wife, or torture and kill his kith and kin. Dostoevsky's *The Brothers Karamazov* tells a true-to-life fable of aristocratic sadism:

A former general had settled into his life as the lord of a manor, home to a thousand serfs and hundreds of hunting hounds. One day a small boy, child of a serf, threw a stone and injured the paw of the master's favorite dog. The gentryman locked the boy overnight in an outhouse. The next morning, he gathered his feudal family in the field, and ordered the boy's mother to stand in front of the assembly. The boy was removed from his prison, stripped naked, and ordered to run. "At him," the master said to his dogs, which caught and tore apart their small quarry, an edifying scene for the great man's servants and their families.

Outrages like this sowed seeds of bitterness over the millennia. For centuries the masses were like victims of the primal scene. They bristled at the embrace between the Classics and the aristocracy. Knowledge of Homer, Plato and Virgil were the pillars upon which inherited Privilege had fortified its mind—at least that part of the aristocratic mind unravaged by *pleonexia,* the morbid, mindless greed for which Thersites had denounced Agamemnon. *Paideia* had become another unattainable credential for acceptance into that association of superior men and (a few) superior women from which most commoners were hopelessly excluded. Classical studies, then, like the aristocrats themselves, stank in the nostrils of the middle class.

Classicists were blamable; for they had too often scorned the uneducated masses, and every insolent gesture refreshed the commoners' rancor. Every new insult reawakened the feeling of exclusion humans find so difficult to pardon.

Commoners passed it down from generation to generation. and their children's children seethed with their ancestors' hatred, as they were absorbed into, and rose with, the middle class. Narrowing economic and political gaps made the masses yet more intolerant of insult and prejudice.

Rising commoners relished the pleasure of sneering, all the way to the bank, at those who once had sneered at them. They tasted, and relished the aristocratic delights so long denied them. Meanwhile, their *ressentiment*, reinforced by private envy, fueled a deathless campaign of revenge.[3] Just as a new regime, intoxicated with unaccustomed power, brutally culls its former oppressors and demolishes their political structures, cultural monuments and symbols, so the new middle class smashed the pillars of the aristocracy. And one of these pillars, particularly from the Renaissance on, was Classical training.

The vengefulness of the excluded, toward which our egalitarian spirit is so sympathetic, is what killed Classical education. The old university ideal—the enhancement of the self, higher education's contribution to mental growth—had collided with the rising demand for economic and social leveling, that is, a more equitable distribution of frustrations.

Within this noble crusade, however, envy concealed itself, corrupting all life's treasures. Social thickening had raised into view the Utopia of Universal Inclusion. This irritated envy back to life, and legitimized its malicious satisfaction. And one of envy's deepest satisfactions was to ruin the humanist academy and corrupt the matrix of great minds past, present and to be.

Wasn't this the satisfaction of the imaginary Achilles, as he listened to the death wails of his Greek allies being cut to ribbons by Trojan swords? It was spite, gaining nothing for its subject, while destroying others. By singing the rage of Achilles, Homer was educating his audience to envy. He was saying, "You'd fear spite more, if you knew your own better."

Envy-Fear in the Modern World

But to recognize one's own spite entails tension-tolerance, in the interest of mental growth. Modernity, however, chose an ethos of mental ease and indifference to wasted human potential. The value once placed on psychological development galled the great collective, which gradually habituated to tension-evasion and mental stagnation.

Hand in hand with evasion of envious spite went an evasion of envy-fear. This needs clarification. Envy and fear of envy are different phases of the

[3] Backed-up envy and hatred, sometimes transformed into self-abasement. Please see Glossary.

same phenomenon, like ice and steam. Envy flips into fear of retaliatory envy. This retaliatory envy, moreover, is less the envy of others, than of our own.

I'll explain this. Envy-fear is largely fear of one's own envy, projected onto others. Our own envy thirsts for the others' suffering. We feel guilty about this thirst, and expect retribution. We ease our apprehension with preemptive punishment, that is, self-inflicted misfortune. That's how suffering calms some people down. The impulse to expiatory self-harm, together with the raw death-drive itself, promotes self-destructiveness in individuals, nations, and humanity.

The dynamics of self-destructiveness are little discussed outside of psychoanalysis. It must by now be clear, however, that public reticence on the topic is in itself self-destructive: It makes envy fester. Only a culture that publicly acknowledges envy can detoxify private envy. Such a culture has the mental security to weave protective myths that shield its members from envy-fear. These mythologies constitute a social defense system.[4]

Remarkably, only one writer has examined the defense systems with which societies manage envy-fear: In his magisterial study of social envy, published in 1966, anthropologist-psychologist Helmut Schoeck described the defense systems that allow cultures to manage the envy excited by superiority, advantage or inequality. Schoeck calls these strategies "envy-suppression." Envy-suppression is a cultural attitude or practice that discourages envious attacks and shields the enviable against the menaces of the envious. Some examples are the idea of an innate cultural elite (aristocracy); traditional or religious sanctions against envious behavior; religious concepts of Fate; or even secular ideas of good and bad luck. Fate and luck randomize talent and prosperity; this exonerates the talented or prosperous individual.

Cultures with weak envy-suppression, like many forager cultures, cannot change because they proscribe inequality. Cultures with strong envy-suppression evolve. They allow gifted individuals to innovate. The community prospers, or suffers, from their innovations. The innovators themselves, safe from malicious retaliation, can enjoy the social, financial and political rewards occasioned by their success. Humanity may thank envy-suppression for its literature, art, music, even mental growth, but must blame it for our world-destroying technology, wealth and population growth.

---

[4] A social defense system is formed through unconscious cooperation among group members to reinforce their private internal defenses against anxiety and guilt.

Envy-fear—not envy-suppression—prevailed in early nomadic societies. Nomads' social propinquity condemned them to perpetual mutual vigilance. Any tribal member who gained the slightest advantage, perhaps merely an extra yam or a longer hoe, risked envious retaliation. Revenge commonly assumed the form of an "evil eye," a sometimes-lethal device of social control.[5] New tools, and, perhaps above all, refinements or expansions of consciousness, could not be born in this poisonous atmosphere.

Envy-suppression protected inequalities, widened socioeconomic gaps and spawned agriculturally based, rigidly hierarchized, aristocratic societies.[6] The privileged, of course, often abused these imbalances and the underprivileged, accordingly, enviously hated them. So, societies curbed malice by canonizing ideological or religious condemnation of envy, or legitimizing unequal attainments with "luck" or "fate." These were social defense systems; they gave breathing space to personal excellence. These emerging aristocratic cultures defused envy with theories of an innate cultural elite; they dispersed envy by evacuating (projecting) it into their gods. They then reduced their own envy-fear of those spiteful deities by appeasing them with sacrifice, prayer, or exaltation. When Homer opens *The Iliad* by beseeching the deity (ἄειδε θεὰ "sing, O Muse"), he deflects his audience's envy from himself by affecting to channel the goddess's poetic genius; he placates her, at the same time, by making a rhetorical bow to her ingenuity.

Modern industrial and technological society, heir to agricultural aristocracy, further enhanced protections for the innovative and diligent. Among the most effective were *positive* (government-established) *law* and the sanctioned right to pursue wealth, influence, and happiness. Such strategies restrained or appeased enough envy to unleash collective learning, especially in science and technology.

Though modern cultures in such ways restrained, distracted, hoodwinked or appeased, they never extinguished, envy. Whenever they blocked envy's direct expression, envy found roundabout gratifications. One common detour, as Kierkegaard observed, is invidiousness, the incitement of envy. As modern society strengthened envy-suppression, envious members abused that

---

[5] Described in Cannon's (1942) classic paper on "voodoo death"; Burrell's (1963) study of "curse death"; and Mathis' (1964) case report on a curse death in modern society.

[6] These appeared after an intermediate horticultural phase, during which foragers "gardened" in forest clearings.

protection, often by provoking envy in others to obscure their own. Invidiousness flourishes today, for example, in the ostentation of smart-phones, cyber-popularity, trophy wives and children, and moral grandstanding.

In moral grandstanding envious spite discovered an unimpeachable indulgence. Historically, spitefulness bided its time until society could contrive respectable strategies for stripping privileged humans of their special gratifications. It jumped unnoticed onto the bandwagon of social justice. Sincere social activists now worked side-by-side, unaware, with expanding numbers of envious confederates seeking to gratify malice under the flag of egalitarianism.

That confederacy is devoted to helping one another disavow their envy, its malevolence, and the penitence envy evokes, by performing rituals of loving kindness toward victims of exclusion. Meanwhile, they attack included people, justifying themselves with the exculpatory credo that the fortunate deserve to be hated and despoiled.

Again, crowding and social propinquity obliged society to adopt more rigorous but ultimately, unsustainable social controls. Egalitarianism grew more imperious, and envy suppression weaker, particularly from the 17th century on. Following the path of least tension, society legitimized the malicious passion, disguising it as moral outrage. This was easy to do, because conscience garrisons the retaliatory force that terrorizes the mind. So, envy suppression evolved into moral pain—guilt and shame. And once begun, this strategy of social control too intensified uncontrollably.

Political correctness, our name for this moral tide, overflowed the banks of reason and prudence, and swept more and more of us into its flood, spreading its immoderate doctrine throughout the population. As we washed out certain inequalities, we became intolerant of those inequalities that remained. As culture enfranchised certain outsider groups (such as women and blacks), others (like the transgendered) further back in the queue of respectability, advanced one by one into the sunshine of public sympathy. More and more, we normalized behavior once considered abnormal. The judgment that once devalued those disenfranchised groups and reinforced their exclusion by censuring their unusual behaviors, was censured in its turn.[7]

For their own part, the modern privileged, like the academic cognoscenti,

---

[7] Censoriousness continues to intensify (Heller, 2016).

fell prey to the guilt, or shame, and above all, fear, of having been prosperous, protected or indulged. For example, baby boom teenagers, the children of unprecedented prosperity, of the diligence of the generations whose blood, sweat and tears had paved their golden paths, lived uneasily with the unearned blessings which had befallen them. Being "free riders," they feared the recriminations of the third world, or civilized underclass, or their own consciences. They had enjoyed a privileged existence that, *in unconscious fantasy*, had enraged the unfortunate, both present and past. Young boomers quickly learned to sedate this anxiety with drugs or expiate their guilt with the reaction formations so richly available in social activism. Schoeck, perhaps borrowing from Nietzsche, describes their condition as "bad conscience."

Bad conscience impaired the judgment of some advantaged people; envy-fear, others. Both flew to social justice and its mission of appeasement. They became, or feigned being, until they actually became, more mediocre in qualities or capabilities. In this way modern society gradually restored the stultifying conditions of Paleolithic cultures, this time on a moralistic plane.

The new morality hamstrung humanist education. Humanism promotes the individual's dignity, worth and capacity for self-realization through reason. Society became uneasily aware that this aspiration raised some people and lowered others. In the zero-sum contest for human worth, a gain for one individual or group entails a corresponding loss for another. Those worthy under the old value system were the few who pursued humanistic goals and had talent, sometimes wealth, enough to reach them.

In *Human Dignity* (2011), George Kateb, Princeton Emeritus Professor of Politics, confronted this contest for human worthiness. He argues that cultural praise for mental breadth, depth and foresight once distinguished the upper levels of ancient culture. This praise unavoidably degraded the common people. *Paideia* exalted humanity's self-conscious capacity to improve itself, a capacity denied to other living things. It glorified the educated, but depreciated the uneducated masses, without respecting their practical contributions. The old value channeled prestige, privileges and wealth to the talented or resolute, and generated formidable social tensions. Society came to interpret this system, with some justice, as exclusionary and cruel. This new ethic gradually overpowered the talented and educated. Now, resentment from below, and guilt and envy-fear from above, tormented the wise and disciplined. So, the academy deconsecrated mental excellence to dodge resentment, guilt and envy-fear.

Then, to stave off self-incrimination for betraying their ideals, academics assumed a lofty posture of civic sensitivity and accountability. This persona silenced their own and public censure while provoking the secret contempt of both.

As Kateb observes, the western transvaluation of values flattered the self-regard of the masses, and eased the tensions generated by the traditional intellectual hierarchy.

But it's had disastrous consequences. By de-stratifying human worthiness and distributing unearned material and psychological compensations, the species has ruined the environment and degraded human dignity. If we want to save civilization, Kateb suggests, we must respect higher abilities even if permanent disparities in worthiness frustrate our deep egalitarian urge to ease cultural strain.

Today, fourteen years after Kateb's book appeared, envy-fear, more than ever, paralyzes education. Today's university even excuses Classical majors from Latin and Greek. How did we get here?

Schoeck, in the mid-1960's, detected envious attacks on advantaged people disguised as social justice. He realized that humanity was gradually restoring envy-fear as the lever of social policy.

Relentless as he was, however, in unmasking envy's influence on human life, Schoeck failed to fully tap the richness of his subject. He respected psychoanalysis, but seemed either not to have read or understood its then-recently published text on envy, Melanie Klein's 1957 monograph, *Envy and Gratitude*. Klein showed that envy originated not, as Schoeck supposed, in sibling rivalry, but in the newborn's complex reactions to the mother's beneficence and her erotic bond with the father. His unfamiliarity with Klein made Schoeck underestimate envy's distorting influence on reality-testing, our ability to assess the authenticity of our perceptions.

He did indeed demonstrate that the fashionable socialist project to create harmony was futile, rooted as it was in the illusion that envy could be eliminated. Yet Schoeck failed to realize that market capitalism, rooted in the illusion that envy could be ignored, was also rotten with wishful thinking. Unfettered capitalism promotes the illusion that Earth is a cornucopia. Schoeck seems not to have recognized that the omnipotent fantasy which sustains capitalism would disastrously expand demand (population).

Schoeck also did not consider that centuries of restraining envy would fatigue the public will. Nor did he contemplate, this being outside his purview, the unacknowledged strain of crowding, and erosion of collective self-respect. These factors—wishful thinking, public fatigue, demographic strain, and collective shame—expedited envy's final takeover. But he would not have been surprised to see envy-fear become the supreme tribunal in every cultural decision, even as humanity gratified the destructiveness of envy by ruining its own habitat.

While Schoeck was exposing envy-fear in the mid-'60's, Kleinian psychoanalysts—spreading from England into North and South America—were showing how envy evoked that which they called persecutory or paranoid anxiety. This refers back to the infant's dread of imaginary retaliatory attacks by mother or father on the baby's body and internal organs, provoked by the baby's envious fantasy-attacks on their bodies.

Schoeck, we recall, had also identified "bad conscience." Its sufferers believe that their own pleasures entail others' pain. Bad conscience corresponds to Klein's depressive anxiety, the agonizing guilt the child suffers over its enviously greedy mental attacks on the mother. The Kleinians thus discovered a causal link between envy and depressive anxiety. So Schoeck seems to have recognized, albeit in social terms, what psychoanalysts call the two psychotic anxieties.[8] These are the fears, as Bion had earlier realized, that drive people into irrational, but reassuring, cooperatives. These often comprise whole nations or cultures; he called them basic assumption groups.[9] Today's whole world is a basic assumption group.

Envy, Psychotic Anxieties, and Self-Envy

The confluence of psychoanalysis and sociology on the disturbing topic of envy occurred at an apparent turning of the cultural tide, after which depth psychology sank in public esteem. So, in the 1960's, 2700 years after Homer first set a poetic mirror before his community, humanity began its final, fatal

---

[8] The psychotic anxieties are the so-called *persecutory* (sometimes called paranoid-schizoid) or *depressive anxieties* of infancy that live on in adults, usually only visible in psychotic states. In the term "psychotic anxiety," "psychotic" refers both to the extravagantly unrealistic nature—relative to *external reality*—and to the terrifying quality of the phantasies associated with these anxieties.

[9] The *basic assumption* is a shared group fantasy, magical and omnipotent, of salvation and gratification. These are grossly unrealistic, psychopathological social defense systems, like a shared fantasy of limitless growth. See Glossary for further explanation.

flight from mindsight.[10] Society's fitful, reluctant, but advancing self-awareness—the momentum of which had carried it forward for fifty years after *paideia* disappeared—stopped and reversed.

Psychologists, psychiatrists, and psychoanalysts in the 1950's and 1960's seemed to have converged on the deeper problem of envy. The role of envy in learning disabilities (Daniels, 1964-65), mental illness (Sullivan, 1956), and a variety of interpersonal disturbances (Farber, 1961; Heider, 1958; Reisman, 1950) attracted widespread attention. And I have already mentioned Klein's pathbreaking 1957 monograph. Western society was now glimpsing the demons of childhood Hell, goblins gratefully forgotten by most adults. From the corner of its wary eye, I believe, the public saw Freud, Klein, Schoeck, Bion and the others shining a light into the tenebrous depths of envy. I think that the unveiling of this recess of our minds provoked an invisible, silent dread. Envy frightens people because it makes them savage their nearest and dearest. These, then, in the enviers' minds, suffer pitiably. This evokes anguished guilt (depressive anxiety). At other times, the victims shape-shift into enraged enemies, evoking terror (paranoid anxiety).

If these explanations strike you as fanciful or, at least, personally inapplicable, you may wish to recall the nightmares or night terrors of your own childhoods. Nightmares are irruptions of psychotic anxieties. By recalling, if you can, the witches, monsters or formless presences that terrorized your childhood sleep, you might more vividly understand why we work so hard, sacrifice so much, and suffer so grievously at our own hands to keep psychotic anxieties at bay.[11]

---

[10] The Rockefeller commission on population gave its report in the early 1970's. Its conclusion, that the U. S. was already overcrowded, was an unusual instance of group self-awareness. Self-awareness raised fears, in this case fears of coercive limits on reproductive choice, equivalent in the unconscious to vengeful attacks on reproductive organs. The public seems to have evaded this paranoid anxiety and the foregrounding of its overgrowth by doubling down on growth. Both limitless growth and stubbornness are *manic defenses* against envy and the psychotic anxieties.

[11] Snow White's envious mother, in Grimm's original version, orders a huntsman to kill her daughter, cut out her lungs and liver, and bring the organs back to her to eat. In the *Juniper Tree,* the stepmother decapitates the stepson, and boils the body for the unknowing father's dinner. Hansel and Gretel, hungry enough to eat a house (a maternal body), barely escape cannibalism by the house's owner, a witch (the personified mother).

The human imagination, also, as Klein discovered, harbors a vengeful breast. Native American Utes visualized giant female Siats, called bapets, with huge breasts filled

It would be impossible to live with ourselves, were we defenseless against these two fears, the envy that evokes them, and the nightmares to which they give rise. But most of us, as I said earlier, manage to distort or forget them; and when forgetfulness fails, we fall back upon social defense systems, described above.

Although this private/public defense apparatus typically suppresses the two psychotic anxieties, the peace of mind thus acquired has a cost. It weakens the group's contact with reality, cripples its ability to learn from experience, and stunts its mental growth. Indeed, rational optimism and the fantasy of perpetual growth, enabled by technology, bewitched late 20th century society. We fell under a spell.

Society's advancing distortion of reality, meant to sooth the group, instead spawned contingent envy, provoking the very terrors it was fleeing.[12] Let's see how this works, using the case of humanity's mismanagement of its overgrowth.

Goffman (1963) and Milgram (1977/2010) pointed out decades ago that crowding, having first beset the city, later the suburb, and eventually the countryside, had overloaded the human capacity for interpersonal attention, recognition, trust, and commitment.[13] "Overload," a term from systems science, is any massive stimulation that overwhelms a system's adaptive functions, forcing it to ignore long-term well-being in the interest of immediate survival. Overloading, I believe, began thousands of years ago. Society escaped overload panic by numbing itself to the growing discomforts of crowding. The late 20th century, trying to survive, closed its eyes to uncontrolled fertility, a disintegrating habitat, and the futility of technology. These massive self-deceptions increasingly warped its perception of reality.

And global self-deception intensified envy. Here's how: We all feel a little shame when fatigue dissuades us from exercise, or hunger, from dieting. Even after trivial acts of cheating like these we envy honesty more, and wish more to corrupt others, to diminish the sum of honesty in the world and

---

with poison milk. Siats eat the hungry children they treacherously suckle. Odysseus, who raided the milk and cheese-filled cave (bodily interior) of the single-eyed (nipple) Cyclops, paid for his plunder with cannibalized comrades. And there is, of course, Jack's giant, who "smelled the blood of an Englishman".

[12] *Contingent* envy. Please see Glossary.

[13] Anthropologist Robin Dunbar (1992) postulated that the size of the neocortex limits our social universe to about 150 people, a figure thereafter called "Dunbar's number."

thereby decrease our envy of it. How much more do we aggravate shame and envy when we twist reality into a never-never-Land of Invulnerability? Every new self-deception more deeply damages self-respect; cheating breeds cheating;[14] lying is a slippery slope.[15]

Analogously, we devalued the generative ideals that once united us in the aspiration for mental growth, because they made us toil for self-respect. Dim awareness of this dodge shamed us. Shame exacerbated our envy of self-respect. Then the culture, having come full circle, but freighted with heightened envy, spawned frightening infantile phantasies in both society as a whole and its members.

So, in this story, when depth psychology ventured into envy, it ventured too far, and society shrank from its enlightenment. Had the group respected the inevitability and power of human malice, it might not have so mindlessly fled its psychotic fears. Then, instead of lurching further into suicidal expansion as it did after 1970, society might have restrained reproduction and immigration. It could have thinned itself out, reduced the pressures of crowding, re-expanded open space, and allowed the natural world to rejuvenate. It could then have pursued a culture of mental growth and contact with reality, the activities promoted by Classical Humanism.

Tragedy, perhaps the most emphatically educational component of Classical Humanism, recognized the primary cause of human envy: Exclusion. Shakespeare's Hamlet and Sophocles' Oedipus personify the rage of the excluded. Exclusionary copulation lies at the heart of *The Iliad*'s narrative: Paris cuckolded Menelaus and sailed away with Helen to Troy. Greece burned the great citadel, the adulterers' love nest, to the ground.

Helpless exclusion, as the Introduction explained, lights the fuse of envy. It provokes fantasies of attack in both infants and adults: Attacks on parts of their own or others' bodies, commonly the breast, vagina, penis, or mouth. Why these? These are the anatomical "copula," the tools of copulation, the instruments of bodily linking. Attacks on these structures are more vicious in the disturbed infant or adult. But envy tempts people to attack all interactions: Interactions between others; between others and ourselves; or even between their own inner voices as they converse and procreate insights. Envy, from which no human being is exempt, makes us attack *the capacity to give and*

---

[14] Ariely (2012).
[15] Garrett et al. (2016).

sustain life, because life consists of inconceivably complex linking. Chapter Nine delves into this phenomenon.

When we cannot gratify our envy by personal attack or by embedding it in the faceless destructiveness of group activity, we turn the envious attack back on ourselves. In 1916 Freud described people "wrecked by success," people who cannot tolerate their own happiness. Thomas Carlyle aphorized this dynamic when he said, for every hundred that can stand privation, only one can stand prosperity.

In preparation for the approaching section, I should mention that self-envy also exists unprompted. Self-envy sounds like a psychoanalytic fiction, but people relate to themselves just as they do to others, regarding themselves with love or hate, desire or disgust, indifference, envy or gratitude. Self-envy is our deprived self—our inner "outsider"—watching the copulating grown-up self we now relish being. Aesop's "The dog and his shadow" allegorizes self-envy: A dog swims across a river while holding a piece of meat in its mouth. Seeing his reflection, the dog furiously attacks the watery illusion, and lets go of his morsel, which is swept downstream.

How did *paideia* survive envy?

The humanistic ethos, an extension of *paideia*, exalted the growth and complexification of the mind; it sacralized humanity's true prosperity, the interior life, and this provoked cultural envy and self-envy.

Greek and Latin students tried to understand the minds and spirits of their cultural parents, rehearsing the music of their thoughts, searching for their latent realities. By their labor and care, if I may licentiously extend my metaphor, Greek and Latin students earned the delights of the ancient bedroom.

Humanist education, which in my view culminated in psychoanalysis, enriches the fabric of the mind. It lays down layers of knowledge into which ideas both new and old can embed themselves. There they evolve, like embryos in the endometrium, and thrive or are shed according to their viability. Such a mind grows clear-sighted, better able to assign proper values to the proper things.

An education of this sort helps by building inner coherence (integrity), which in turn builds self-esteem, which in turn makes one less susceptible to pathological contingent envy. But successful management of envy needs more than this. And that "more" is psychoanalysis. In the psychoanalytic setting, envy is vividly experienced in the here-and-now of an emotionally crucial relationship. The experience exposes the defenses used to hide envy's baleful effects on the patients' life. But even psychoanalysis has limits: It cannot extirpate envy. It can only help recognize and manage envy.

How did the Greeks, without psychoanalysis, handle the vexatious passion? The envy that finally killed *paideia* must have plagued the ancients no less than it plagues us. This makes us wonder how *paideia* could have managed to be born, let alone last so long.

Here is my speculation: Initially, *paideia* gratified, more than provoked envy. *Paideia*, in its early Sophist form, jabbed a thumb in the aristocratic eye. It asserted excellence by effort, not just birth. When *paideia* appeared, the Greek nobility, back on their political heels, judged a battle over education as impolitic. In this galling innovation, moreover, the aristocrats recognized their own ancient devotion to *arête*. So, with a divided heart, they spared *paideia* at its birth.

Of course, in democratic Greece, social propinquity steadily advanced, hand in hand with envy's menaces. Against those menaces, the Hellenic religious and ethical system deployed several envy-suppression measures.

Greek religion was one. It was flexible system of lifelike Olympian gods whose omnipotence was curbed only by impersonal Fate. The divine family was a sink for their votaries' envy. The gods' rancorous Olympian councils, their jealousies, and their mutual treacheries dispersed the pernicious emotion.

Fate, as a disinterested distributor of fortune and misfortune, also suppressed envy. It legitimized disappointment, this being one person's lot, and happiness, that being another's. This calming cultural vision redefined inequalities as the emanation of distributive justice, an allotment beyond human control and, accordingly, beyond envy. Fatalism, too, emboldened the Greeks to excel: If a man's lot was to prosper and suffer nemesis (punishment for success), he may as well strive on.

Perhaps the Hellenes also pacified envy by diffusing among themselves, more than other cultures, a sense of shared cultural achievement, a collective pride, a splendid "we-image." Group pride soothed personal deprivations, mortifications and resentments. Their cultural cohesion both reduced overall stress, as it does for the long-lived Japanese (Marmot, 2015; Pilling, 2017), and facilitated the radiation of civic pride. There's evidence that most Athenian residents, even many non-citizens—women weaving in their homes; resident aliens dickering on the streets of their adoptive Athens; and even slaves harvesting olives—basked in the reflected glory of their country's luminaries.

Gratitude also neutralizes envy. And, as Pericles' famous funeral speech makes clear, the Athenians appreciated their good fortune.[16] They cherished their sublime artistic, philosophical, scientific and political achievements. The Golden Age Athenians and their allies adored their patroness Athena despite deepening religious doubt, for having "held her hand over Athens in times of trouble." So, the Greeks' capacity for gratitude may have helped preserve *paideia* from instant destruction.

But perhaps even this formidable array of envy-suppressing strategies, in view of the ferocity (attested by Herodotus) of Greek envy, would have inadequately protected *paideia*. The key to Humanism's birth may lie in the remarkable, to us almost bizarre Greek candor about envy: Homer sang a song of envious rage; the Hellenic philosophers and dramatists exposed envy unsparingly; and the Athenians even practiced the public gratification of spitefulness: Ostracism allowed the six thousand Athenian citizens, annually, to cast out of the city, for ten years, anyone who might be guilty of nothing more than talent, happiness or prosperity.[17] Plutarch described the proceeding as "a humane way of assuaging envy."

And that's apparently how *paideia* survived. In the revolving years, however, Greek self-control relaxed and the Greek will to manage envy waned. Psychosocial regression wore away the luster, then corrupted the core, of Greek identity. And as the stewardship of their lofty achievements fatigued the people, they seem gradually to have forsaken their educational ideal.

Socrates may have been an early casualty of the cultural fatigue. The Athenians' self-destructive over-expansion of their nation, thought to have been a preemptive power grab in response to *fear* of Sparta's growing *envy*, was probably another. Justinian's closure of the pagan Academy, much later, in 529 AD, may have been a third. These and other attacks, if attacks they were, didn't kill Greek learning; but they did postpone its diffusion throughout Europe until the late Middle Ages.

---

[16] At the same time, perhaps being wrecked by success, they let their blessings slip away.

[17] Ostracism existed in other Greek cities at various times. Ostracism differed from exile (as used in Rome), which typically punished a crime and dispossessed the exiles of their property and status.

The Greek strategies, and their historical residua, were meant to suppress envy and fortify the endurance of the tensions generated by unequal lives. They did not survive the rise of modern science and the Enlightenment's altruistic, if obsessive push toward political egalitarianism. Society's attempt to spread education to the masses proved impossible. The quiet ideal, the cultivation of mental growth, the ideal which seemed to justify that push, degenerated into a howl for unconditional equality.

By the late 1800's, envy had the upper hand; envy-fear had cowed the human soul; and self-deception concealed their double mischief. Eventually, the Classical humanists let their own ideas be turned against themselves. Later, psychoanalysis followed suit, recanting its hard lessons. Humanity, seeing its teachers turn tail, despaired of bearing the strains of life, and let itself die.

Late twentieth-century society implicitly understood that envy-fear had irrecoverably weakened it. It no longer had the sinew to produce a self-aware, self-possessed leader who could make prudent decisions. So, it turned to a small group of mindblind people insensible to envy-fear: These became our autocrats.

The rise of strongmen

In November, 2024, America elected President Donald Trump for the second time. In January, 2025, he embarked on a presidency he'd resolved to debase into strongman autocracy.

A strongman concentrates the power of the state in his person. Strongmen autocrats rule with absolute power; they demand complete obedience. We think, for example, of Alexander, Napoleon, and Idi Amin. Autocrats have infested society since its agricultural revolution 10,000 years ago.

Democracy, however, began to prevail among governments at the beginning of the 20th century. By 2000, well over half the world's countries were under electoral or democratic rule. But then, they fell like dominoes. And today, over 70% of the world's peoples live under autocracy. Now, even the first pre-modern democracy is sliding into autocracy.

How autocracy prevailed

Modern society guaranteed the autocratic resurgence when it rejected the ideal of mental growth. By that choice, the public consigned its collective mind to regression and what I call mindblindness. And now the consequences have come home to roost in many world capitals.

Envy-fear had subdued the wholesome impulse for mental growth. It preyed on the mind of the regressed body politic. It made the Left strive for an Idealized Future purified of exclusion and envy. It made the Right strive for an Idealized Past of envy-suppression. But they united to make eternal economic growth and universal wealth seem plausible; ecology dismissible; catastrophic overpopulation invisible; and an envyless world achievable.

Signs of our timid incapacity to focus on group survival appear everywhere: Citizens can't discipline or regulate themselves; leaders can't mandate vaccination. They can't enforce climate change mitigation. They can't make depopulation policy. They can't repudiate the delusions of unconditional inclusion, perfect equity, or even self-determined gender identity.

And so, day by day, the world more deeply loathed itself for pusillanimously ignoring the approaching catastrophe, and neglecting self-protection.

Society, like an infant, craves protection, comfort, and reassurance from a powerful and coherent figure. Fainthearted democracies, over time, made the infantile masses thirst for strong leaders to restrain and guide them. But authoritative (not *authoritarian*) strength was becoming a distant memory. A world destitute of humanistic education could no longer breed strong statesmen. Envy-fear had made cowards of us all.

So, by default, society chose leaders seemingly immune to envy-fear. And these were the mindblind, narcissistic, power-thirsty men, and some women, keen to embrace the disgraceful role of autocrat. So, we installed these strange simulacra of strong leaders to tighten borders, secure resources, and suppress envy.

Freud's resurrection

The strongman resurgence, and in particular Trump's election, had one healthy effect: It forced society to conclude, at last, that it couldn't understand its baffling behavior without psychoanalysis. This was a social sea change.

Even Trump's first election in 2016 raised journalistic pleas for Freudian enlightenment. American psychotherapist Gary Greenberg wrote an article for *The Guardian* (10/12/18) called: "Analyze this: What Freud can teach us about Trumpism." He said "Trump offers an even easier, more primitive way, to dodge grief, limits, emotional wounds and helplessness…"

More recently (6/3/24), Merve Emre wrote in the *New Yorker:* "What does Freud still have to teach us?" Emre lists the recent appeals to the former pariah: "The past few years have given us a Freud for the pandemic, a Freud for Ukraine, a Freud for Palestine, a Freud for transfemininity, a Freud for the far right, and a Freud for the vipers' nest that is the twenty-first-century American university."

Shortly after (10/27/24), the leftist *Jacobin* printed "Confronting the Death Drive in Trump's America" by Eric Reinhart. Reinhart drums away on unconscious motives, especially destructive ones. He asks us to see the malignity on both the Right and the Left; he believes both express Freud's "Death Instinct." He says society will fail until it acknowledges "…. the …. destructive human tendencies that manifest ….throughout history."

The following month (11/20/24), the *Atlantic's* Elizabeth Bruenig wrote "Another theory of the Trump movement: Who else to help explain but Freud?"

Of course, they plead too late. Long ago, our anti-psychoanalytic society decayed into a gigantic collective Personality Disorder beyond the reach of depth psychology.

But let's enjoy what comfort psychoanalytic understanding might offer us in these frightening times.

The strongman's addiction

We'll probe the strongman mind.

Strongmen confuse good with bad, right with wrong, truth with falsehood. Though this handicap troubles everyone to some degree, it utterly dominates those who suffer Personality Disorders.

Personality Disorder is an intractable mental illness. But (excluding so-called Borderline Personality) it's nearly painless. Personality Disorders, a diagnosis we nominalize for convenience, don't suffer; they make everyone else suffer.

Personality Disorders are common among autocrats (Burkle, 2019). More specifically, autocrats have *narcissistic* Personality Disorders (NPD) (Post, 2015). NPDs are people who see other people only as extensions of themselves. Pathological envy—no surprise—rules NPD.

Pathological envy curtails mental growth almost from birth. Envy sabotages the foundational distinction between "good" and "bad," the critical mental divide between the good, loved mother from the bad, hated mother.

Later in life, envy confuses richness with barrenness, truth with falsehood, integrity with corruptibility.

Here's how that happens: The morbidly envious baby not only wants the breast all to itself; it must put badness into the breast. So, it spoils the breast with imaginary excrements to make it unenviable. "Piss on her," an envious woman says of her glamorous rival.

By relieving envy, "bad" spoiling becomes *good.* The "bad" excrements, by fouling the breast, briefly ease envy and, accordingly, suppress retaliatory fantasies. So, execrable behavior gives *momentary protection, relief and deliverance.* "Bad" has become "good."

Future autocrats idealize their tools of protection: Deceit, avarice, inconstancy, and intimidation. By such corrupt and corrupting devices, NPD strongmen blunt awareness of both their envy and fears of retaliation. Every successful escape makes them high.

Elusion is the opiate of the autocrats.

Autocrats are Gambling addicts

NPD autocrats are addicted to the exhilaration of eluding self-destruction. They're gambling addicts, hooked on the gamble of hubris: How many limits can I violate and escape retaliation? How many outrages can I commit, without being destroyed?

Autocrats' emotional stability depends upon an endless pattern of goading the world and dodging its blowback. Successful evasion is so addictive because it represents, to them, escape from superego retaliation. For them, *worldly requital symbolizes retaliation* for their unconscious envious attacks on mother and father.

They endlessly replay this drama on the world stage. They attack, then escape. They taunt the world, then elude its punishment. Every escape intoxicates them more deeply.

The autocrats are hooked on Russian roulette with the world. Every misfire enhances their illusion of invulnerability, and reassures them against psychotic anxieties. When reassurance is not at hand, these anxieties approach their consciousness. On those occasions, NPDs evacuate their anxieties into others, by bullying them. Trump's Greenland and tariff gambits exemplify this defense.

The autocrat's inner gang

Like autocrats, real gangs bully and gamble, and autocrats have a deep connection with the gang mentality. They even seem, in fact, to form gangs in their heads.

It's a subtle operation. All infants personify their mental structures: Memories, wishes, fears, identifications, defenses. Just as farm children name their animals, infants "name" their mental contents: "bad dependency," "good denial," "bad helplessness," or "good, protective spoiling."

Similarly, NPDs personify their avarice, arrogance and mania. They organize these personified defenses into a protective union, like a "gang." This mental gang fortifies strongmen's sense of security. The gang martials its collective power against extreme envy and extreme envy-fear. Autocratic mental gangs, like real gangs, despise helplessness and dependency, feelings which would expose them to envy-fear.

That scorn makes NPDs notoriously hard to help in psychoanalysis. Their mind gangs sneer at help as weakness and humiliation. They'd prefer to die, rather than depend upon the analyst.

And just as real gangs beautify themselves with good aspects like loyalty, mutual concern, and protection, the mind gang edulcorates itself with charisma ("attitude"), strong opposition to bad elements (outside gang members) in their territory, and national (neighborhood) pride.

Gang of gamblers

Autocrats are not only gambling addicts with internal gangs; they form real gangs of gamblers.

Autocrats recognize their pathology in each other. This sick sympathy drives Trump's cloying bromances with Putin and Kim Jong Un.

They copy and learn from one another. They cooperate through networks, sharing economic resources and investing in one another's economies. They share security services to suppress popular dissent, and interfere in one another's elections. They also use a common group of legal and political specialists (Real and Menjivar, 2024).

Ganging up fortifies their protective might.

Autocratic natalism

The whole world, by and large, is natalist. But the autocratic gang are natalists on steroids (India's Modi is a possible exception). Natalist autocrats incentivize or even coerce their subjects to make more babies. Russia's Putin, Turkey's Erdogan, Hungary's Orbán, China's Xi and our own Trump are just a few of these.

Consciously, strongmen natalists think they are fortifying their nations: They think they want more good, native insiders, not bad, unwashed outsiders, to sustain their national economies and identity. And they think they are beefing up their gang.

Preconsciously, though, natalism is highest-stakes gambling. It mocks Mother Nature. The autocrats, like everyone else, feel the tightening noose of ecology. This threat evokes in them the psychotic retaliatory anxieties. It inspires them to make the most perilous wager: They bet they can escape the biophysical reality, the reality that preys preconsciously on every mind, the real limit of carrying capacity.

So, perhaps this was our destiny: To grovel, in our end days, before mentally ill masters who accelerate Nature's project of self-destruction and gratify our tragic species' darkest wish.

3.

Classical Education and Tension-Tolerance

We've introduced the tragic forces of envy and envy-fear and, in a preliminary way, self-deception, which lets envy run riot. We've seen them play out in Homer's ancient imagination and the 21st century's autocratic surge.

Classical education exposes envy, envy-fear, and self-deception: That exposure is crucial to cultural mental growth. Classics also exposes hubris. Hubris puffs its victims up, elevating them above the painful tensions of envy and envy-fear, while sustaining them with self-deception.

The exposure of one's hubris can be transformative. I know from experience: By the mid-1960s, a faint memory of the lost treasures of the university somehow survived in my father's mind. He believed that northeastern men's schools valued, almost as a sacred attainment, a Gentleman's Education. And so, I, an eighteen-year-old Ohio rube, went to a small Eastern men's school in 1967.

In a year or two, I'd drawn aside the mystic veil of the East, having found nothing of the transformative magic I'd gone there to find.

But I couldn't give up my, or perhaps my father's, idea that college should educate and transform. So, late sophomore year, before the window of opportunity closed, I pleaded my case to a professor, who suggested what at that time in this country was an unusual experiment: Stop going to classes; organize a team of tutors to guide you through junior year, and read the great philosophical, theological and literary works of the Western World. Then, take first semester, senior year, to write about it all.

I became a junior, immersed in solitary study. I was proud beyond my deserts. Something critical was missing, but I didn't see it until a therapeutic mortification peeled the scales from my eyes.

I'd come to reckon myself an *intellectual*. So, I presumed to hobnob with several Greek and Latin students. Inevitably, one evening, over several bottles of beer, they punished my vanity. One of them suggested we choose an article at random from the *Encyclopedia Britannica*, close the book and each discourse upon the subject, to the limits of the speaker's knowledge. Volume I fell open to "avatar."

I shrank into my chair. The eggheads hardly hesitated. "The term is Sanskrit," the first said, "and means the 'descent' of the god into a human body, an incarnation, like Jesus. But in Hindu mythology, yoga masters sometimes unite with god and become avatars. The word 'yoga' itself means 'union,'" he pointed out, then gamboled through its lush etymology: English "yoke," the Latin "iungere" (to join) and the Greek "ζεύγνυμι" ([sounding something like zdeygnumi] "to yoke together").[1] He noted their common "y-g/k" sound sequence.

The second student picked up from there and drew parallels between an Indian philosopher's upward passage to the Divine Spirit and a Platonist's ascension of the ladder of love to contemplative union with the Eternal Forms. He quoted from Plato's *Timaeus* and *Symposium*.

The last speaker, by acclamation, took the palm. He started with the Hindu-Platonic concept of Divine Oneness degenerating into the Many and showed us how it reappeared in one intellectual discipline after another. Even science was slave to its unseen influence, the senior classicist said, and pointed to the Big Bang theory (only twenty years old then, in 1969), which implies that all the transient diversity now swirling around us emerged from a unified something that obeyed unsearchable physical laws. I remember that he then, to the delight of the Greek students, said that the great George Gamow, one of the first proponents of the theory, arranged for authorship of the pathbreaking Big Bang paper to include the physicist Hans Bethe and Gamow's actual co-author, Ralph Alpher. In evocation of the first three letters of the Greek alphabet, the theory was called ever after the Alpher-Bethe-Gamow theory.

In this way the Classics majors frisked away two or three hours. Afterwards I skulked through the dark, back to my dorm, dazed as a duck hit on the head. How could I call myself a college student? It wasn't just their ability to instantly retrieve, organize and combine material from different disciplines to make their points. It was the liveliness in their learning, the playfulness in their exchanges, the confidence in their memories. How could I have missed so much? Why hadn't anybody told me I was missing it?

---

[1] I couldn't remember the Latin or Greek words he used, but I remember "yoke" and the sound sequence; so, I've taken the liberty of supplying iungere and ζεύγνυμι.

Without knowing it, I had been transformed. But, obeying the law of convenience, I forgot my questions, resumed my dash toward professional graduate school and didn't pause until eighteen years later. That's when I remembered that night, and how violently I'd envied my schoolmates. That's when I realized that the intervening years had done nothing to remediate the ignorance that the accursed Greek and Latin students had exposed. I thought of the great writers, scientists and statesmen who had learned the ancient languages. I envied them too, each for their distinctive genius. But this time around, I tried to avoid easy tension-evasions—the evasions of spite, of withdrawal of interest, of devaluation—by pursuing a more laborious tension-evasion: Emulation.

And so, when I was thirty-eight, I embarked upon the ancient languages.

An Argument for Studying the Classics

Puncturing hubris is only one way Classical study teaches tension-tolerance.

We can better appreciate the others by first clarifying the nature of tension-tolerance (TT) and distinguishing it from tension evasion (TE). The two would seem to be entirely distinct conditions. But tension-tolerance is actually tension evasion by a more rigorous route. In comparison to TE, TT manages tensions more than evades them. TT is more oriented to reality; it is prospective; it understands that instant TE creates greater tensions later, when pressures for TE will have risen, and be manageable only by yet more arduous TT, an effort the overmatched subject often cannot muster, leading to a vicious cycle of TE leading on to more TE, as in vicious cycles of addiction or morbid habits of self-deception. TT is the child declining a single marshmallow now, in exchange for two marshmallows later. It is the runner having endured an extra 400-meter sprint yesterday and resolving to do it again tomorrow, for a personal record in the 800 meters a week later, avoiding self-criticism. TT is the middle manager, acknowledging her personnel mistake today, to become a more discriminating judge of character tomorrow, avoiding demotion or yet more shame. TT is the student memorizing Greek declensions an extra hour, every day for a week, in order to comprehend

Μῆνιν ἄειδε θεὰ Πηληϊάδεω Ἀχιλῆος

the next week, avoiding frustration, despair of learning, and envy of the learned.

We also exercise TT when trying to reform society, synthesize information, work for depopulation, and seek self-knowledge.

The compulsory study of ancient languages and their literature could have fortified society's TT to fulfill those four tasks. How?

1) Classically-educated people used TT-demanding ancient Western cultural models to inspire their own societies. They venerated the Athenians, who overthrew tyranny in the late 6th century, forged a limited democracy, and far outpaced neighboring autocracies in advancing human rights.[2] The Greeks wouldn't have called it "human rights." But they, much more than the surrounding cultures of their time, understood and pursued justice and equality. The 7th century Ionian Greeks had already displaced their aristocracy with a more democratic polis, and the 6th century Athenian Solon revised the Draconian laws in the same direction. By the fifth and fourth century, the polis Greeks no longer tolerated aristocrats trampling the necks of the common man.

2) The Greek philosophers, alone among the ancients, focused on humanity's tendency to deny the limits of its power. This tension-tolerant focus alone might have humbled human exceptionalism and curbed ecological overshoot. Their worldview, the *tragic* vision, informed, and was informed by, the novel scientific view of the 6th and 5th century Ionian philosophers that certain natural laws regulate the behavior of matter and energy. This is a perspective without which, for better and admittedly worse, western science and technology might never have developed.

3) Greek and Latin, compared to most other languages, make heavier demands on, and thereby better fortify, the memory and the synthetic faculty, the capacity to collect, collate and make meaning of scattered bits of information.

4) Greek literature and culture exalt self-knowledge as the basis of wisdom.

The long list of its illustrious students make these four tension-generating educational features of Greek and Latin learning seem useful, or almost

---

[2] Throughout this book, "Greek," except as otherwise specified (for example, "Homeric Greek") refers to the Athenian language, culture and government from the 6th through the 4th centuries B.C. Greek society was the product of migrants from the northern steppe lands and Near East, whose cultures, over hundreds of years, converged and blended on the Aegean peninsula.

necessary, for great and honorable achievements. But history can't prove that they ever actually improved anyone.

Greek declensions, Latin conjugations, or the contemplation of Plato's dialogues don't make dunces brilliant or criminals honest. After all, many of the Nazi SS were Classically-trained lawyers. And hadn't the great historian Edward Gibbon, a sharp observer of human behavior, said, "The power of instruction is seldom of much efficacy, except in those happy dispositions where it is almost superfluous."? Didn't Plato himself try to educate a corrupt Sicilian tyrant into a philosopher-king who then, by one account, sold his teacher into slavery?[3] In other words, isn't character more powerful than *paideia*? The correlation between Classics and great achievements, so impressive on its face, might be meaningless.

Nevertheless, at the turn of this century, a group of writers argued that the old educational tradition had saved civilization. *Who Killed Homer* (Hanson and Heath, 2001), *The Devil Knows Latin* (Kopff, 2001), *Climbing Parnassus* (Simmons, 2002), *Sailing the Wine Dark Sea* (Cahill, 2003), and *Love, Sex and Tragedy* (Goldhill, 2004) all testified to the community's need for Classical knowledge.[4]

They agreed that Classical education uniquely improves the growing mind. How, according to these scholars, does it do this?

It starts by impressing on the students the uniqueness of Greek wisdom and Hellenic values. These are not just different from, but antithetical to any other civilization of Greece's own time or space: They are not predicated on race; they are not Mediterranean but anti-Mediterranean; the polis is neither African- nor Asian-inspired but deliberately opposes Eastern approaches to government, literature, religion, war, individual rights, citizenship and science.

The core Hellenic values, rooted in a devotion to mental growth, as defined in this book, are unique, unchanging and non-multicultural. The Greeks of the polis bound all of its racially-diverse residents to a common

---

[3] Aristotle, though, managed to excite a yearning for knowledge [πόθος (pothos)], in Alexander.

[4] At publication: **Hanson** was Professor of Greek, U. Cal.-Santa Clara; **Heath**, Assoc. Prof. Classics, Santa Clara U.; **Simmons**, journalist and literary critic; **Kopff**, Prof. Classics, U. Colorado; **Goldhill**, Prof. Greek, Cambridge U.; **Nicholson**, prize-winning author of scholarly books for general readership; **Cahill**, best-selling author of the *Hinges of History* Series and other books.

value system and common pride in humanity's higher powers and sentiments. Hanson and Heath catalogued that system's values: The acquisition of knowledge is free from religious and political authority; military power is subordinated to civilian control; religion is subordinate to political authority; the polis trusted neither the rich nor poor, but the average citizen; the polis assumed free dissent and open criticism of government, religion and the military. These lofty political values and Greece's ethical autonomy from its surrounding cultures partly explain both the dynamism and durability of Western Culture, the heir to Hellenic culture.

The Hellenes organized these values into a novel political system. Barbarism, autocracy, or inherited aristocracy dominated their era. But the Greeks extended education and human dignity to a greatly expanded portion of the self-disciplined and talented. The Athenian franchise, although limited to about 20,000 of the 100,000 believed to have lived in the city, paved the way for the parliamentary and representative democracies we have prized.

Then, by framing our intellectual lives, by meditating on the concerns of a freer society, and by prizing self-knowledge, as Professor Goldhill showed, the Greeks gave us the tools for both individual and group self-understanding and mental growth.

Without mental growth bodies politic degenerate into ugly tyrannies, despotisms, autocracies, or totalitarian behemoths.[5] Public mental growth depends on a critical mass, however small, among the people, of cultural sophistication, intellectual elegance, and emulousness for truth; Classical training systematically educates to all these. Simmons asks: We moderns have been free to use this system; why haven't we?

Whatever our culture's spirit is, it was, Professor Kopf writes, surely born in the language community's past. Greek and (especially) Latin—in addition to Anglo-Saxon and more modest contributions from German and French—contribute about 60% to the vernacular English vocabulary, and 90% to the scientific. Insofar as a community's members lose the sense of their common heritage, they grow indifferent to their government, their laws, their institutions and their responsibilities. This, the citizens of the United States have done over the last 75 years.

These authors support my impressions: What we learn through the study of ancient Greek and the Classics is rigorous concentration, mental agility,

---

[5] As society has done in the 21st century, the phenomenon described above.

and respect for limits. By such gifts, *paideia* stimulates mental growth, orients its students to reality, and helps them tolerate the grievous tensions of life.

And to recover this heritage—returning here to my own vision of education—a society must provide general accessibility to Classical education. Indeed, Classics serve no specific class, because none monopolize talent or energy. So, everyone with the requisite ability, intelligence, curiosity and doggedness for detail is welcome.

But we abolished the Classical university. Accordingly, our mental growth has stagnated, our minds have regressed, and our capacity to grieve the intellectual, political and environmental casualties strewn everywhere around us has withered.

We happen to have some simple metrics which might buttress these claims: Standardized exam scores and documented performance in professional schools.

Students who major in Classics Languages and Classics are among the best performers on the Graduate Record Exam (GRE), rivalling even physics and astronomy students, and do as well or better than such students in being accepted into and performing in professional and graduate schools. It is possible, of course, that those who major in Classics are simply smarter than most other college students, and that their intelligence, not their Classical educations, explain their success.

On the other hand, high intelligence can be sharpened by academic rigor, or dulled by academic ease. If, after four years of education, a Classics major can perform almost as well as physics students—whose educational rigor is undoubted—on some common measures, and exceed them on others, then we might reasonably conclude that Classics is almost as effective as a demanding scientific and mathematical curriculum in stimulating mental growth. This is what we will see. It will justify our skepticism toward the STEM bias of the current university, and refute the idea that Classics are merely a form of cultural studies.

In his study entitled "Classicists are bright!" (*Discover Magazine*, Jan 25, 2012), Razib Khan, geneticist and public educator, analyzed GRE scores by intended graduate school concentrations, or fields. Kahn chose 105 fields for which at least 100 students took the test. Keep in mind that grad school (together with pre-med and pre-law) applicants tend to be the cream of the college crop.

We can, of course, rank the "aggregate smarts" of the average student in each concentration by summing their verbal and math scores.[6] Kahn found that physics students, as expected, topped the 105 concentrations, Classical Language students (those planning to study Greek and Latin, plus Hebrew, Sanskrit, Tamil, Arabic and Chinese) were 7th, and Greek and Latin ("Classical" Classics students) were 14th.

But now, to measure the students' relative "intellectual balance," Khan converted the average verbal and math score for each discipline to standard deviation units away from the mean (SDUM).

The standard deviation, in common language, measures the difference between—in the case of the GRE—an individual student's score and the average of all scores on the test. The SDUM value must be zero or more standard deviation units above (positive) or below (negative) the average. Khan made this conversion in the process of "[correcting] for disciplines stronger in math .... because math averages are higher all around."

After this intellectual balancing, Khan found—once again—physics students at the top, but Classical languages students second only by a hair (-.03 SDUM) and Classics students now 9th, just -.13 SDUM behind Physics students.[7] And among the "intellectually balanced" Top Ten Titans, only

---

[6]
1. Physics 540/743: 1283
2. Astrophysics 540/727: 1267
3. Mathematics 523/740: 1263
4. Atomic Physics 522/739: 1261
5. Solid State Physics 514/743: 1257
6. History of Science 596/661: 1257
7. Classical Languages 619/633: 1252
8. Biophysics 523/727: 1250
9. Physics, Other 519/723: 1242
10. Planetary Science 545/694: 1239
11. Materials Science 509/728: 1237
12. Astronomy 525/706: 1231
13. Operations Research 483/743: 1226
14. Classics 609/616: 1225

[7]
1. Physics (+0.85)
2. Classical Languages (+0.82)
3. History of Science (+0.82)
4. Astrophysics (+0.80)
5. Mathematics (+0.77)
6. Atomic Physics (+0.77)
7. Solid State Physics (+0.74)

students of Greek, Latin and the other Classical languages represent the humanities.

The Classics students' performance bewildered the author. This speaks sociocultural volumes. In explaining the high scores of Historians of Science (3rd among the "intellectually balanced"), Kahn comments: "I think I know why: Many of these individuals have science backgrounds, but later became interested in history. They are by nature relatively good generalists." As to Classicists, he says "*I have no idea* (my emphasis) why people drawn to traditionally Classical fields are bright, but I wonder if it is because these are not 'sexy' domains, to the point where you have to have a proactive interest in the intellectual enterprise."

So far has the public forgotten the means and the meaning of education.

Public ignorance, cultivated during the 20th century, has not stopped 21st century Classics majors from scoring highest of any major on the Law School Admissions Test (LSAT) and, once they enter law school, law school grade point average. (Derek Muller, Pepperdine University School of Law [2013]), They have the highest success rates of any majors in Law School. (*Harvard Magazine*—Princeton Review 2014) And if they choose, it seems, they can excel in science: According to gustavus.edu, Classics majors scored the 2nd highest overall on the Medical College Admission Test (MCAT) and had a 50% acceptance rate to medical school.[8]

So, Classicists can learn science as well as dedicated science students. Not so accessible to science students, however, is the ability to step outside their physical and social environments, and look back on them. Classics students were taught to see them holistically and experience what Classicist Liam Kinney (2015) called "Matrix Moments," or paradigm shifts which correct widely accepted misunderstandings.

Finally, Classics students learn how to understand why people do what they do. These two lessons—how to see the human world holistically, and how to understand human motives—are scant in the educations of Physics students, or of any other STEM major.

---

8. Biophysics (+0.73)
9. Classics (+0.72)
10. Planetary Science (+0.71)

[8] Dr. Charles Austerberry of Creighton University gathered specific data on the performance of Classics majors in 1997.

Perhaps, by now, this is clear: Classical education imposes nearly as rigorous an intellectual challenge on its students as the most rigorous scientific education. But if mental growth is the progressive understanding of *both* the external and internal worlds, then science students are cheated of the most important half.

4.

Lost in Translation: Mental Growth

So far, in our analysis of *paideia*, I have praised the scholarly rigors and content of Classical studies and literature. And I have even introduced, just now, another gift of *paideia*: Holistic education. But this integrating effect goes deeper—psychophysiologically speaking—than the relatively superficial human psychology imparted to Classics students; this effect actually harmonizes body and mind.

The beauty and power of the ancient Greek world is contained in the language itself: Its music, precision, and efficiency. It is not enough to understand Greek ideas, one also has to understand them *in Greek*.

The university knew, or should have known, the centrality of Greek to a humanist education. When it abandoned its ancient language requirements, the university and the culture began to decline. The university rationalized its abdication, and overlooked its decline. The late 19th and early 20th century academy denied, to itself most of all, that it had fawned upon a peevish public, and abandoned its educational responsibility. It even concealed its abdication with a promise to teach the great works in translation. It claimed that the pleasures and treasures of Homer are available in translations. Translations, the educators insist, adequately transmit the genius of the originals.

In its zeal to flee mental strain and economic insecurity, society applauded the new policy. It was relieved and pleased that the flower of its youth, thirsting for job training, would no longer wilt in arid Greek and Latin classes, but bloom with mental vigor. Far from depriving them intellectually, the academy said, it would edify its students with translations. This rationale even today justifies the "Great Books" curriculum, a course of study in which students read translated works of the ancient thinkers, the pride of exclusive schools like Columbia University.

If the "translation rationale" turns out to be invalid, however, then it must truly be a rationalization, that is, a *strategy of self-deception*, and its unmasking will make us suspect that other self-deceptions too are propping up the reputation of the modern university.

This claim—for the educational adequacy of translations—calls for a candid response. Frankness, maybe even vehemence, is needed because this claim, on the surface, seems like pointless academic quibbling. But it actually exemplifies that type of destructive behavior that looks directly at a patent reality and denies seeing it, a type that includes denials of evolution, and on a more serious scale, the Holocaust and overpopulation. Behind such behavior lurks magical thinking, the unrelinquished infantile strategy of merely believing things into or out of existence, the strategy of omnipotence.

The magical claim that translations into the vernacular produce good liberal educations seems even on the face of it so wrong that we cannot be blamed for wondering how anyone, without blushing, can make it. Some of its claimants are good and intelligent people who teach that the sound and the sense of every line of English literature are indissolubly united. Then they forget that their doctrine should apply to all literature, including Homeric Greek.

I'm hardly the first to point this out. When Alexander Pope asked the renowned Classics scholar Richard Bentley to grade Pope's new translation of *The Odyssey*, Bentley replied, "It is a pretty poem, Mr. Pope, but you must not call it Homer."[1]

Why the Original is Important

An English teacher once invited me to recite some Homer for her ninth-grade students. They had been reading *The Odyssey* in translation. I could only meet with them after school and so I expected my young audience to be chafing in their chains. But the recitation spellbound them from the first alpha to the last omega. Their teacher told me afterwards she'd overheard them effervescing to their friends: "You wouldn't believe what we heard!... spooky!... awesome!..."

Of course, this proves nothing. Maybe Homer's unfamiliar sounds or lively rhythm intrigued them. Then again, maybe original is to translation as the nightingale's song is to the crow's caw.

Others have certainly thought so. Tennyson, writing of Homer translated into English:

> These lame hexameters the strong-wing'd music of Homer! ....

[1] What is lost in translation, Robert Frost said, is the poetry.

When did a frog coarser croak upon our Helicon?

There's just no squirming out of it: English translations, however beautiful and evocative, are not Homer. They use entirely different sounds to narrate the original work. A typical English translation of *The Iliad*'s opening words, "Sing, Muse, the rage ..." is acoustically alien to the Greek: "Μῆνιν ἄειδε, θεά..." (This phrase sounds something like "ma-a-neen ah-ehh-dei tei-ahh..." with the first two a's sounding like French ê's.) The Greek line has seven sounded vowels and four consonants; the English reverses that ratio. These differences alone play discordantly different notes on the emotions of the reader.

All languages but Homer's own mutilate the poet's creation by destroying his music. Our language, rich as it is, has no distinctive musical pitch accents. Our words are distinguished from one another by spelling and stress accents. For example, if we stress the first syllable of "record," we mean a disc formerly played on a record player. If we stress its second syllable, we mean the act of recording music on that disc. But in Greek, pitch accents distinguish the word. For example, the Greek word "βίος" means "life" when you raise the pitch on the first syllable, but "bow" (βιός) when you pitch the second. In English we only pitch-accent our words to modify their meaning to suit the occasion. For example, one Yale student asks another if she is going to major in Classics. The other replies, "No-o!" with an upward, then downward melisma (this is, by the way, how the Greek circumflex accent sounds) on the long "o." This tonal addition means, "Don't be ridiculous." But the tonal variation does not (as the accent in βιός denotes "bow") *denote* the word "No."

Thus, every word of Homer is a little song. But not in translations. Abandon all hope of hearing Homer, you who read translations.

The belief that one can learn Homer in translation, and avoid thereby the trouble of learning Greek, is a fume of wishful fantasy. Who learns Mozart by reading an English libretto of *Don Giovanni*? To degrade the Homeric songs to speech, change their sounds, shift their word-order, and annihilate their meter and rhythm, is to blast the poetry and, together with that, its emotional, psychological, and conceptual significance. It is especially true of the Homeric songs that, as Fellini said, "A different language is a different vision of life."

You may argue that, owing to our vast cultural and temporal distance from the Greeks and our inability to perfect the ancient pronunciations, no one can recapture the spirit of Homeric poetry, the Greeks' "distinctive way of experiencing the world." It's hopeless to think a 21st century American can apprehend Homer's full beauty and meaning just by learning Ionic orthography and vocalizing the Homeric sound and rhythm.

And I must confess, no, we can't fully appreciate Homer's richness. But we can *refine* our appreciation. We can come much closer to Homer now. We've discovered the pitch accents, the correct pronunciation of the Greek vowels (α, ε, ι, η, ο, υ, ω) and Greek diphthongs (αι, αυ, ει, ου, ευ, ηυ, οι, υι, ωυ). Diphthongs are known as "sliding vowels," sounds formed by combining two vowels in one syllable. They begin as one vowel and slide toward another, as we hear in "l**ai**d," or "l**ou**d." We also know the Greek aspirates (θ, χ, ϕ), the letters produced with a slight exhalation, essentially an "h." Aspirates sound like the p-h in "to**p h**at." That is the sound of ϕ. θ is t-h. χ is k-h.

We can also now properly apply syllabic quantity (the duration over which we vocalize certain vowels). Diphthongs and certain vowels (to use our familiar musical language) typically extend for a whole note, and the rest, only a half note.

Furthermore, we better understand the importance of euphony. Euphony is simply pleasant spoken sound that is created by smooth sequences of phonemes.[2] It's a matter of taste, perhaps. "Let me not to the marriage of true minds admit impediments" strikes me as euphonious. All these refinements brought the sound of ancient Greek closer to the modern ear. Fifty years ago, Greek pronunciation was grossly incorrect.

Aristophanes, on hearing our refinements, might snort in derision, but he would nonetheless understand them as actual Greek. On hearing students barbarize with the traditional mispronunciation, however, he would just stare at them, uncomprehending.

The translation problem doesn't end, of course, with Homer. Even after the rosy-fingered Homeric dawn of Western letters, when the Greek mind was illuminating the expanding Hellenic world, other Greek writers still irradiated their words with music. Some pre-Socratic philosophers composed, like Homer, in dactylic hexameter (A rumba-like rhythm repeated six times per verse). By the melodies of his prose, Plato—according to Longinus, a first century A.D. rhetorician—strove to match the sonorities of Homer. The plays

---

[2] A phoneme is any perceptually distinct unit of sound.

of Aeschylus, Sophocles, and Euripides, ringing with choral music and arias, prefigured opera and inspired its creation in late 16th century Italy.

George Hall writes in the *Guardian,* "[t]hough various ways of bringing music and drama together had been explored over centuries [opera happened when] a group of Florentine intellectuals called the Camarata decided to recreate the original form of Greek Drama …. and accordingly, one of them, Jacopo Peri, composed *Dafne*" (1597).

And there's this from the *Britannica*: "The Florentine Camarata…. sought to revive ancient Greek drama and music…. the Camarata used music to heighten the poetic qualities of the dialogue."

It is impossible to separate the meaning of Greek thought from its aurality and musicality. The Greeks knew it themselves and emphasized it in their writing. We deceive ourselves in thinking that we are teaching Homer, or Plato, or any other ancient, if we are only teaching translations.

Music unites mind and body

The music of the ancient Greek language is not merely ornamental or rhetorical in a shallow sense. The musicality of the language gives it a deeper power: It unites the mind and body. In this way, Greek harmonizes our very being; it gives us greater knowledge of, and command over ourselves.

What made the ancient authors so mindful of their music is still debated, but it appears that most of their readers *read out loud.* For centuries, silent reading—among antiquity's few readers—was, at least, unusual; history names only Julius Caesar, a couple of senators under Augustus, and Saints Ambrose and Augustine. They read silently, but only on occasion.[3] So, ancient readers didn't just *think* their texts; they *intoned* them, that they might hear and feel the mind of the author whose text lay before them. They knew that phonemes broadcast their influence beyond the ears; they resound throughout the whole body. For example, the letters "p" and "b" require slight bursts of air, more than, say, the letter "d." Researchers used turkey basters to puff on peoples' necks.[4] Capitalizing on synesthesia—the ability to transduce one perceptual modality, like touch, into another, like audition—they asked their

[3] St. Augustine learned silent reading from his mentor, St. Ambrose. In the *Confessions* Augustine observed of Ambrose, "His heart searched out the sense, but his voice and tongue were at rest."

[4] 2009, National Public Radio.

subjects to tell which consonants they "heard" the most. The subjects answered "p" and "b."

This musical feature of ancient Greek makes it a richer and more enriching language than most others, because it more widely engages and challenges the brain. Mandarin Chinese is like ancient Greek in having musical pitch-accents. In 2002 researcher Sophie Scott showed that the intonations of Mandarin make its speakers use both the right and the left temporal lobes to communicate while, in contrast, speakers of stress-accent languages like English only use the left.[5] Other researchers (Etienne, 2003) question this interpretation, but even their own work shows that musicality in speech increases inter-lobal coordination. Cortical centers in the right hemisphere, named Broca's and Wernicke's, are dedicated to the prosody, or music, of speech.

So, the sonic effects of Greek literature go beyond those of most other literatures, ancient or modern. Ancient Greek, owing to its pitch accents, is imbued with song; the distinctive function of song derives largely from music; music plays a unique role in human life; and because the musicality of literature incommodes apologists for translations, we will look at some defining characteristics of music.

Maybe I personally overvalue music. But musicologists seem to agree that music, with its melody and rhythms, adds an expressive dimension to speech and text. As composer and lecturer Robert Greenberg says, music can reveal truths beyond the written word; when we marry words to music, as opera does, we make a whole greater than the sum of its parts; we evoke thoughts and feelings incommunicable by words alone. The ancient authors were not merely evoking the incorporeal cognitions and subvocal reflexes to which we silent readers are limited today, but were engaging the reader's whole body—ears, lungs and vocal systems, facial and postural muscles. Then, in a kind of perceptual echo, the feedback from vocal exertion would re-stimulate the entire sensorium. This phenomenon corresponds to what cognitive scientist Benjamin Bergen (2012) calls "*embodied simulation*," the sights, sounds, feelings and actions we inwardly experience every time we hear a word. Only from the pitch accents, the true vowel sounds and poetic rhythms can we retrieve the sonic embodiment (Butler, 2015) of the authors' intentions. Infants relax in response not just to their own mother's lullabies,

[5] *The Week*, 7/10/02.

but the songs of unfamiliar singers, languages and cultures. This suggests some powerful evolutionary role in vocal music (Bainbridge et al., 2020). This psychophysiological, self-feedback performance art underlies all western scholarship, but is now lost, a casualty of the drive to make life easier.

It is true that ordinary speech—by its native virtues of lexical variety, syntactical rules (grammar), symbolic amplifications, vocal inflections (as distinct from pitch accents), and modifications of syllabic emphasis—can express and communicate ideas and inner needs with great virtuosity. However, had prosaic language been able to adequately represent inner experience and sentient life, humans would not have bothered to develop alternative tools of expression. Poetry stretches language to its expressive limits, trying to describe or evoke the passional sphere. Even poetry, however, remains land-bound to its lexical substrate, that is, the fixed meanings of its words. Poetry lacks the amphibious versatility to play in the moving currents and eddies of conscious and unconscious emotional experience. No literary genius—not Shakespeare, not Milton, not Dante—is so skillful in shaping his stories, in cadencing his verses or in finessing his syntax and vocabulary, as to faithfully simulate the purely musical elements of wordless experience as they flow through the mind, commingling and separating, perpetually changing each other by their unique effects. And much less so can any discursive, expositional, scientific prose adequately conceptualize the motions of the interior.

Others have identified the educational importance of musical language on a neurobiological level. British-American literary scholar Frederick Turner is a much-cited pioneer in the neurobiology of aesthetics. With German neuroscientist Ernst Pöppel, he discovered that we thirst, neurobiologically, for certain artistic effects, such as poetic meter and visual patterns, because they promise new harmonies, new emergences, new complex understandings of reality to the brain. These artistic inducements to new organizations of the mind he calls "neurocharms" (Turner, 2002).

Over all cultures and all times, Turner wrote, neurocharms harmonize various functional areas of the human brain. "...... meter is so neatly attuned to the functionings of the brain itself, it can [stimulate and reinforce] those mental capacities that together contribute to and compose what we term understanding, in the fullest sense of the word" (Turner and Pöppel, 1983, p. 71-72).

So, reading Homer without meter and pitch accents together, like reading an aria, mutilates the art, and to read him in translation obliterates much of what is unique and profound in this literary treasure. This isn't really controversial: Linguists have long known that what distinguishes human language from other natural sounds, say birdsong, is language's systematic patterned links *between meaning and sound* over a potentially infinite range of meanings and sounds. For almost one hundred years, defenders of translations have insisted that unlinking meaning and sounds isn't fatal to education, and have even implied that the reader of Homer in translation has acquitted every scholar of his obligation to learn Homer.

For nearly a century, professional academics, never reading ancient Greek, never hearing or rehearsing the cadences and sounds of Homer, gradually forgetting their intellectual heritage and sometimes despising it, have nonetheless claimed their places in the ancient community of masters and scholars. But the Greekless scholar is to the Classical scholar as a coroner is to a surgeon, both knowing the parts of the body, one dissecting a carcass, the other cutting open a breathing person with a beating heart.

I have deliberated on the difference between translations and the original text because it exposes the illusion that higher education, by dismissing Greek and Latin studies from the heart of its curriculum, has cost society nothing that actually matters. As it used to be said,

Traduttore-Traditore! (Translator—Traitor!)

If the popular belief that translations are adequate is false, why does it persist among the educated? Maybe something deeper than the taste for convenience, more daemonic than the desire to avoid the time, toil and trouble of learning the ancient languages, has been misleading the defenders of translations.

Mental Growth Through Rigor and Dexterity: A demonstration

That ancient Greek must be sung, and thus engage the whole mind and body, requires unique skills. Ancient Greek, more than other kinds of study, challenges the mind, and by that challenge, generates mental growth.

Mental Growth is a psychical transformation from incoherence to coherence, stimulated by exposure to truth. The mind cannot grow unless a person recognizes, tolerates and reflects on reality, even when reality causes pain—pain such as anxiety, regret, sadness, shame, guilt or even boredom—rather than evades it. Mental growth is a transition from the evasion, to the acceptance, of such realities. When we tolerate a painful reality, thought emerges:[6] we scan our memories; we perform a rational analysis of the meaning of the pain; and we make predictions. Thought is intended to manage the pain and understand it—its cause, quality, and course.

Mental growth is also the discovery that certain events are constantly conjoined, that is, always happening together. All learning entails this recognition. Subsequently, the mind reflects on these conjunctions, and forms novel ideas, abstractions, or concepts to explain them.

These conceptual innovations bind the conjoined phenomena and prevent their dispersal back into mental chaos. The bound conjunction instantly generates an expanding penumbra of meanings. Those touch other perceived or remembered events, turning up more potential conjunctions to be recognized and bound, and radiating new penumbras of meaning. We recognize this process when a scientific discovery is followed quickly by an elaboration of the discovery into an intellectual system, comprising a cascade of new insights.

Learning Greek and Latin improve the mind's binding ability in other ways: To master the Classical vocabularies by extensive drilling and memorization, fortifies the powers of attention, memory and reflection, extends the scholar's English vocabulary, and irradiates English derivatives with the spectra of their ancient meanings. Those who, when young, learn the Greek κῦδος (kudos), for example, or Latin *gravitas,* forever hear overtones of their earlier meanings whenever they encounter their narrow modern meanings of "praise" and "weight." They hear in κῦδος not only "glory and fame," those transient blessings we seek from the external world, but also "pride," an internal condition. In *gravitas,* they hear not only "seriousness and depth," but "consequence, pressure, pregnancy of meaning, creativity and power." They even hear counter-tones of "dullness" and "faintness."

Translation of Latin and Greek into English forces the student, on one hand, to fix the meanings of words; this requires a solid understanding of inflections. Inflections are short suffixes, like the Latin –ae, -os, and -u; these signify grammatical functions like subject, indirect object, direct object and

---

[6] This is one of countless evocations in this book of *hormesis* (see *Glossary*), the positive biological response to stress.

so on (English indicates most of these functions with word order). Translation also, therefore, requires accurate knowledge of the parts of speech and appreciation of grammatical relations, all within the contexts of the specific passage being examined and the work as a whole. Because of the continuously changing context, translation must often suspend judgment, backtrack, review earlier decisions, and revise those decisions as new material accumulates. Good translation restrains premature foreclosure. The process strengthens and refines analytic and synthetic mental functions.

But even though modern languages aren't so heavily inflected, doesn't their translation still require just as much mental exercise? Well, let's put Greek and Latin toe-to-toe with French. For the purpose of the contest, we'll borrow Simmons' example, the Latin phrase, "Vellem mortuos," and expand his analysis.

First consider the French equivalent, "Je voudrais qu'ils soient morts." How many mental steps are required to translate this into English?

Having four independent words and one contraction, the sentence requires six word-recognitions (those being the first six mental steps in translating the sentence) plus four grammatical identifications, consisting of the persons 7), 8) and voices 9), 10) of *voudrais* and *soient*, then recognition of 11) *qu'* as *que*, a conjunction introducing the clause whose subject is 12) *ils* to which 13) *morts* is in apposition. Since French, like our native English, uses word order to indicate grammatical function, we already recognize subject and object. So, with thirteen discrete cognitions—good mental exercise, no doubt—we can translate the French sentence correctly as "Would that they were dead."

Now we consider "Vellem mortuos." Understanding this sentence will require twenty-one cognitive steps. Looking at "vellem," the Latin student must 1) determine, right off the bat, whether it is a verb or noun, because its suffix, *-em*, though possibly verbal, is also identical to the endings of certain nouns in the accusative case. This predicament obliges him to 2) remember what cases are. Then, to establish *vellem* as a verb, he must know 3) the person [1st, 2nd, or 3rd] 4) number [singular or plural] 5) Voice [indicative, imperative, subjunctive, or infinitive] 6) tense [present, future, imperfect, perfect ... etc.] and 7) Mood [active or passive] to which this verb may correspond.

But we still haven't determined whether vellem *is* a verb. The translator must recognize 8) that *vellem* could come from "volo," meaning 9) "wish," that 10) the *–em* ending and the word's internal change from *vol-* to *vell-*

suggest the subjunctive voice, and that, in this context, 11) the subjunctive has a particular shade of meaning, before he can fit all the pieces together and conclude that "Vellem" means "Would that …"

The word *mortuos* tasks the intellect at least five more times. The student must 12) realize that the word is in the accusative case. "Accusative" describes a noun acting as the direct object of a verb—*sometimes*. At other times the accusative is used in a grammatical construction called "indirect statement," a usage common in both Greek and Latin. The translator must therefore 13) determine which usage of the accusative is needed here. Along the way he must 14) remember the *declension* of "mortuus." Latin nouns, if mortuus *is* a noun, are divided into five declensions, each forming their various cases by adding the *inflections* specific to that declension. This knowledge will help the translator determine if *mortuos* is, in fact, accusative.

It's hard for Anglophones to appreciate how much meaning can be compressed into two or three letters, and this particular inflection, *–os*, is as densely packed as it can be. The Latinist must recognize *mortuos* as 15) plural and 16) masculine, that it 17) derives from *mortuus*, and that *mortuus* 18) derives in turn from *morior,* meaning 19) "to die."

Having recognized that last derivation, the translator is suddenly 20) flooded with light, slapping his forehead, and exulting in his own sagacity, for he has just realized that *mortuos* is not a noun at all, but a participle (a verbal noun, like a gerund, which is declined like a noun). If he can now only 21) understand why the accusative form of this participle is necessary (it is necessary because the sentence is an *indirect statement* of the form "I wish that …."), then he can confidently construe "Vellem mortuos" as "Would that they were dead."

Now the reader can appreciate the Latin Student's Lament:

Latin is a language
Dead as dead can be;
First it killed the Romans,
Now it's killing me.

But for all the eloquence of that complaint, the translation of the Greek equivalent, ὤφελον τεθνηότας (my rendering), is yet more demanding. In addition to those 21 mental tasks requisite to the Latin, the Greek phrase requires its translator to 22) understand an alien alphabet; to have mastered 23) a strange apparatus of pitch accents and 24) breathings; and 25) to understand reduplication (the doubling of a sound standing at the beginning of a word: τεθ–). This particular sample does not require the additional steps of recognizing 26) poetic elisions and 27) so-called Greek particles.

The final score: Greek, 25 (27); Latin, 21; and French, 13.

Classical study is rigorous, and though we still value rigor, those who will submit to it are growing less common. Yet, for this tolerance of rigor there is no substitute; without it, intellectual life is doomed to shallowness and futility. Long, close reading of Greek and Latin is one of the best ways to build that tolerance and enable the mind to acquit itself of hard intellectual tasks with creativity, satisfaction and elegance.

Latin is orderly, and ideal for recordkeeping and aphorizing. But it can, in the hands of a genius like Virgil, climb to magisterial heights and mesmerize the reader with its euphony. This refines Latin readers' aesthetic for linguistic sound, and this refinement flows over into their vernacular.

Greek is an even more powerful tonic for self-expression. Cahill characterizes Greek as more fluid and luxurious than the terse "desert talk" of Hebrew, more literary and complex than Latin. He compares this beautiful language, to a "vast orchestra of diverse instruments, able to produce modulations of extraordinary refinement" (201). He lovingly describes ancient Greek as proceeding

> in a naturally discursive style, constantly turning this way and that in elegant riffs and delicate variations, like a spring river running to tributaries, curling into rivulets, bubbling into pools (201).

Greek engraves new patterns of expression that its readers consciously and non-consciously follow, diversifying and adorning the patterns of their own native languages.

For similar reasons, Sir Richard Livingstone, a classicist of the early 1900's, wrote: "... not to know Greek is to be ignorant of the most flexible and subtle instruments of expression which the human mind has devised..."

The dance-like character of Greek syntax discourages rigid or fixed forms of expression. Its liveliness inspired Virginia Woolf to say that

> no language can move more quickly, dancing, all alive, and yet controlled. Then there are the words themselves—so clear, so hard, so intense, that to speak plainly yet fittingly, without blurring the outline and clouding the depths, Greek is the only expression.

There once was a time when educated people thought it obvious that such mental exercise inured the student to the austerities and complexities of any worthy intellectual work. There was a time when educated people assumed that the reading, hearing and speaking of ancient languages and the cultures reflected in those languages sophisticated the mind. Once, we knew we could properly evaluate contemporary ideas, arts or inventions only by examining them in the context of their intellectual history. Can we now be trusted to assess, for example, the true personal and social value of computers?

Goethe said, and cultural leaders at one time believed, that whoever doesn't have 3000 years to draw upon is living hand to mouth. Without the ballast of cultural and historical knowledge, we are mental featherweights, blown by all the breezes of fashion and group fantasy.

But a long time ago even educated people abjured these beliefs. And the results are before us: Media professionals confuse pronouns; Americans countenance presidents who can't form sentences; few of us can recite poetry from memory; forty-year-olds can't do long division; and increasing numbers can't write cursive.

Once, the Classical humanist university forced its students to blaze new cognitive trails by learning a strange alphabet (in Greek), new vocabulary, unfamiliar sounds, and an alien syntax. They forced them to re-tune their minds to the elegant languages of other eras and to accommodate ideas that discomposed their habits of thought. By these compulsory adventures, their students could annex mental territory and acquire a level of intellectual endurance unknown to most modern students.

What are we without Greek?

5.

Self-Knowledge and Tension-Tolerance

I have already named the highest Greek value, mental growth. And the hardest part of mental growth is self-knowledge—but what is that? In order to grasp how *paideia* lays the groundwork for alert, mindful and responsible citizenry, we need to know what it means to teach self-knowledge.

What I mean by "self-knowledge" is more a verb than a noun; more a pursuit, like fluency in a language, than an achievement. When someone asked then ninety-year-old Pablo Casals why he still practiced cello so carefully, he answered, "Because I'm making progress." The practice of self-knowledge is like that, a lifetime work in progress. The mind, having been found out, or suspecting self-surveillance, will try still more cunningly to redeceive itself. I will try to show that the Western tradition intended self-knowledge to mean a lifelong habit of searching for signs of self-deception; for one's characteristic strategies of self-deception; and for ways to read those signs and interrupt those strategies. Ultimately, self-knowledge is reality-testing of the inner world.

Know Thyself

I'll introduce the unique Western contribution to self-knowledge by analyzing the famous inscription above the entrance to the temple at Delphi: "Know thyself."

Classical scholars, mindful of the Greek preoccupation with the dangers of grandiosity, have understood the inscription as "Know your limits." This makes the phrase into either a general command to humanity ("You're humans; don't try to be gods.") or advice to individuals ("Know your limitations; stay within yourself").

Werner Jaeger was one such scholar. He seems to have adopted these two interpretations, further explaining that the famous saying reflects the "doctrine of sophrosyne." He is referring to the Greek word σωφροσύνη (sophrosyne) the concept of psychological equipoise. The word has various meanings, including soundness of mind, prudence, discretion, and sanity; moderation in sensual desire; self-control and temperance. Jaeger's view implies "If you know your limits, you will be prudent, sane, discrete and moderate in your actions and reactions." Many classicists have agreed with Jaeger's perspective and with this implication, but waver on this sensible but superficial view of the Greek insight. Jaeger himself says that the "... philosopher works on his understanding of the nature of the psyche" (1928, Vol. 3, p. 22). Elsewhere he acknowledges depth psychology among the ancients, calling Plato "… the father of psychoanalysis… [because he was] the first to disclose that… the lewd desire to have sexual intercourse with one's own mother was part of the unconscious personality" (1928, Vol. 2, p. 343).

I think that Jaeger and the other "limits" interpreters perceive a connection between awareness of limits and awareness of self.[1] People or cultures that cling to an illusion of *omnipotence* tend to deny their helplessness to invisible inner forces. This connection explains the modern group intuition that labelled psychoanalysts "shrinks" (Because analysts *shrink* grandiosity). On the other hand, the "limits" interpreters are wrong to overlook, in "Know thyself," its exhortation to seek the invisible springs of human thought and action.

The Greek text of the inscribed phrase is γνῶθι σεαυτόν. Even allowing for its untranslatable overtones, the translated phrase doesn't come close to "Know thy limits." γνῶθι (gnothi) is the imperative of γιγνώσκω (gignosko) ("I know, understand, am aware of, examine") and σεαυτόν is an intensive personal pronoun ("yourself") in the accusative case—that is, an object of the verb γνῶθι. The phrase translates, therefore, as "Know Yourself."

Consider next the context of the Delphic command. It sat among three inscriptions on the façade of the same temple. A second inscription reads μηδὲν ἄγαν (meden agan), or "Nothing overmuch," or, as often translated, "Everything in moderation." The third was a mysterious single letter, "E."

---

[1] Contemporary philosopher Galen Strawson, reflecting on Iris Murdoch's thought, said "I share Murdoch's doubts about Socrates' famous claim that the unexamined life is not worth living, when it's taken to be equivalent to the Delphic injunction "Know thyself," and both are taken (wrongly) to recommend minute self-analysis. That way, she thinks, lies fantasy and delusion and (anyway, as she says) 'an unexamined life can be virtuous'" 7/12/19 *Times Literary Supplement*, (*TLS*).
Surely Murdoch didn't think that self-ignorance leads to truth and clarity. And we may well admire a virtuous, self-ignorant life, I think, without agreeing that a human life unaware of its motivations is worth living.

Plutarch believed it stood for the word ΕΣΣΙ (essi), a second-person indicative form of the verb "to be": "Thou art." If Plutarch was right, this could be an early existentialist statement, meaning something like: "Remember that you are responsible for the decisions that make you who you are, the decisions which determine the course of your life."

On the other hand, neither Plutarch nor any other ancient commentator has explained why "E" could not represent ΕΣΣΟ (esso), an optative imperative "Be!" In this case, E could mean something like: "You have no choice but to be who you are, so Be (true to) Yourself." As Pindar writes, in his 2nd *Pythian Ode:* γένοι' οἷος ἐσσὶ μαθών ("Having learned, become such as you are") or Nietzsche: "Become who you are."

These speculations, if true, would explain why the author, or inscriber of "Know thyself," would have had no need to burden his locution with the superfluous duty of telling humanity to know its limits; "Nothing in excess" does most of that work. And either essi or esso would remind its readers to live authentically. The three statements, taken together, warn humanity not to let hubristic grandiosity, on one hand, or hubristic contempt for truth (in pretending to be someone you aren't) on the other, distract it from the care, cultivation, and contemplation of the self. These three teachings constitute the context of "Know thyself."

Finally, we take a historical perspective. In all times and in all places, humans must have wondered why their personalities were different; why some took harrowing risks while others avoided the slightest dangers; why some recalled nightmares every morning while others slept peacefully and dreamlessly. A primitive person who reported seeing visions would have prompted his family or tribe to try to explain those visions. They would sometimes have believed they were divinely inspired. Later, as the species became more self-reflective and realistic, it substituted sublunary, for supernatural, explanations of individual differences. The Greeks especially, as they adopted a more rationalistic, scientific perspective on nature in general, realized that the diversity of human behaviors and beliefs derived from the diversity of antecedent human experience and the impressions those experiences carved into the personality. They realized that the springs of personal motivation lay deeply in one's private history.

Already in the 8th century B. C. Homer was moving the locus of human motivation from gods to men. Before Homer, god was the actor and humans were his mindless tools. But Homeric man, although not yet master of his fate, was becoming an unconscious collaborator in shaping it. Two hundred years later, Sophocles (496-406 B.C.), had elevated Homer's souls—the wan life-spirits that inhabited men and, after their deaths, aimlessly trod the asphodel in gloomy Hades—into the inner springs of human motivation and meaning.

Sophocles used the myth of Oedipus to explore the perils of both self-ignorance *and* self-knowledge. Sophocles intuitively understood that certain unconscious truths about the self, truths that, in becoming conscious, could mobilize hatred and violence toward the self. At one point in *Oedipus Rex*, Teiresias the seer tells the shocked Oedipus that Oedipus had murdered his father. The Theban king's denial and outrage yielded in time to a terrible realization that the seer might be right. Soon after, Oedipus learned that Polybus, the man he'd thought to be his father, had died of natural causes. Jocasta, wife of Oedipus, former wife of King Laius, did not yet know that she was the mother of Oedipus. So, she jumped on this news, perhaps because she'd grown uneasy with the way the story was unfolding. Sophocles, knowingly or not, may be personifying, in Jocasta, both what Freud would have called Oedipus's "signal anxiety" as well as the impulse to self-deception that signal anxiety mobilizes.[2] She presented the news to Oedipus as incontrovertible evidence that he had *not* killed his father and married his mother, something predicted long before by the Delphic oracle. In her reassuring speech, she implies that Oedipus's dread of the oracle is due to a common male fantasy. She says,

πολλοὶ γὰρ ἤδη κἀν ὀνείρασιν βροτῶν
μητρὶ ξυνηυνάσθησαν.
("For many a man has already in his dreams lain together with his mother"
(translation mine. OIDIPOUS TURRANOS (*Oedipus Rex*, lns. 981-82)

Sophocles' irony shows his awareness that dreams reveal unconscious truths about the self.

By the time Sophocles had become an old man, the centrality of the soul, so strongly implied in his plays, had reached its fullness. This we find too in the thinking of Socrates, whose prime directive to all humanity was to care for the soul.[3] Socrates argued in the agora, the gymnasium, and the homes of his friends that neglect of the soul made people think they knew more than

---

[2] Please see Glossary.

[3] Sometimes ψῡχῆς θεραπεία , as noted earlier; sometimes ψῡχῆς ἐπιμέλεια (caring for the soul), as in *Apology* 29d-30b.

they actually did. Socrates was also aware that people had characteristic habits of self-deception (Moore, 2015), though he did not understand their unconscious dynamics. The Platonic-Socratic texts insist that self-knowledge is a lifelong project of self-rectification, demanding continuous reflection and face-to-face conversation and argumentation. This, by the way, is an irreplaceable function of the brick-and-mortar lecture hall, classroom and campus (Ibid., 2016).

Meanwhile, on the Athenian proscenia, the first true psychologist was staging his new plays. Euripides, only eleven years younger than Sophocles, had begun to confront the turbulent inner world of human passions and drives. In drama after drama, he portrayed mental conflict, the collision between irrational inner forces and the intellect. Euripides recognized that people were often not aware of these conflicts or of other inner realities. He also recognized the danger of not knowing oneself. His studies of the mind followed the rationalist path first taken by the Ionian philosophers and scientists, later by the Athenians. This path led through both geophysical and conceptual spheres into previously hidden territories. Euripides now blazed it into psychological frontiers, discovering how tensions arising from sexual disappointments, betrayals and other severe frustrations lead to psychopathology. He illustrates these morbid processes in both his *Medea* and *Hippolytus*. In *Hecuba* Euripides specifically contemplates the unconsciously corrupting effects of mental pain on the character of a high-minded woman.

The Greeks, then, in the fifth-century B. C. E., understood that the human mind was in conflict, waging an internal civil war, pitting a rational part against an impulsive, irrational part. Plato allegorizes the conflict in *Phaedrus* 253-256, with his famous metaphor of the mind as a charioteer trying to control an unruly horse, the irrational drive. This universal condition, Plato implied, obliges all individuals to know their own minds, lest the unseen power of greed, rage and lust surprise and overwhelm the rational part.

The great philosopher also understood something deeper than this almost obvious predicament. He realized that unconscious needs, thoughts, and fantasies exist in everyone, and that many of these appear only in dreamscapes. In Book IX of the *Republic* Plato says that "the lawless desires .... are awakened in sleep when the rest of the soul .... slumbers ...."[4] Then, perhaps recalling Sophocles' lines, he continues, "the savage part ...does not

---

[4] 571c.

shrink from attempting to lie with a mother …" and follows with "… there exists in every one of us … a terrible, fierce and lawless brood of desires, which it seems are revealed in our sleep."[5]

The actual author of "Know thyself" may still have been alive back when Sophocles was born. One possible author of the saying is Chilon of Lacedaemon, one of the Seven Sages of the ancient world. He was *ephor* (magistrate) at Sparta in 536 B. C. The earliest intuitions of the Greek psychological enlightenment may have informed his celebrated exhortation. It may have germinated in Chilon an embryonic notion of a hidden inner life that could blindside its unsuspecting victim. He may or may not have consciously intended to remind his readers to search their minds in the way we can today. But in the spreading light of subsequent cultural education, the Greeks would have been increasingly conditioned to read his message as a warning: Search your souls for personal meaning and the hidden motivations driving your behavior and emotions.

Perhaps, then, some of the "limits" interpreters have overlooked or dismissed this evidence. This would make it harder for them to believe that an ancient scribe or his primitive readers could conceive of a hidden inner life. Or perhaps they reject the psychological view of "Know thyself" because a philosophical or sociological interpretation of the phrase doesn't threaten their sense of self-mastery.

The Cambridge Classicist Simon Goldhill, in contrast, adopts the psychological view. He cites Euripides' tragedy, the *Bacchae*, in which Thebes' young king Pentheus fails to recognize the god Dionysus, and imprisons him. The god challenges Pentheus: "You do not know what your life is, nor what you are doing, nor who you are." Unable to accept this truth, Pentheus lamely recites his patrimony.

At the climax of the play, Agave, Pentheus' mother, catches her disguised son spying on some women maddened by Dionysus. She grabs him, and Pentheus, understanding her grisly intentions, strips off his disguise and pleads, "I am your child, Mother, Pentheus … pity me…!" In her derangement, she couldn't recognize her own son. She tears his arm from its socket and then, with her daughters, dismembers the rest of his body. According to Goldhill, the drama says: "Self-ignorance is oblivion and disintegration."

---

[5] 572b.

About the phrase "Know Thyself," then, he concludes:

> For both individuals and states, the inscription gives a stark warning. Self-knowledge is the first and last necessity, if you are to understand the questions and answers of your life. This injunction from the god at Delphi has lost none of its power. Without self-awareness, without self-understanding, there can only be a fragile grasp on the questions that matter (Goldhill, 2004, p. 8).

It is probably true that the ancient Greek thinkers did not understand the stubbornness and evasive cunning of unconscious defenses. But the textual, contextual and historical evidence suggest that they recognized a hidden inner life and its role in self-deception as well as—probably better than—our era does.

The Origins of Self-Deception

Self-deception opposes self-knowledge. With what kinds of self-deceptions were the Greeks battling? The answer, I think, lies in the origin and nature of self-deception.

The danger of self-deception might seem less ominous for us moderns than it did for the Greeks or, even more so, primitive foragers. For them, quick and horrible death was as close as the next denial. Suppose our Paleolithic parents chose, owing to fatigue, for example, to ignore the unpleasant adrenalin rush stimulated by a telltale snake's scent, or a twig snapping behind them, or a big cat's fresh scats.

Though the modern costs of ignoring unconscious motivations often come due more slowly and intangibly, they are self-destructive all the same. Unconscious motives can ruin careers, finances, mental health, and perhaps above all, the authentic life.

To care for the soul, one must bear the tensions required for careful attention to inner and outer signals. The bearing of such tensions is the crucial element of reality-testing, the faculty that sees and foresees internal and external dangers.

Maintaining contact with reality was probably the original purpose of self-reflection.[6] This function grew increasingly necessary as the mind grew more cunning. In a late phase of hominid evolution, the brain grew rapidly,

---

[6] Self-reflection might have a rudimentary form in every animal's ability to "check back" on its initial perception of a stimulus.

thickening its neural networks in parallel with the social network, as though brain and society were reciprocally complexifying each other. Increasingly, sexual success depended more upon craftiness, cooperativeness and poise, and less on physical prowess. Increasingly, people learned to hide selfishness behind sociality.

Social awkwardness would have betrayed an imperfect control of selfish impulses and undermined the credibility and prestige of the speaker or actor. Those who learned poise would rise in status.

How does one gain poise? Duplicity causes tension that the deceiver involuntarily betrays by incongruent pitches or timbres of voice, facial grimaces or bodily awkwardness. Detectives and criminologists have long known this. As Freud famously wrote:

> He that has eyes to see and ears to hear may convince himself that no mortal can keep a secret. If his lips are silent, he chatters with his fingertips; betrayal oozes out of him at every pore (1905, pp. 77-78).

Primitive humans were probably good detectors of such cues. So, what would deceivers do? They would suppress revealing signals by *not knowing* they were being deceptive; they would obliterate awareness of their own lies. Self-ignorance would have reduced the liars' uneasiness and smoothed out the edgy signs of that uneasiness.

Here, then is a plausible evolutionary story: Skill in self-deception enhanced social and sexual success. Evolution selected mutations that strengthened the traits or capacities that supported self-deception. One of those capacities, consciousness itself, emerged more to improve self-deception than to refine reality-testing.[7] Here's why: Effective lying required self-deception. This, in turn, required a kind of inner television, or radio, which could broadcast misleading scenes or voices to the liar's consciousness, interposing these scenes between the subject and reality. Distorted consciousness helped liars persuade themselves of the truth of their lies.

It was perhaps inevitable that such schemes of self-deception would also injure the mental apparatus and endanger social groups by corrupting the knowledge upon which they exercised their judgment.

I suggest that the rise of self-deception required a countervailing function. This function rehabilitated distorted mental representations and retrieved

---

[7] Badcock, *Ibid.*, p. 72.

distressing memories previously banished to the unconscious. Evolution selected for a faculty for self-reflection.

Evolutionary psychologists have traced out a history of human consciousness, unconsciousness, intelligence and language. It is based in nature's propensity for "dishonest signaling," a deceptiveness all creatures use to gain reproductive advantages (Alexander, 1975 and others).

Primates, for example, not only had to heed leopards, but fellows of their troops who, to win food or sexual status, might want to harm them. Altruism among kin offered some protection to potential victims, since the genetic advantage of kindness to kin ensured its widespread practice. But even kin generosity, when long-unrepaid, will eventually flip into retaliation. Furthermore, altruism toward non-kin only makes sense if the beneficiary is likely to return the favor. And here is altruism's fatal flaw: Any beneficiary may opportunistically fail to reciprocate ("gross cheating") or may reciprocate incompletely ("subtle cheating") (Trivers, 1971).

Cheating is a way to get "free lunches" of status and reproductive opportunities. There is a kind of male fly which, by puffing out its abdomen, fools the female into thinking he is laden with food, and so she offers herself to him. By the time she realizes the imposture, the deed is done. He has debauched her by dishonest signaling (biological lying), a strategy even plants practice. Similarly, cheating and deception by conspecifics made primates guard against their own kind, as well as against predators (Dunbar, 1996). This naturally required much more cognitive work.

So, primates' growing need to monitor and detect cheating, while practicing (very) discriminative altruism, rapidly enhanced mental power, an element of mental growth. Humphrey (1976) and others have postulated this very thing, that intraspecific (same-species) conflict, deception, and the consequent need for sophisticated mind-reading, drove the evolution of hominine intelligence. Those better able to identify deceit and elude exploitation gained more reproduce success. Moreover, every innovation in deception or deception-detection created selection pressures for a counter-innovation. This process generated an upward spiral of interactional complexity, a kind of arms race between deception and detection.

Intelligent deceivers are acutely aware they might be detected and, accordingly, suffer severe and possibly fatal reprisals. Their anxiety, betrayed by non-verbal signs, would increase the likelihood of detection. So, again, unconsciousness of their deceptions, as Trivers (1985b, 415-16) suggested, helped deceivers succeed.

Trivers' logic requires that the unconscious not only take over social planning (deception, manipulation, etc.), but also scrutiny of the victim's behavior: Effective deception requires sharp moment-to-moment monitoring of the victim's responses.

The victims of deception were also under selective pressure to improve their ability to hide their awareness of the *deceiver's* intentions, gaining a strategic advantage by counter-deception. This too would have fed an endless paranoid loop of deception-innovation, exhausting the species of energy needed for food, personal hygiene, mutual grooming, reproductive activities and waste disposal.

Because unconscious social perception should be biased in favor of the subject's interest (so as to enhance the subject's reproductive success), virtually every interaction ought to become "paranoid" with respect to others: Better to fight or flee, than wait-and-see.

As hominine groups expanded, then, individuals became more cleverly armed against one another with strategies of deception, self-deception, and deception-detection. Fellow hominines became the principle hostile force of nature—the principal cause of the individual's failure to survive or reproduce (Alexander, 1987: 78). *Homo homini lupus* (Plautus): Man is wolf to man.

This is a plausible portrait of human history. But isn't the evolutionary triumph of deception and self-deception missing a piece at the end of its story?

Without a corrective principle, humanity could have died early, its reality-testing consumed in this maelstrom of mendacity. Without such correctives, the species could have fallen into a vicious cycle of intensifying paranoia.

Paranoia, no doubt, lurks behind our social personas. But we also enjoy a certain level of trust. We could only have achieved that with enough self-insight to recognize our hunger for the reassurance of friendly relations. Then we could count on similar motives in others. This is not the only selective pressure that might account for a psychoanalytic instinct, nor even the most important. But perhaps it's the most obvious: Without selective pressure for self-knowing, we would have trapped ourselves in a dystopian, paranoid world and perished before our time, which is coming soon enough.

So, evolution would have selected traits or tendencies that supported self-knowledge, the ultimate psychological refinement. Sanity, good judgment and wholesome social contacts depended upon a balance between self-ignorance and self-knowledge.

But self-knowledge restores dissonant, painful, or inconvenient truths, and inflicts fresh tensions. The disagreeability of such tensions, compared to the agreeable narcosis induced by self-deception or group inclusion forever handicaps self-knowledge in its contest with self-ignorance.[8]

Humans needed an educational strategy to redress that disadvantage.

The Values of Self-Knowledge

Classics students will be reluctant to retreat from self-knowledge when those they admire esteemed it as the highest value of all. The students of ancient wisdom must at least watch themselves shrink from the challenges with which their daily reading confronts them. And if, even once, just for a moment, they notice an aversion to self-awareness, they will have begun the process of self-discovery.

In this process, the Classics student experiences exactly what the Greeks meant by self-knowledge. Several guiding principles, or ideals of *paideia*, ideals bearing upon self-knowledge, emerged from the political and cultural freedoms of the early Classical period. Let's consider a few of these foundational ideals, starting with self-determination and perfection of the inner-life.

a. Self-determination

By the mid-5th century BCE, the notion of individualistic freedom was securely lodged in the Greek mind. This ideal had developed slowly, though, in the northern Mediterranean from 800 BCE-400 BCE. Homer was writing, we think, in the 700's BCE, when monarchical society was passing away. In this era, the city state was displacing the tribal monarchy. The monarchy and aristocracy were colliding, even as the commons were challenging the aristocracy. Those contests led to the great tyrannies and, in some places, democracy.

---

[8] To repeat: we associate *inclusion* (belonging) with reassuring relationships, calmness, pride and identity cohesion; *exclusion* with separation, shame, identity fragmentation, anxiety, agitation and thoughts of death. We use inclusion to regulate anxiety. See Stacey (2003).

The transformation began in Ionia, the central sector of the western coast of Anatolia, an area corresponding to modern-day western Turkey. From there it spread to mainland Greece.

On those same Mediterranean shores, perhaps a century after the great epics were written down, the Ionian city-state emerged. It abolished class privilege and established the liberty of all its members to pursue the free development of their potentialities (Jaeger, 1945, I, p. 137). This new political freedom seems to have counterbalanced the tightening grip an emerging legal system was imposing on the behavior, impulses and passions of its citizens.

I have already mentioned the Ionian philosophers of the 6th and 5th centuries BCE. The Ionians' realistic legal system had created among them a new security, safety and political freedom of thought and speech. This unaccustomed freedom encouraged adventures in naturalistic science. Individualistic freedom may also have inspired Ionian and Aeolian poetry.[9] The poets might now instruct the audience in self-determination, while performing their traditional educational role.

The concept of self-determination is first visible in the lyric poetry of Archilocus (~675 BCE~635 BCE) of Paros (one of the Cyclades Islands). It was Archilocus, according to Jaeger (Ibid., p. 125), who first "formulated the idea that a man could be free only in a life chosen by himself." Homer's Sarpedon, for example, puts Honor above Death. He adhered to the old aristocratic code, and wouldn't consider returning to his fellows without his shield. Archilocus, however, offers a self-interested alternative: In his fragment, "On his shield," Archilochus writes, "One of our Saian foes is exulting over my shield, ... which I left unwillingly beside a bush. But I ... escaped death. Let the old shield go." His writing suggests a new, self-reliant, self-possessed and defiant—if perhaps less heroic—man.

Ionia's governance and cultural practices spread to Athens and Attica in the mid-7th century BCE. This included fashions like the ἀρχαία χλιδή (archaia chlide), the ancient luxury in clothes, hairdressing, and social manners, a "soft" lifestyle. But the new Ionian ideal of individual freedom had not yet swayed the Athenian soul.

The Athenian individualistic ethos evolved reluctantly until Solon came of age in the early 6th century BCE. Solon was a poet, statesman, political

---

[9] Aeolia was a group of cities on the west coast of Anatolia, and included the islands of Lesbos and Tenedos.

scientist, civic leader and above all, educator. He apotheosized the spirit that raised his native city, in less than a half-century, to humanity's most brilliantly intellectual culture. Ancient Greece considered Solon one of her Seven Sages. For a century, schoolboys learned his poems by heart, and orators in the public assembly quoted the great lawgiver to validate their understanding of Athenian citizenship.

As Athens learned to respect individual spiritual activities, she channeled them into the life of her community. Athens was the first to balance the energy of the individual with the unifying power of the state, subordinating individual talents to the economic, political and cultural aspirations of the city-state. By assimilating self-determination into their communal identity, Athenians, unlike the Ionians, mustered the strength to defy the Persian threat and rise to unequalled greatness.

b. Perfection of the Inner-life

When the Romans codified Greek learning, they named this codification the *artes liberales* ("liberal arts"), because they considered these arts necessary to liberate the mind from practical preoccupations and turn it toward a contemplative life. The liberal arts taught the Greek life-view, an outlook that placed wisdom, truth, and perfection of the inner life above wealth, reputation and honor.

We all have some idea of what is meant by wisdom and truth, though they resist definition and acquisition. But *perfection of the inner life* seems impossible to define or acquire because we, as living, evolving, complex creatures cannot perfect anything, least of all our minds. Nonetheless, Humanism promulgates this notion of some ideal consummation of character development, and we, as heirs to that tradition, are obliged to understand that ideal.

But the ideal we are to understand here is a moving target. Inner perfection, on one hand, refers to the empowerment and refinement of the mind, the improvement of memory, judgment and discrimination, as explicated by the authors I've cited above. But perfection of the inner life also refers to the improvement of self-knowledge, by which the ancients meant both knowledge of one's own culture, and of one's own person.

Cicero, for example, believed maturation and civic usefulness required cultural knowledge. The great Roman orator said, "If you do not know where you come from, you will always be a child." That is, you will lack power and authority (*gravitas*) and be useless to society.

c. Mental growth

No body of literature, outside of psychoanalysis, encourages self-examination more generously and insistently than the literature of the ancient Greeks. And, as described, *paideia* drilled its students in the use of words, concepts and logical approaches to problems. It habituated students to intellectual discomfort, and valorized that habituation. *Paideia* gave them the tools to consider tensions thoughtfully and restrain impulsive action, lest they hurt themselves or others. The Classical humanist university supported this kind of self-development and character-building with incentives and sanctions.

Self-development is the consolidation of the *ego*, directed by the individual, supported by family and culture, and intensified in university education. Character building is the *structuralization* of the ego, the person's lifelong process of organizing a more and more complex network of mental links. Structuralization proceeds below consciousness, but advances by conscious, secondary process thinking, exemplified by disciplined learning.

Neuroscientist and psychoanalyst Mark Solms (2002) has given us a neuro-psychoanalytic description of structuralization. He attributes these reality-testing functions to the ego and the prefrontal cortex (a neural component of the ego): Inhibition of unprocessed reflex action (impulsiveness) and instantaneous tension-evasion, binding of the energy saved by inhibition, and repurposing that bound energy for thought. By thinking, the individual or group adapts to tensions in the moment or anticipated in the future. Thought helps the subject tolerate discomfort, delay action, and effectively manage external and internal realities.

Classical educational ideals also restrained tension-evasion. By assimilating the Classical ideals of discipline and exactitude, students consolidated their identities as scholars. Emulation of their teachers and the great Classical figures further fortified their tension-tolerance.

Higher education, by advancing mental growth, is meant to help make lives worth living. A worthy life is not only productive and dutiful; it not only includes friends, lovers and satisfying careers; it also enjoys intellectual achievements, beautiful music and art, magnificent intellectual systems, and elegant literary creations.

The Status of Self-Knowledge Now

The Classical call to self-knowledge taught discipline and awareness, it taught reality-testing and understanding of one's limits and possibilities. These rewards flowed from hard study and practice.

Social leveling has delegitimized those rewards. Rewards are based on values, and values imply that some ways of being and thinking are better than others. As this implication grew culturally improper, the university, in envy-fear, concealed the value of mental-growth. And now, having grown comfortable with self-deception, shifted the privilege of distributing rewards and punishment from its professors to its students.

Education, even elite education, underestimated human resistance to mental growth, and forgot that the development of the human personality could only advance until it collided with the wall of self-deception. The siege machine of liberal education had limited effect against that wall—so stubbornly reinforced with cherished personal illusions.

The group builds its collective illusions, its social defense systems, upon the personal illusions of its members. A group cannot liberate itself from collective self-deception—religious fanaticism, for example, or the fantasy of limitless growth—unless its members understand their personal self-deceptions. People deceive themselves into believing that they are free from collective illusions when they are not. Understanding self-deception presupposes, in turn, a refined awareness of *how* one avoids being aware of self-deception—the specific psychological defenses one deploys. The university could not teach how to investigate personal unconscious defensive strategies. But so long as it mandated Greek, it encouraged students to prepare for such investigation. The Classical Humanist university encouraged its students to beware their mental tricks. It also implied, by emphasizing dialectic, the value of an observer, a second mind, to superintend the subject's project of self-discovery.

What applies to Classics students, applies to the culture. Without a cultural commitment to the responsibility of self-knowledge, the communal mind is helpless to the incursions of self-deception. This is where we are today. But what got us here? How did Greek *paideia* reach the humanist university? And what made *paideia* wither, reducing the university to a vocational school, research lab, and social reeducation camp?

6.

Birth and Death of the Humanist University

We've identified the ideals of the Classical culture: Mental growth, tension-tolerance and self-knowledge. Now, we'll explore the history of the institution which embodied that culture, a culture so crucial to the survival of humanity. First, we'll follow a kind of time-lapse history of the whole 2500-year story of Classical education through a personal moment in Northwestern's brief 150-year history.

A school of middling size, in the middle of the country, ranked among the country's most selective schools and one of the earliest in coeducation, today a respected research university, Northwestern epitomizes both the modern university and liberal arts college. My father and brother were both graduates. That family connection, together with the school's reputation, commended it to me, and I suggested it to my unsuspecting daughter.

Northwestern's founders had required all entering students "to demonstrate... a reading knowledge of Greek and Latin" (Williamson and Wild, 1976, p. 19) and the college even set up a preparatory school in 1855 to feed qualified scholars to the university. Ten years later Northwestern trustees voted to admit young women to classes "upon the same terms and conditions as young men" (Ibid. p.23).

This was Northwestern at its nativity, and when I learned these facts, I wanted to know when the school had revoked the Greek and Latin requirements. Since the written histories of the school were silent on that matter, I called the Northwestern library and asked the archivist if he could tell me, or discover, the year of the fateful change.

"That's an untoward request!"

"Really?"

"Yes!"

"But people in your office said they would gladly look up whatever I couldn't find on my own."

"Yea, well, they're just assistants. I'm their boss. It's way too much work. We'd have to search through years of early catalogues. Anyway, I think you're wrong. I doubt there ever were such requirements."

"But two books from your own university press say there were."

"Uhhh ... well ... I don't think so. Look... send me a letter saying what you want."[1]

Shortly after Northwestern's birth, its founders began to offload their educational responsibility onto students' backs. They let them choose one of three courses of study: Classical, scientific, or elective. Both the first and third required four years more of Greek and Latin. Science students, however, were excused from Classical studies if they studied modern languages. Several decades later, the school offered the same privilege to every student at the school.

But at its birth, Northwestern obliged every candidate to breathe the spirit of the ancient mission of the university. I had assumed that the institutional memory of Northwestern and of every other scholarly community had kept that spirit faintly alive. The following story makes clear how profoundly this and most other universities have forgotten their founding ideals.

My idealization of the selective university made me think that Northwestern, one of our country's most selective schools, would accept my daughter. Abby's class ranking and the quality of her extracurriculars were slightly below that of the average successful Northwestern applicant, but her SATs were slightly higher. Her "legacy" was stronger; minority, geographic and socioeconomic distinctiveness average; and essays (so she was told) stronger. On these qualifications alone, Abby's candidacy seemed merely viable.

But admissions people always say: "Give us the applicant with the rare angle." Their hearts go out to the student who writes a poignant family tragedy or has triumphed over poverty. They warm to the applicant who plays the horn, slings the forward pass or balances on the beam.

---

[1] The 1856 *Circular of the Trustees and Faculty of the Northwestern University*, published by The Rounds Premium Printing Establishment (Chicago) says that candidates for admission will be examined in Greek and Latin. Despite this prerequisite, the university, in its second year, seemed already to have begun excusing applicants for the Scientific Course from the Greek and Latin admission and curricular requirement.

So how about this angle: The ability to sing Homer in the original. Surely this distinction, and the scholarly discipline it implies, would dazzle those responsible for populating an institution of higher learning?

But… hold on. Just how distinct *was* this angle? I talked to the Harvard Dean of admissions in 2002 to get some numbers. She told me that, of Harvard's 20,000 applicants, about 300, or 1.5%, had studied a year or two of Greek. How many of these had studied the language outside of school? About 1/10 of those, she guessed. So, the number drops to about 30 applicants, or .15%. And not to make too fine a point of it, but how many of these thirty had mastered the ancient pitch accents and done public recitals of Greek passages from *The Iliad*? My friendly source couldn't think of a single one.[2]

So Northwestern, which at that time was admitting 5000 students from 16,000 applicants, probably hadn't a single applicant who did what Abby had done with Greek. That's fewer than those with double 800's on their SATs, and far fewer than those with perfect GPAs. She may have been the first in the school's history who'd done what she'd done.

So, I was convinced that Northwestern—or any school—would leap at the chance to get her.

How remote, as the reader already knows, was my conviction from reality.

The Basis of the Humanist University

Many of our collective convictions—like limitless Growth—are similarly fantastic, meant to evade the tensions associated with unpleasant truths of the inner or outer world.

Modern society seemed sure that its frustration tolerance, foresight, and self-awareness, the sinews of civilization, would stave off the corruptions of prosperity; its mental powers wouldn't need constant exercise and repair. But those virtues withered as society pursued ease and immediate gratification and universal inclusion, and surrendered to the corruption of crowding.

Pre-modern society, on the other hand, appeared to anticipate the approaching rot. So, it created collective education, a kind of giant support group against regression, an "incitement to the conquest of the pleasure

---

[2] In 2002, only a few Greek *professors* had mastered the pitch accents. Later, it caught on: by 2015, fifteen American colleges or universities were training the restored pitch accents.

principle, and to its replacement by the reality principle" (1911, p. 224), as Freud described it.

Let's survey the history of this support group, a story of the rise and fall of humanist education, the institutional embodiment of Classical ideals: Tension-tolerance, self-knowledge and mental growth.

Every spring, Greece's olive groves burst into spectacular flourishes of white flowers. In antiquity, one of these orchards overspread the hillside of Colonus, a modest prominence rising along the western perimeter of Athens. The old Greeks had dedicated the plantation to an obscure hero named 'Ακάδημος (Academos). In 387 BCE, in this pleasant stand of sacred trees, Plato embowered his first school, and perhaps lectured in their shade. His Academy survived almost nine hundred years.

Plato thought the mind should be a tool of truth-finding, not a weapon for political conquest. That's why he rejected sophism. Sophism, a brilliant form of mental training, had appeared 30 years before the Academy. It was an egalitarian program (unlike the earlier medical training of chosen disciples at Cnidus and Cos), open to anyone with the requisite time and money. It taught its students to argue and persuade, that they might win political contests in the emerging Greek democracy. Students learned gymnastics (training of the body, hygiene and dietetics); music (dance, choral and solo singing, poetry, playing of the lyre); and literature, Homer above all, with eloquence as their final goal. Advanced students studied rhetoric for five to six years, cultivating their oratorical grace.

The Academy selected and trained only the best young minds, although how the school rated them is not known. Its curriculum included gymnastics and abstract thought (mostly mathematics, up to *thirty years*). Its rigor was meant to expose, with a view to expelling, half-hearted, weak or perverse students, and to establish a clerisy of philosophers and meritocrats.

Plato saw education as both transformative and salvational. Without proper education, neither the individual nor the city-state was viable.

The city-state would offer, in effect, two educations: One for ordinary citizens, and another for boys and girls with the talent to become guardians or philosopher-kings, rulers of the polis. The first would merely train the citizens to read, write, manipulate numbers and machines and learn trades, the kind of education we have today. The second would be more arduous, an education meant to transform the soul, to liberate it from the chains of irritable acquisitiveness and impatience for transient pleasures. It would create leaders more dedicated to the welfare of the citizens and the hygiene of their minds, than to political power.

The education of the guardians, in Plato's words:

> οὐκ ὀστράκου ἂν εἴη περιστροφή, ἀλλὰ ψυχῆςπεριαγωγὴ ἐκ νυκτερινῆς τινος ἡμέρας εἰς ἀληθινήν ......
>
> (*Republic, VII*, 521c); "would not seem to be a [mere] spinning of the oyster shell, but a turning round of the soul from virtual night to true day ..." (my translation)

In the *Republic*, an eloquent treatise of suppressed, bitter rage and disappointment at the loss of Athens' future, Plato outlines his educational program for the philosopher-king, the visionary ruler without which every state must at last disintegrate. His educational program makes nakedly clear the distinction between the ideal statesman and the politicians who presided over Athens' decadence.

Education, as described, and prescribed, in the later *Laws*, would begin even before birth. Expectant mothers were to concentrate on rhythmic motion, presumably dancing and walking. They will continue the post-natal gymnastics by rocking their children, and singing to them, with kindness, tenderness and cheerfulness. All citizen children, both boys and girls, from the ages of three to six, will gather to play supervised games together in village temples. Supervisors will punish misbehavior, always respecting the child's dignity.

After the age of six, the state will separate the sexes, but give them identical lessons in riding, archery, javelin-throwing, slinging and other military arts and drills. The state would also teach them singing, harp-playing, rhythms, scales, and choristry. The schools will introduce gymnastics, dancing, stand-up wrestling, and whatever drills and exercises that conduce to their mastery. Children would learn all upper body skills with both left and right hands, like our best modern basketball players.

All children will learn letters, for at least three years, or until they can read and write; then arithmetic, reckoning, measuring length, surfaces, solids and the motions of the heavenly bodies. And they will learn poetry by heart.

Throughout their early education, some of the children, male or female, will show special talents; the state will separate these from the rest, and craft their education more carefully. The rest will take on non-governmental functions for society. To facilitate their acceptance of this hierarchy, the state will tell the children a "noble lie": The gods mold people into one of three types: Guardians, workers (producers: Craftsmen, miners, etc.), or auxiliaries (soldiers). We note that the noble lie would perform the crucial social function of defusing envy.

The guardians' education understands that its students' minds and souls are initially enchained to the material values of the world, and preoccupied with change and impermanence. It will try to make these minds receptive to the immaterial, the abstract, the eternal ideas and concepts. To this purpose, the proteges will study mathematics, beginning with numbers and number theory, proceeding to linear, plane and solid geometry, and moving on to theoretical astronomy and harmonics.

Mathematics is not, however, the consummation of the guardian's education; it is an orientation to the process of finding and defining eternal truths, the changeless concepts, concepts that are clear, distinct, universal and objective. For example, the trigonometric ratios or functions (sine, cosine and tangent) will always represent the relative lengths of certain sides of a triangle. The triangle will always exist, with or without the changing, material world. Mathematics also habituates the future guardians to logic and deduction. The guardian trainees will be forever bonded, both by their common pursuit of mathematical truths and their knowledge that these truths are not matters of opinion.

Imagine now that concepts like "justice" or "beauty" could attain to the axiomatic character of mathematical objects like the triangle or hexagon; imagine that justice could be brought into the light—clear, distinct, established with flawless logic and irrefutable demonstration. What if justice, like the 180 degrees of a (Euclidean) triangle's internal angles, could be a settled matter? Just government would then also become a settled matter. Government is typically an interminable, rancorous, futile, often fatal argument among the multitudes. And the multitudes are lightly educated, unaccustomed to deep thought, hostile to reasoned argument, or intractable to governance of any kind, including self-governance. They doom their state.

So, the culmination of the guardians' education is not mathematics. It is dialectic, a systematic course of question and answer—Socrates' métier. Dialectic aims to delineate ideals, or Ideas like justice. Because dialectic is powerful, and must be used carefully, it is dangerous to teach to students too early, because they'll want to use it everywhere, on everyone. Dialectic irritates conventional people; it also enrages those who, like Plato's character

Thrasymachus, can't do it well. Socrates himself was envied for his mastery of dialectic.[3]

Except for physical exercise and training, the students selected for guardianship will have hardly done anything but study until they are twenty years old. After that, they will study mathematics for ten years. Only at thirty, and for the next five years, will Athens' future rulers be allowed to study dialectic. Then, at 35, they'll be forced to go down into the city for fifteen years. There, they'll apply their learning to practical matters, like commanding soldiers and serving in public office. This apprenticeship makes the future guardians worldly. Their urbanity, incidentally, could forestall the demeaning gossip that philosophers are terminal adolescents, skulking in the corners, muttering about the meaning of life.[4]

At 50, those who have survived all the tests are promoted to the order of Masters. They are educated to turn their souls upward and contemplate the Good. Then, as kings or queens, they are to organize their city upon this sublime pattern, engage citizens with it, and regulate themselves by it for the rest of their lives.

I've expounded on Plato's education, to answer this question: Could Plato's training of the guardians, a pattern for Classical humanist education, have really "turned their souls" to mental growth?

We need definitions. Let's define "turning the soul" as changing the character qualitatively and define qualitative character change as the permanent reallocation of power and influence among the triumvirate of the mind—the ego, superego, and id.

There are exceptions to this rule, but most people, to turn their souls, must understand the unconscious strategies by which they deceive themselves. This entails life experience and arduous psychoanalytic work.

A successful analysis, however, also involves a great struggle between hatred and love. Analysands must at some point recognize their spite, their bitterness, and their destructiveness. They must acknowledge how their hatred has damaged their relationships and their communities. They must endure the contrition this acknowledgement evokes. They must undertake repairs. Only

---

[3] As I point out later, Socrates may also have provoked people with his irritating personality, but more innocently, I add here, by his friendship with Alcibiades, who ended up betraying Athens.

[4] I owe this diverting image to political philosophy professor Melissa Lane.

these steps can securely establish their self-respect, mitigate guilt, and save them from self-defeat.

Plato's education recognizes this struggle and tries to solve it in a different way. It capitalizes on the universal human need for a sense of inner goodness. That sense encompasses a feeling, object, or conception inseparably linked to coherence, inclusion and satisfaction. Any teacher, ancient or modern, can invoke this link to commend their students to mental growth.

Plato invokes this link when he exalts the eternal Forms or Ideas, the Good, and its emanations. He is appealing to the innate search for inner unity and goodness, once so critical to the infant's survival and development.

As we recall, infants destitute for confidence in a good *object*, a person that cherishes the infant, will languish and sometimes die. It's not enough for a mother to keep her baby fed and warm. She must convince it of her devotion, be it ever so narcissistic, to the baby's happiness.

Psychoanalyst Rene Spitz's famous studies (1945, 1946) on hospitalism in infants established the deadliness of passionless mothering. Without this experience, infants are exposed to the terrors of the primitive superego; they live, unprotected, among nightmares of menaces and monsters, groping for loving guardians, and interpreting their absence as a directive to die.

All babies accomplish Goodness of this kind imperfectly. Throughout life we try to repair that wound. We feel it as a lingering sense of incoherence, fragmentation, unworthiness, exclusion. The false repair typically involves neurotic and psychotic maneuvers. One of the less drastic strategies, observed in the author, is *idealization*, the unrealistic exaltation of the parent, or parent symbol. Idealization, most visible in adolescents, adopts this mental weapon against inner badness. It reassures and stabilizes the idealizer, but also leads him into error.

All our lives we search high and low for inner Goodness. Like rag and bones men, we find bits here and pieces there from which to cobble together unified lives. This is Plato's educational insight: Mental growth consolidates this sense of worthiness by showing students how much they can do, and endure, in pursuing personal transformation. As a civil institution, education can enroll its students in a Good and noble community dedicated to the welfare of every citizen. An educated community watches the progress of every member's mental growth, like St. Matthew's God, who marks the fall of a sparrow and numbers the hairs on our heads.

The achievement of worthiness, even when derived from group pride, could plausibly "turn" individual souls and produce lasting character change. It could adjust the relative influences of id, ego and superego, the inner mental relationships that determine equanimity and resilience.

To that degree, then, a rigorous educational regimen might modify character. But the regimen of detecting self-deceptions is much more powerful. This, a rigorous education cannot adequately offer, and so instead might produce highly educated, highly intelligent, politically prudent, socially valuable zombies.

Even this unsatisfactory outcome, however, would lift the (imaginary) Platonic dialectician far above cultists and religious converts. Plato's dialecticians confront, rather than evade, inner and outer realities.

Classical education, the offspring of Plato's academy, also immerses its students in the problems and the solutions of the Athenian democracy and Roman republic. It teaches them to grapple with the problems of complex group living and to practice critical political analysis. *Paideia* understands that rational thinking, clear expression, and familiarity with an ideal educational society cultivate responsible citizenship.

The Academic and sophist educational currents probably converged in Aristotle's Lyceum, the "peripatetic school" founded in 335 BCE. Aristotle believed that ἐπιστήμη (episteme—knowledge arrived at by dialectic), although necessary, was insufficient for a life of action. Επιστήμη cannot meet life's occasional requirement for sudden and spontaneous action and speech, guided by mere beliefs and appearances (δόξα: doxa) uninformed by the dialectic process.

Aristotle supplied the last piece of Greek higher education. His Lyceum de-emphasized the Platonic intuition of basic truths. It valued systematization of natural observations. But Lyceum students continued to study mathematics, music, and literature.

These, then, were the original aims of higher education: Eloquence and persuasive skill developed by literary and musical training; mathematical and philosophic habits of thought, secured by self-reflection in underlying realities; an empirical spirit; physical vigor; and a capacity to systematize knowledge.

Education in Rome

In its beginnings, Roman education emphasized national and family tradition. Young children were taught first by their family, then a family friend who served as master, and finally the military. Education seemed to have been practical and moralistic. It taught, on one hand, the proper management of family land and other holdings, including slaves and tenant farmers and, on the other, the rural values of frugality and austerity. Older students also learned Roman law which, being more formal and technical than Greek law, entailed extensive study.

All this changed quickly after Rome's conquest of Greece in the second century BCE. Horace captured the subsequent cultural transformation in his celebrated phrase: "Graecia capta ferum victorem cepit et artis intulit agresti Latio" (*Epistles*, ii, i., 156) ("Captive Greece captured her savage captor and brought her arts into wild Latium"). Before this great introjection, the Romans had no school of philosophy or even a Latin word for that discipline. Cicero was the first to say that the educated person must know both Latin and Greek, and the noblest Romans, such as Marcus Aurelius, wrote in Greek. The best of Roman thought was Greek, and the Romans knew it.

By 500 CE, the barbarian invasions had destroyed most Roman institutions, including Greco-Roman education. Europe, now deprived of primary Greek texts, lost contact with the language of Homer and Plato. The new Christian church, imbued with the Hellenistic tradition of Byzantium, fanned the fading embers of scholarship by teaching Greek ideas to its clergy. But a shadow of ignorance spread over the continent.

In this great cultural upheaval, the barbarians were Envy Incarnate, destroying a gigantic social network and extinguishing, in continental Europe, the sublime Hellenic spirit from which it first emerged. The existence of the Roman Empire, for hundreds of years, had tempted the invaders' greed with its measureless wealth and clement climate. And it had galled their mental pride, which recognized the Romans' superior intellectual commonwealth.

But the blaze burned brightly in Byzantium itself, which devoured Greek learning in every respect but its paganism. In 425 CE, as Rome was disintegrating, Theodosius II, in the empire's new capital of Constantinople, created perhaps the world's first true university. He endowed it with 31 Professorial Chairs. These included: Letters, Rhetoric (both Greek and Latin), Philosophy and Law. The life of this university, which embodied the best of

Classical education, spanned the entire European dark ages, surviving until 1453. Other Christian schools of late antiquity, most prominently those in Alexandria, Antioch and Beirut, taught the literature, science, and philosophy of Classical Greece. They preserved ancient Greek learning and extended it into foreign lands: Russia; India (Akbar the Great supplemented study of the Hindu Classics with Greek works); the Caliphates; and even the Chinese Mongols (1206-1368 CE).

The Classical tradition would not recover in continental Europe for almost five hundred years. In a slow and fitful pincers-like movement, as we will see, scholars and soldiers from the north and the south converged to restore Greek education. By the end of the Middle Ages Classical learning was rising again to preeminence on the shoulders of the new European university. Let's trace its resurrection, focusing first on the southern, then northern influences in Europe. Finally, we'll cross the Atlantic and follow the university's career in the United States, from the mid-1800's to the present day.

Humanist education after the Empire

In the aftermath of the barbarian conquests, as noted above, European monastic and cathedral schools preserved some ancient intellectual relics. But because these schools subordinated Classical learning to religious indoctrination, scholarship steadily degenerated. When Charlemagne ascended the Frankish throne in the eighth century, he was disgusted by the condition of Latin among the clergy. His influence improved Latin scholarship and brought Greek to the monastery.[5] He recruited the best minds in the world, scholars from whom he himself learned Latin, a little Greek, mathematics and astronomy. The great warrior's enthusiasm for learning, his insistence on rigor, and his forays into Greek wisdom inspired a thirst for education throughout his kingdom. During his brief fourteen-year rule (800-814 CE), Charlemagne distinguished his Frankish kingdom as one of the few states in history legitimized chiefly by its leader's efforts to raise the cultural level.

By 834, only twenty years after Charlemagne died, his administrative, economic, and military empire had disintegrated. But his vision had prepared

---

[5] We know, for example, that a monk was traveling to Chartres about 991 AD to study the *Aphorisms* of Hippocrates of Cos.

the continent for a scholarly revival. His reign's elevated intellectual, political, and religious values spawned the first (Carolingian) of three increasingly powerful renaissances. When, in the 1100's, Arab intellectuals seeded medieval Europe with Greek ideas, the Little Renaissance in Italy sprouted from already fertile ground. The Western intellect thrived in this climate until the early 1900's, and proved one of Charlemagne's court poets prescient in having called the emperor *rex pater Europae*—King Father of Europe.

Before the Little Renaissance, Muslim scholars had been translating Greek texts into their own language. Their intellectual beneficiaries brought ancient learning to Italy before 1000 CE. Most of these teachers were Spanish Arabs. Latin renditions of Ptolemy, Aristotle, Euclid and the Greek physicians then appeared. After five hundred years of intellectual sleep, southern Italy woke to a new dawn of Greek learning.

This was the story of the western university up to 1600. It was launched by Muslim scholars in southern Europe; but without Irish scholars, Classical Humanism might never have reached the modern West.

As early as the 5th century CE, when the Goths were demolishing Roman culture, Greek and Latin flourished in distant Ireland. The Emerald Isle, probably in the prior century, had become a refuge for masters and scholars. We know that two pre-Patrician (before 432 CE, when Saint Patrick returned to the island) Irish scholars were already teaching back on the continent. This fact implies the anterior development of a culture of learning in Ireland.

How did that culture arise? When the Roman Empire crumbled, both secular and monkish scholars from Gaul fled imminent death, torture or enslavement and, having safely reached the Irish shores, gratefully imparted their Latin and Greek to natives and fellow refugees. Throughout Europe's "dark ages," every corner of Ireland was a hive of learning, buzzing with students ardent for enlightenment. Two of the largest schools enrolled up to 7000 students each. Clonmacnois, in the center of the island, and Armagh (founded by St. Patrick), forty miles southwest of present-day Belfast, taught Greek, and had taught it for centuries, when it had been forgotten elsewhere. Even Gregory the Great (540-604), a highly educated Pope by the standards of southern Europe, didn't know the learned language. Europeans came to assume, that if you knew Greek, you'd come from Ireland.

Long before the early medieval Arab teachers, and even before the Carolingian awakening, Irish knowledge was spreading to the continent. It typically sprang up in large urban centers where, in the Middle Ages, the first

European universities emerged and the Renaissance later took root. We know that the Irish inspired Charlemagne. His chief court scholar Alcuin corresponded with Colcu Macua Dunechda, professor at Clonmacnois. One letter from Alcuin calls Colcu "my dearly loved father and master," and informs him that he and the emperor are each donating fifty shekels of silver to Colcu's famous school. The Irish astronomer Dungall may have visited Charles to teach him the structure of the heavens. Later, the king's grandson, Lothaire, put Dungall in charge of the educational system in Pavia.

Columbanus, a monk at Bangor for twenty-five years, was born in 540 in the province of Leinster. He was the most productive of the scholar-missionaries who spread Classical learning back into Europe. Europeans widely celebrated his preaching and teaching. When Columbanus approached the Eternal city, it is said, "all the bells of Rome rang out." He is thought to have founded between sixty and one hundred monasteries in France, Germany, Switzerland and Italy from 590 to 615 AD. Many other Irish teachers sojourned on the continent, preserving the pulse of a moribund European civilization.

In *How the Irish Saved Civilization*, Cahill concluded that the Irish saved most of our ancient intellectual treasures. Scattered communities of Jews would have delivered the Hebrew Bible to us. But without the Irish, we would have had to hunt down and, only by luck, recovered the Greek Bible, Greek commentaries, and most ancient Greek literature. Except for the Irish, all these works, during the Dark Ages, would have been sequestered, and perhaps sepulchered, in old Byzantium. Without the Irish we might have lost Latin literature, and without the Irish example, Europeans might not have developed their vernacular and national literatures. Had Ireland not cultivated the continental mind, Muslim scholarship might have been sown on barren soil. "Beyond that," Cahill says, the Irish preserved "the habits of mind that encourage thought."

Inevitably, lawless peoples preyed upon Irish prosperity. The Vikings discovered Ireland in the late 8th century. Sometimes—contrary to popular belief—the Vikings traded peacefully with the Irish natives, or stayed to farm the Irish countryside. But just as often, they raped and robbed. They destroyed monasteries and denuded, of their gold-chased and jewel-encrusted covers, the priceless books the Irish scholars or their predecessors had calligraphically copied out.

The Scandinavian raiders did not, however, meet pushovers in Hibernia. The Irish obstinately resisted Viking takeover for 400 years and, in 1014, finally vanquished the Danes in the Battle of Brian, named for the 73-year-old Irish king present at the battle. If the Irish had fallen, the Danes might have used the island to found a vast northern Viking kingdom centered in London. What Irish scholars did for the Western mind, then, Irish warriors may have done for Western culture.

Although the glory of Irish learning never recovered its earlier brilliance, its legacy survived on the continent, not least in the Greek and Latin books that the monks and teachers had sent there for safekeeping.

It seems, then, that Classical learning did not disappear with the Roman Empire, as we commonly think, only to be revived by Muslim scholars around 1000 AD. Instead, throughout the Dark ages, plantations of Irish scholarship sprang up on the landscape of Europe. However, because of slow, inefficient and unreliable pathways of communication, the frail network they formed there failed to crystallize into a coherent culture. To educate and unite Europe with ancient Greek and Roman learning was left to the medieval universities and the European Renaissance.

The medieval and early modern European universities, like Plato's Academy itself, were hybridizations, centers both for mental growth and vocationalism. From remote locations men gathered to form schools: First in Bologna, and then, no later than 1100 AD, in Paris (arising from the cathedral school at Notre Dame). These were collections—colleges—of students and teachers living together. Their common love of knowledge and the way in which they organized its pursuit formed the basic structure and definition of the university: *Societas magistrorum discipulorumque* ("a society of masters and scholars").

Like the carpenters, cobblers, or candlestick makers before them, the scholars organized guilds for self-protection. For no sooner had they gathered in their various locations than local profiteers began to soak them for room and board. So, the students organized against the townspeople, and brought them to terms. They called their guild a *universitas* ("all, whole, or every"), a term originally meaning only a group or corporation in general.

Similarly, when teachers, the *magisteres* (masters), neglected their teaching, the students moved against and sometimes boycotted them. The masters retaliated with a guild of their own, requiring for admission the successful completion of an examination. Success won the *licentia docendi*, a license for teaching and a certification of the student's knowledge, the first academic degree. The old system survives in our Master's (from *magister*) and Doctoral (from *docendi*—"teaching") degrees, the Latin terms originally being synonymous.

The medieval university left us this legacy:[6] An association of masters and scholars leading the common life of learning; the concept of curriculum *specified as to subject and sequence* and tested by examination, with a view to a degree; the faculty with its deans and officers; and finally, the college. But the real glory of the medieval university was, as 19th century Oxford philosopher Hastings Rashdall described it, the Consecration of Learning.

Scholasticism and the Birth of Humanism

The medieval university organized itself according to Greek educational ideals. Long before, 5th century AD scholars had conceived what eventually became the academic curriculum. Those scholars, having rated their abilities inferior to those of the Greeks they themselves studied, condensed ancient knowledge into a form accessible to their more modest talents. A North African writer and poet of that time, Martianus Capella, divided ancient learning into the *trivium*—grammar, rhetoric, and logic—and quadrivium—arithmetic, geometry, astronomy, and music. He packaged up this regimen like a time capsule, to be opened later by the medieval cathedral and monastic schools. But medieval educational culture could rise no higher than this curriculum required. And having lost, or rejected, its secular Greek moorings, it gradually drifted into barren scholasticism.

Scholasticism, a school of thought founded in the 11th century, evolved from the religious impulse to reconcile revelation with reason. Although it revived the Greek notion of intellectual discipline, and on this credential ruled the early medieval university, scholasticism clung to superstition ("How many angels can dance on the head of a pin ...?"). In time, the sterility of an education trembling before God, whetted the European appetite for the more secular *societas magistrorum discipulorumque* of the university.

But the rough winds of *useful* education bruised the flower of the Societas even at first bloom. There appeared, in the 13th century, a class of opportunistic professors called *dictatores*. They pandered to the students' vulgar instincts for quick results. Their teaching, in Haskings' words, was

---

[6] Keith Thomas, in the 5/7/10 *TLS* summarizes the modern university's history.

"short and practical, with no time wasted on outgrown Classical authors, but everything fresh and snappy and up-to-date, ready to be applied the same day if need be." The *dictatores* taught students how to write the sorts of letters and documents usually asked of notaries and secretaries of that day. The most popular professors taught the priceless art of writing letters home, asking for money.

Through the lens of history, the early university, *dictatores* aside, looks like a medieval vocational school. It was charged with preparing a select group of students for the service of church and state. Yet we can detect in medieval academic policy, from our distant prospect of 800 years, three values undetectable today, even on close inspection, in the modern academy: Learning for learning's sake; inner enrichment; and self-reflection. Respect for mental refinement suffused the quadrivium and trivium; and when medieval clergy and courtiers learned these seven liberal arts, they absorbed that respect.

And from the liberal arts medieval students also absorbed the Socratic ideal of education as care of the human soul. And a surprising ally now reinforced this value: Augustinian Christianity justified, even sacralized, the project of self-reflection.

Early Christian apologists had proffered the visions of equal human liberty and "equal souls"; they portrayed the new Christian community as a free association of morally equal agents. All human beings—master and slave, Jew and gentile, father and son, mother and daughter, man and woman—were now to be seen as individual souls sharing a common fate and endowed with equal moral status.

Oxford Lecturer in Political Thought, Sir Larry Siedentop (2014), showed that these powerful ideas undermined forever the ethos of born elites. They offered, but did not guarantee, personal dignity to every human being. They renewed the old sophistic assumption that education, an expression of self-respect, should be open to all. They reasserted the concept of earned elitism, a creed fundamental to a sustainable civilization. They did not insist, however, that people perpetually re-earn their dignity by practicing self-reflection. This omission left the educational community open to corruption.

Though Christian superstition no doubt corrupted the search for truth in the medieval university, Christian Humanism elevated and ennobled the institution and facilitated the transmission of *paideia* to the ministers and civil servants of the age. Absent the church, the humanist academy might not have championed self-development and individual conscience.

So, the medieval marketplace never engulfed its university. Although Greekless, the school strictly preserved Latin, the obligatory language of the students, whether discoursing in the classroom, making merry at the local pub, or prattling in their rooms at night. To enforce this directive the university employed student "wolves" to prowl among their peers in all their haunts—reporting all infractions to university officials.

Intellectually sustained, then, by the Capellan curriculum; turned inward by the humanistic spirit of this curriculum and the self-examining Augustinian strain of Christianity; and immersed in Latin; the medieval student forged an unbreakable bond with ancient Roman learning, which was Greek at heart. Many of her graduates, inoculated against radical utilitarianism—the creed that humanity must dedicate every effort to its own ease, an early expression of Bacon's concept of "charity"—earned their places in the Societas.

In the Renaissance university the latent ideal of *paideia* fully reemerged, and from about 1400 to 1600, displayed its brightest colors. The reappearance of Greek texts in Italy in the 1400's launched Classical Humanism in Europe. There were two migration waves of Byzantine scholars: The first following the sacking of Constantinople in 1204: And the second, the fall of Byzantium in 1453. They brought Greek and Greek texts to their scholarly Western counterparts.

As the late Denys Hay, British historian of the Renaissance tells us, Barlaam of Calabria (1290-1348) and Leonzio Pilato (both born in Calabria, southern Italy) were educated in Greek and deeply affected the first Renaissance Humanists (1976).

Humanists aspired to a citizenry able to speak and write with enough eloquence and clarity to inspire others to virtuous and prudent action. Humanism resembled ancient sophism, except that Humanist education, unlike early sophism, aimed at virtue and prudence. Their humanist education was later crucial, to repeat an example, for early feminists. Drawing on their Greek and Latin training, Elizabeth Cady Stanton, Alice Paul, Lucy Stone, and Helen Keller, among others, wrote erudite and eloquent essays and speeches showcasing their brilliance. They demolished the myth of female feeblemindedness. They amazed and sometimes shamed the male opposition, and exposed women's exclusion from the franchise as absurd.

Prefigured in the 1300's by Petrarch and Boccaccio, Renaissance humanists, as described by Charles Haskins (1957/1923), first academic medieval historian in the United States, now worked in a white heat to apprehend the thought of the past. They mastered both Latin and Greek, that they might inhabit the minds of the ancients, trace the old sages' thinking patterns, and in that way acquire a "new historical and critical consciousness" with which to better understand themselves. They rejoiced in their liberation, the liberation of the mind from the chains of theological dogma and unthinking morality. It was, overall, deep education.

The study of humankind became central again, and for the next three hundred years the scholars of Europe savored the literary, philosophical, social and scientific richness of the ancients.

Humanism flourished in Renaissance Italy. The country's new classicists widely taught ancient Greek. They established a Platonic Academy in Florence in the late 15th century. They cultivated a new philosophy of liberal studies which explicitly excluded a view of education as a stepping stone into the lucrative professions of law and medicine. And they founded boarding schools: These rejected utilitarian or vocational education and concentrated instead on revisions of the *trivium, quadrivium*, and philosophy. Teachers gave all instruction in Latin, and students mastered both this language and ancient Greek.

Humanism gained enthusiasts more gradually in England, France, Spain, Holland, and Germany. Erasmus (1469-1536), its paladin in northern Europe, believed that Classical literature, the most important of all studies, was suitable only for a minority. He thought the masses should restrict their learning to training in an occupational skill. He believed science unnecessary for a cultured man, but religious instruction necessary for everyone. He concluded, and concluded well, that a healthy society valued schools and teachers as highly as soldiers and generals. He opposed instruction of unwilling or passive students and took a sympathetic interest in the psychology of children.

English Humanists, led by Thomas More (*Utopia*) in the late 1400's and early 1500's, prepared superb texts for studying the Classical languages. They sometimes clashed with the "Trojans," scholars adhering to the religiosity of medieval scholasticism, resisting Greek and the secular philosophy its promulgation represented.

Christianity and the University

The new Protestant university modified the traditional B.A. course. It still emphasized Classical literature but deemphasized logic and rhetoric. The evolving academy retained its vocational—or professional—function. It aimed to improve writing and speaking skills of 16th century society's governing elite: The lawyers, gentry and civil servants. Like sophism, the Reformation university neither advertised, as a marketable commodity, nor valorized, as a guiding principle, the enhancement of the self. This describes the Reformation university treading water. It was holding onto life, temporizing, waiting for society's next signal: Cultivate minds? or indulge magical thinking?

Martin Luther, well aware that successful reform depended upon the support of the masses, promoted an educational system open to everyone, even peasants and miners. His program broadened elementary education and established the vernacular in schools. Reformation educators, in training children for a trade (never before considered part of education), scorned "useless" [Classical] books. Nevertheless, Greek education survived. Luther, respecting the Christian tradition that valued cultural literacy, insisted that the schools teach Greek, Latin, and Hebrew. Language study also enabled the pious to read the Bible themselves, uncorrupted by priestly interpretation.

The Christian universities of the medieval and early modern eras both extolled the inner life and pandered to the public thirst for gainful employment and social status. They indulged this impulse more than the ancient academy but much less than today.

The Christianization of knowledge reinforced the value of knowledge and preserved the Greek respect for the inner life by sacralizing the soul. Post-Classical developments—Platonism (Philo), middle Platonism (Albinus) and Neo-Platonism (Plotinus and Augustine)—saturated pre-scholastic medieval higher education. They fixed Plato and Aristotle as luminaries in the Western educational firmament. The Christian academy supported tension-tolerance in all these ways. But its superstitions also supported tension-evasion by distorting knowledge of the soul and other natural phenomena.

The medieval academy implied that mental growth was intelligible only in the context of Christianity. The school subordinated the dignity of self-knowledge to Grace and, in that way, diminished and devalued it as a Good in itself. The Medieval university allowed students to expand their minds if and only if the scholars placated an envious God by their collective devotion. This arrangement presumably deflected the imagined shafts of His, and the public's, envy.

Scholasticism blended St. Thomas Aquinas's (1225-1274) theology with Aristotle's metaphysics and empiricism, forging a compromise that endured for 500 years.

Christian domination of the medieval and pre-modern university obscured or at least delayed the progress of secular, rational, free, inquiry. Knowledge was not expanded awareness in the service of individual autonomy, but of God's magnification. The medieval university's purpose was to rationalize faith. That is why the church's cathedral schools taught logic: To test Catholic theology. The epistemological instinct is the drive to know, the urge for knowledge. Ionian thinkers, in their new cultural freedom, had celebrated this precious endowment 1800 years before. But the Christian academy subjugated this potentially subversive drive to the Higher Power.

Society, then, had backtracked, a process distressingly common in human history. Two recent examples from my field: Psychiatry's restoration of somatic treatment and psychology's restoration of cognitive-behavioral treatment in the late 20th century. Here, the medieval university, following the earlier Byzantine and Muslim universities, had returned society to a more primitive strategy of tension-reduction. Compared, however, to the witch hunts of the late 15th through early 18th centuries in Europe and America, the religious appropriation of knowledge was a better regulated, more evolved, less primitive expression of paranoid anxiety.

The Christianization of medieval and early modern universities was not, however, merely the conservative persistence, and institutional inertia of the earlier monastic and cathedral schools of Europe, or even Byzantine and Islamic schools.[7] The educational diapause in the West, after the Roman Fall, had opened a niche for a secular humanist state. But a fractured society hungered for religious consolation. Moreover, the lonely monasteries, during the long darkness, were virtually the only European educational venues, save perhaps aristocratic estates. The monks could at least teach reading, writing, and some Latin. And they spent enormous amounts of time copying out

[7] After the collapse of the classical Mediterranean, Indian and Chinese cultures, we note, Christianity, Islam and Buddhism overspread the world, unimpeded by national boundaries. Perhaps society was seeking consolation in religion for the lost security, identity and other satisfactions of inclusion in great polities.

ancient manuscripts, the very texts that would someday sit in the stacks of the first European university libraries.

This magnificent social maneuver, the church's annexation of humanist learning, pandered to humanity's fantasy of omnipotence.

When Catholicism secured a spiritual alliance with the omnipotent Christian god, it sought to procure *political* omnipotence. The church's failures to conquer the nations of Moses and Mohammed had awakened it from the (omnipotent) dream of religious hegemony. Partly to compensate for this mortification, it annexed the empire of the intellect. The conquest also fit Catholicism's plan to absorb, and control, the secular world, embracing every being in God's omnipotence.

This strategy was, however, about to fail. The Scientific and Cultural Revolutions of the 17th and 18th centuries withered the stature of religion. And as the pious illusion lost its power—as God died—the tensions associated with limits to human life, limits to human happiness and power, intensified. The cultural drumbeat for omnipotence grew louder and more insistent.

Science and technology would eventually answer this call. By the 18th century, the stars of inductive science and vernacular languages were rising in European education. But Latin and Greek remained a prized attainment, a presumed goal for the educated person. Every man wanted to be a secular, enlightened, and cultured gentleman, someone who might warm his slippered feet before the evening fire, reading Euripides in the ancient tongue.

Through the first half of the 19th century, even as mechanical aids to human toil proliferated, the European university clung to the core of the Renaissance model. This model prized the mental growth of an intellectual and social elite. Classical learning retained a *spiritual* hold on European universities, and became, in England, the very foundation of national virtue. Even before 1800 in England, Greek superseded Latin as the criterion of an educated person.

Across the pond, in the late 19th century, the American sun began to set on the traditional curriculum, a gift imported from Europe. Even so, colleges here, as in Europe, were producing highly educated citizens in increasing numbers. Liberal arts institutions and many professional schools still required Greek and Latin. At the turn of the century, for example, the University of Maine required, of all its *agriculture* graduate students, two years of ancient Greek. But this cultural condition, which produced an elite from whose ranks prudent citizens and leaders might arise, could not last much longer; the clamor for useful and inclusive education, the supposed antidotes to envy, was rising.

So, as the 19th century closed, our country dumped this system of enrichment. The educators and administrators of that time were like de Tocqueville's French, as they pursued their Revolution: Being halfway down the stairs, they threw themselves out of the window in order to reach the ground more quickly.

The Americans' self-defenestration, like the Europeans', consisted of the legitimization, even glorification, of research universities, whose essential elements were an elective system and specialization at the undergraduate level. The American academy was answering less to democracy, whose survival, as Jefferson believed, depended upon an educated citizenry, than to market capitalism, which only survives on more and more people trained to burn energy. This utilitarian culture, once it had conquered the larger universities, rapidly annexed smaller institutions. By 1920, the gods of usefulness and inclusion had driven compulsory Classical curriculum from all of higher education.

The collapse was global, swift, and bloodless. The 19th century vocationalization of traditionally humanistic schools describes higher education's transformation across the globe. In the process, science education eclipsed "liberal" studies.

In the United States, engineering colleges multiplied from 13 in 1862 to 126 in 1917, and their enrollments from a few hundred to more than 30,000. This increased the need for scientists and science courses in the American University. 1883 was the last year in which the Classical languages were compulsory for Harvard freshmen's admission. By 1892, matriculated Harvard students were allowed to substitute, for Greek and Latin, advanced studies in mathematics or natural science (Greenough, 1892). By 1900, just eight years later, less than a third were electing Latin, and a sixth, Greek.

To slake the nation's thirst for training and to feed its growing economic appetite, Congress passed the Morrill Act of 1862, establishing land-grant universities. These institutions offered practical courses of study ("agriculture and the mechanic arts") at low cost to a wide group of applicants. Then, as occupations in the late 1800's became professionalized, colleges in this country too, eyeing their European models, remade themselves into research universities and credentialing bodies, to arm students for victory in the marketplace.

The group pulse began to pound for wealth and thrilled to the sight of approaching prosperity. Innovations proliferated. The use of coal spread. Petroleum's discovery excited scenes of a black gold rush. Industry extracted, consumed and burned ever more energy resources. And humanity's numbers swelled.

At the same time, society began to devalue the contemplative life, previously a useful inspiration for the classically taught schoolchild. The learned interpreted this withdrawal of respect as an envious shot across the academic bow and leapt for the water.

In the post-World War I era, the Massachusetts Institute of Technology took a startling step, committing itself to industrial innovation and commercial interests. It was perhaps the first of what later would be called "entrepreneurial universities." After World War II Stanford University copied this model. In 1951 Stanford gave land and facilities in the spacious Stanford Industrial Park to companies like Hewlett-Packard. Since that time more and more universities have assumed this shape. They pursue research contracts from industrial, pharmaceutical and military concerns, and encourage their faculty to act as consultants. Other countries followed the same course, England adopting the entrepreneurial model in the 1980's. Countries made their universities into economic muscles and, as it seems, excretory organs of their national minds.

Meanwhile, the influence of humanist education steadily diminished. However, Humanism continued to offer society a solace more rational than rational optimism and unconstrained capitalism: Self-development and cultural mental growth. The humanist program cultivated intellectual power, explained the external world, taught the mental strategies for knowing that world, and supported civic self-regard. However, both the limitations of its public pedagogical format[8] and group resistance barred Humanism from the psychoanalytic study of the unconscious strategies of self-deception.

---

[8] Claims have been made, however, for self-knowledge from large group (up to 500 people) interaction when conducted along psychoanalytic lines (Foulkes, 1948; de Mare, Piper and Thompson, 1991; Brown and Zinkin, 1994; Nitsun, 1996).

A Psychological Overview of the University's Decline

To recapitulate: The social covenant uniting the goals of self-knowledge with Classical knowledge must have been shaky from its birth. The early Athenians hated Socrates for exposing their intellectual self-deceptions, let alone unconscious conflicts.[9] The clashing impulses to confront, and to avoid, the self, seem always to have tormented humans. The old Greeks probably disliked it as much as we do. What their culture did that ours does not, however, was to affirm tension-tolerance and self-reflection.

The species must have learned early how to anaesthetize the mind against inner tensions. Self-exploration, on the other hand, sensitizes the mind by exciting unpleasant tensions. This makes us antagonistic, or at least ambivalent, toward self-knowledge. So, society converged on a soft strategy of mental cultivation and cultural self-exploration. It rejected a remorseless attack on individual self-deception, perhaps inwardly understanding that too few of its members could endure that austere regimen.

Yet even this soft strategy ennobled and included those capable of mental growth; it degraded and excluded the rest. The inequity generated tensions, a time bomb which envious people detonated in several historical catastrophes. These crises reawakened psychotic anxieties in the enviable, western society, anxieties identified as fear of divine wrath. Accordingly, after the Germanic conquest of Rome, medieval European culture, believing it must not press its luck, sweetened its contract with the deity, whose love is conditional and vengeance, swift. The culture believed that He to whom it bent its knee might condescend to protect *paideia*, if *paideia* exalted Him, and assuaged His envy.

Paideia had to be cautious. It was subversively secular, historically pagan and, left to its own devices, apt to outrage the Infinite Mystery by reconceiving it as an infantile illusion. So, to protect *paideia*, the European universities subordinated mental growth to the glory of God.

In this narrative of *paideia's* historical struggle against envy, we can describe the progress of *paideia's* antagonists. The Germanic peoples first directed their envy at Roman material, cultural and intellectual wealth, and its Greek educational heritage. Centuries later they embodied their envy in Hitler's misappropriation of Greek racial identity—though emphatically not

---

[9] Various writers have adduced, however, as reasons for his persecution, certain of Socrates' infuriating personal qualities. See, for example, Wilson (2007).

its contemplative ideal. The Germans hungered to undo their national humiliation, identity confusion, and self-doubts, envious of the richer heritages and military prowess of neighboring European states. We could plausibly interpret the Final Solution as a psychotic attempt to exterminate threats to its exhilarating illusion of Aryan purity.

Islamic envy at first emulated Greek education, then devalued it and regressed to religious omnipotence. Centuries later, it took malicious gratification in 9/11's destruction of a vulgar symbol of American economic might, and finally prevailed, by hanging the threat of a permanent Fatwa over intellectual freedom. Such freedom is, of course, a basic condition for mental growth.

We can now trace out education's envy-driven transformation from an institution of mental growth to one of wealth-creation. The expansion of prosperity, today drawing slowly to a close, was essentially a crusade of Human Imperialism, omnipotence and the extinction of envy.

In the early 1600's Francis Bacon launched his assault on scholasticism, crowing that his scientific method would extend "the power and dominion of the human race itself over the universe." (*Novum Organum, I.CXXIX*). Bacon whetted humanity's appetite for liberation from all tensions, and prepared the collective mind for the overthrow of *paideia*. Riding Bacon's long coattails, 250 years later, in the late 1800's, another hypomanic man, much beloved, extended omnipotence's triumph over humanist holdouts. He led the progressive movement, considered a broadening and deepening of university education and a raising of secondary school standards. Society celebrated him as an educational hero.

Over his forty-year presidency at Harvard, which began in 1869, Charles William Eliot dismantled the Classical curriculum, piece by piece, at our nation's premier university. In 1887 he dropped Greek as an *entrance* requirement for Harvard.[10] Widespread congratulations fed his hunger for more, so he excused even his matriculated students from compulsory Greek. Nor had he gratified his appetite for innovation, destruction of his heritage, and popularity, when he left Harvard in 1909. Like his anti-classicist predecessor Benjamin Rush—distinguished by his clinical habits as the Great Exsanguinator—Eliot slipped into a *furor sanandi* (curing frenzy), and

---

[10] Small schools seem to have resisted for a couple more decades. Middlebury College required Greek for admission until 1908. And the great Oxford dropped its Greek admission requirement in 1920 (Latin lasted till 1960).

purged, of its tired blood, the educational system entrusted to his care. In 1915, as a prominent member of the steering committee, he helped the new Lincoln School of Teachers College in New York exclude Latin and Greek from its curriculum. In 1916 Eliot was still opening veins, publicly insisting that vocational utility—and not liberal education—was to be the rationale for undergraduate instruction (Eliot, 1917). Crucial to his mission was the elective system. "It is a straight line," Kopff (2001) noted, "from the introduction of the elective system in high schools and colleges, made possible by the banishment of Greek and Latin from the humanities curriculum, to the current woes of the behemoth university."

President Eliot may have dimly understood this himself. When leaving Harvard, he produced the 50-volume *Harvard Classics* (1909-1910). It was as if, in unconscious contrition, he was returning to an injured world the carcass of the humanist education he had drained of its lifeblood.

> There is not perhaps in all the stores of ideal anguish, a thought more painful than the consciousness of having propagated corruption by vitiating the mind ... (Dr. Johnson: *Rambler*, no. 31)

By the 1920s it had come to pass: Vocational training, in the once hallowed halls of learning, had replaced education. The academy weeded out courses useless to that training. And the courses most conspicuous in their uselessness were Greek and Latin. Classical education became an elective, and few elected to learn Greek.

As I said in the Introduction, humanist education tackled tension-evasion only halfway. Humanist education animated the part of mental growth mediated by what we call *secondary process* thinking, that is, logical, controlled, largely conscious thinking.

But psychoanalysis, by confronting the unconscious strategies of self-deception, promotes mental growth more comprehensively; it expands education to internal reality. Psychoanalysis, as we will see, familiarizes the analysand with *primary process* thinking. This is the far greater part of our mental life: Instantaneous, unmediated and uncontrolled, irrational, wishful, hallucinatory thinking, thinking characteristic of dreams.

Humanist education and psychoanalysis strengthened tension-tolerance, each in their own way, to expedite mental growth. So, just as an envious society destroyed the university, it came for psychoanalysis, too.

7.

Psychoanalysis and its Malcontents

Academic Humanism, as we've seen, made an indispensable contribution to collective mental growth. But it left many private truths invisible, cloaked in self-deceptions.

Unconscious self-deception is humanity's Achilles' heel. Since psychoanalysis grapples with unconscious self-deception, it was humanity's best hope, possibly its secular redeemer. But collective envy cowed psychoanalysis, too.

Here's what provoked the collective envy: Psychoanalysis engages two people in psychical intimacy, an infuriating analogue of the primal scene, and this in itself provokes social envy and hatred. But worse, psychoanalysis exposed those to whom it is useless—the incurably fearful or obtuse—and the world could not forgive this mortification.

Psychoanalysis exposed the self-deceptions that bar humans from their private, vivid, psychophysiological worlds, worlds inaccessible to consciousness. This was to be the final advance in humanity's great historical struggle for mental growth.

Many-faced malice creeps through every historical culture, stalking the enviable, and in the 20th century it fastened on psychoanalysis. With exquisite subtlety, malice sabotaged the Liberator of the Mind. Slaves to fear can't bear their envy of people who confront it.

The forces that attacked psychoanalysis are those that brought down the university. But the anti-analytic forces expressed and fulfilled themselves in more guileful ways. They resisted detection, as they do in dreams, panic attacks, tics and stuttering. They even recruited saboteurs working within the field.

So, historically, after the university fell, the promise, threat and exclusiveness of psychoanalysis awakened envy's full fury. We'll understand better the collapse of the university after looking at society's attack on psychoanalysis: This lays bare the ugly psychology that undermined the total humanistic project.

First, let us look at what psychoanalysis—a method, treatment and science—was intended to be, so that we can compare this with what it has become, eroded by over a century of tension-evasion.

Generally defined, psychoanalysis is the science of the mind, a life science grounded in psychobiological drives. We divide these drives into two categories: One dedicated to life, love and creativity; the other to hatred, death and destructiveness. Freud invented some 200-300 other concepts, like primary and secondary processes, to explain mental phenomena.[1]

Psychoanalytic science specifically investigates the interaction of conscious and unconscious processes. It formulates laws ruling the mental system. The laws are rooted in this axiom: *Unconscious fantasy, patterned upon infantile experience, infiltrates everyone's struggle to meet the demands of the internal and external worlds*.

But is psychoanalysis science? Most people don't think so. But few of them know the following story:

The late Adolf Grünbaum was a leading philosopher of science. Throughout the 1980's and '90's he argued that psychoanalysis was unscientific because its fundamental hypotheses defied experimental verification. Grünbaum traveled the world, to persuade receptive audiences of his conviction.

Meanwhile, the late Howard Shevrin, psychoanalyst, and his University of Michigan research team, were doing neuroscience. They aimed to verify, beyond doubt, this fundamental psychoanalytic theory: Unconscious conflict causes or contributes to discrete anxiety symptoms. After three experiments, Shevrin contacted Grünbaum, who said Shevrin had shown correlation, but not cause-and-effect. On reflection, Shevrin agreed.

So, Shevrin did a cause-and-effect study (Shevrin et al., 2013). Grünbaum accepted it. He conceded that, indeed, fundamental psychoanalytic concepts can be tested empirically, his litmus test for science.

So, psychoanalysis is a science, but also a powerful therapy. Successful therapeutic psychoanalysis has six typical features: 1) the development, elaboration, and resolution of a regressive transference neurosis; 2) the undoing of the infantile amnesia; 3) the modification (so far as possible) of psychic structures; 4) the development of the individual toward genital primacy; 5) the exploration of the primary process, and 6) the controlled

---

[1] Freudian and psychoanalytic concepts of later coinage are catalogued in the Glossary.

interpretation of unconscious strategies of resistance, transference and desire, including destructive desire. Symptom-relief is common, but is not the analytic aim. The analytic aims are heightened awareness and mental growth.

These aims are unattainable without a method. This method entails a faithful observance of the Fundamental Rule of psychoanalysis: Patients must try to say everything that comes to mind, no matter how shocking, embarrassing, or offensive. They lie on a couch, usually perpendicular to the analyst, who sits in a chair, two or three feet behind them.

The Fundamental Rule also applies to the analyst: The analyst tries to maintain free-floating (sometimes called evenly-hovering) attention. Free-floating attention surveys the analysand's stream of speech, without focusing on any one detail of that speech. It also surveys the analyst's feelings and fantasies—no matter how shocking, embarrassing, or offensive—evoked by the analysand.

Analytic success depends upon rigor. Because the defenses (tension-evasions) are tenacious, psychoanalysis began as a five- or six-day weekly practice. The "Monday crust" was Freud's phrase for Sunday's reassertion of the defenses. In the early years, however, treatment was short, lasting only one or two years. Defenses had only to bide their time until treatment ended, then reconquer their lost territory. Analysts began to realize, or concede, that the mind is more reluctant to dismantle its fortifications than Freud at first understood. So, treatment grew longer. Longer treatment did not, however, excuse the analytic pair from the same frequency of meetings, the same rigor, as before. After all, defenses grow only more guileful under scrutiny. And they have grown more impudent (consider anti-vaxxers and anti-Darwinians) as the ambient culture has more widely indulged self-deception. So, effective analytic regimen is at least daily.

The sequence of 50-minute sessions is unbroken except for the analyst's vacation and the rare holiday. It continues indefinitely, usually for decades. When analysts miss sessions, for whatever reason, they should replace them. Patients must pay for every session scheduled, whether they attend or not. All this encourages discipline, keeps both parties aware of the hour, and ensures the analyst is paid for reserving the hour.

Both parties submit to a systematic investigation of unconscious strategies of self-deception. Analysts understand that they can deceive themselves. If they recognize a self-deception and see it has confused or hurt the patient, they must openly acknowledge this and then privately analyze their evasion.

The relationship between the analyst and analysand is central to this investigation. How do the parties deceive themselves or each other about the thoughts and emotions they have toward one another? The analysis focuses, of course, on the patient's deceptiveness. But sometimes countertransference phenomena—that is, the analyst's attitudes toward the patient—interfere with the process. For example, a patient's relentless rumination might discourage or anger the analyst, who then withdraws. Here, again, the analyst must analyze his despair with the help of an outside analyst.

As the participants relax their rigor, the relationship grows superficial, the communications more barren, the defenses more imperious, and the treatment less effective.

Psychoanalysis understands cultural changes not as realities, but as social adaptations, infiltrated with fantasy, to changes in reality. Psychobiological laws, in contrast, are changeless.

For example, biology imposes gender; culture doesn't get to choose it, except in fantasy. Psychoanalysis recognizes, of course, that genetic abnormalities can express themselves as hermaphroditism and other gender ambiguities. As a group these chromosomal peculiarities are called intersex variations. Scientists estimate their incidence ranges from .018% to 1.7% of the population (Sax, 2002).

Let's compare the high number, 1.7%, with the 7.6% of people today who identify as LGBTQ+ (*Gallup News*, 5/13/24). Can we reasonably infer, from this ~6% gap, that many non-intersex LGBTQ+ people have taken a *psychological* path to their condition? Isn't it plausible they have been psychologically compelled—rationalized as choice—to assume one or more LGBTQ+ roles? On that plausible assumption, psychoanalysis believes those 6% non-genetic sexual variations to be unconscious adaptations to early adverse experiences.

Similarly, Classical psychoanalysis believes that conception consigns all non-intersex zygotes to maleness or femaleness. Subsequently, gender shapes our psychologies. Examples: Males are more sensitive to fantasies of castration; females, to internal mutilation. Males envy the potent or pleasure-giving parts of the female, and vice-versa.

Cultural indignation can silence public discussion of taboo psychological realities like inescapable heterosexual predispositions, but cannot cancel the realities themselves. Other unwelcome realities include psychogenic autism; psychogenic psychosis; and, of course, the primal scene. Tension-fraught realities trouble our inner lives no less than our outer lives.

The Power of Psychoanalysis

> *One of the boys threw the other down. ....* [*The dreamer*] *hurried toward the offender with his stick raised, to chastise him. The latter fled for protection to a woman, who was standing by a wooden fence, as though she was his mother. She was a woman of the working classes and her back was turned to the dreamer. At last she turned round and gave him a terrible look so that he ran off in terror. The red flesh of the lower lids of her eyes could be seen standing out* (Freud, S. S. E. IV, p. 201).

This is what I read, two months into my freshman year, from a book lying open on a friend's desk. The book was *The Interpretation of Dreams.* The sample dream in this instance illustrated the mind's recruitment of childhood experiences, in an effort to solve its conflicts. Before reading Freud's discussion of the dream, I guessed the meaning of that last sentence, and was pleased, on reading further, to find my guess confirmed. The dreamer told Freud that he had rushed toward some boys who had *thrown each other down* and were fighting and, seeing him approach, *fled.* Later, walking along the Danube, the dreamer found an isolated spot, and urinated against a *wooden fence.* The woman in the dream stood in the same attitude he had assumed when urinating. Then an elderly woman addressed him, and asked him to visit her. The patient also told Freud that when he was a boy, he had seen little girls' genitals (*the red flesh of the lower lids*) on two occasions: Once, when a girl was *thrown down*, and again when some girls urinated in his presence. He remembered that his father had once *chastised* him (as he had the boys) for his sexual curiosity.

Point by point, Freud connected the tangible world with the intangible truths of the dreamer's mind. From a hodgepodge of memories, recent and remote, the dreaming mind made such links effortlessly and instantaneously. It stitches together a hallucinatory drama in which the competing wishes of its different agencies achieved a momentary reconciliation. The agency of desire once again ogled the female parts. Simultaneously, the agency of constraint – conscience—exacted its expiatory pound of flesh, in a single, unforgettable image. The dream, as in fact all thoughts and actions do, negotiated the clashing claims of drive and defense. The first insists on the immediate satisfaction of its wishes. The second insists on minimizing anxiety, the sense of danger (the father's anger) that wish-satisfaction might occasion. The mind is trying to minimize three tensions: A wish-tension; an anxiety-tension; and a tension of conflict between the two claims. All in all, the dream is obeying our Principle of Least (Expectable) Tension.

The law of minimal tensions derails analysands trying to comply with the fundamental rule of psychoanalysis, the rule to free associate. They must repeatedly inhibit themselves to placate their consciences. This is a typical sequence: Free speech; faltering speech; silence; interpretation of silence; renewed spontaneity; halting speech renewed; and so on.

Almost always, we can trace disturbances of speech to forbidden thoughts concerning the analyst. But over time, analysands grow bolder. More and more they confront their inhibitions, sometimes before the analyst does. They more comfortably recognize and reveal intimate ideas about themselves in relationship to the analyst. They can openly explore deep, ever-changing fantasies about who is doing what, to whom, and why. They've gained the freedom to explore their interior landscapes, mapped onto the psychoanalytic relationship. It could be said that analytic patients enjoy a freedom unequalled in any other human relationship.

To emancipate the mind from the fetters of ignorance and error had been the Humanist mission. Seen in this way, the *fundamental rule* is Classical Humanism's ultimate ethical extension of the maieutic, or Socratic inquiry, the free investigation of the creations of the soul; it is humanity's Emancipation Proclamation.

Humanity cannot understand itself without psychoanalysis. It doesn't know what it is, or could have become. Psychoanalysis is a vision of both humanity and its potential. It provides a conceptual framework for all the other human sciences: Anthropology, economics, history, sociology, literature, psychiatry, biology, physiology and medicine.

As soon as economists, or sociologists, or even physiologists venture into human intention, they stand perplexed before a mare's nest of disguise, deceit and self-deception. Uninformed by depth psychology, they either abandon the problem before them, believing it too complex to resolve with science, or they veil their confusion with superficialities. We'll presently look at one example of this in economics.

It outrages some people to hear it said, that only psychoanalysis could have saved the human mind from superficiality. Surely, we have other ways to study one's psyche: Neuroscience, literature and art, Greek Tragedy, and so on.

But two conditions set psychoanalysis entirely apart from these other worthy approaches to self-knowledge. Psychoanalysis alone proceeds in the living, breathing, here-and-now context of a private human relationship. And even the deepest private friendship cannot, as psychoanalysis can, systematically and relentlessly investigate unconscious self-deception—so slippery, so elusive, so devious. Psychoanalysis is not unique because it delves into the unconscious: Literature, art, philosophy, and music do that too. It is unique because it analyzes the unconscious strategies of self-deception, methodically, systematically, persistently, within a private relationship, over very long periods of time. These two unique features of psychoanalysis oblige us to say that, without psychoanalysis, without a culture that protects psychoanalysis at all costs, human superficiality is assured and society is unsustainable.

And further, if you can believe that we all want the intimate pleasure of penetrating our own and others' mental and emotional realities, the pleasure enjoyed by analysts and analysands, a pleasure accessible only through habitual scrutiny of self-deception, then you'll understand why the world envies analytic pairs.

The inexhaustible source, therefore, from which our culture draws the power to generate *New Yorker* cartoons—the ones which let us innocently trespass the boundaries of privacy, "get inside" the analyst's office, and laugh—not to mention the power to excite its intelligent critics to mock, distort and attack psychoanalysis, need never be a mystery again.[2]

The light of psychoanalysis reveals some celebrated intellectual achievements to be tinkling brass. Consider the achievement of the psychologist Daniel Kahneman, who won the Nobel Prize in Economics in 2012. His seminal paper, "Prospect theory: An analysis of decision under risk" is the most heavily cited article ever published in *Econometrica*, a first-tier economics journal. The student of psychoanalysis wonders why.

Kahneman had shown, contrary to traditional economic theory, that people don't make rational economic choices based on self-interest. They use rules of thumb, like fairness, past events, and aversion to loss. Psychoanalysis

[2] Laughter pleasurably releases energy, previously inhibited, energy associated with unattractive and asocial preoccupations, as Freud explained in *Jokes and their Relation to the Unconscious* (*S. E.* VIII, 1905)

could have shown the economists that Kahneman was shadow-boxing. The theory he was debunking is the theory of rational self-interest, an axiom in the economists' stable of concepts. This had always been a hollow concept. It ought never to have been taken seriously. It served only to conceal the *unconscious* compulsions that determine our choices. Kahneman, it is true, pummeled his zombie opponent. He exposed its weakness by naming the *preconscious*, irrational, trouble-saving, tension-evading cognitive-biases upon which we seem, to superficial observation, to make decisions. He landed a stroke for surface knowledge; but he left rational self-interest standing at the final bell.

Early in his career Kahneman was exposed to psychoanalytic thinking at Austen Riggs Psychiatric Center. But it didn't quite take, and he pursued the surface-dwelling cognitive psychology of the late 20th century. So, he was able to overlook economic man's enslavement to *moral masochism* (the flight from unconscious superego tensions). Unconscious superego anxiety provokes moral masochism, not mere lazy or wishful thinking. But it's lazy and wishful thinking that Kahneman assigns to the cognitive biases he has exposed. Moral masochists weaponize those cognitive biases, using them to smoothly mislead themselves into self-defeating errors. Unconscious envy-fear is closely related to moral masochism. It hides behind cognitive biases, provoking self-destructive decision-making.

Envy-fear and moral masochism inhabit a deeper level of reality, one increasingly remote from economists, non-analytic psychologists, and the general public. The number of those deprived of such concepts is mounting in a world that misprizes psychoanalysis. They are condemned to grope in Plato's νυκτερινῆς ("virtual night"), grasping only fallacies and part-truths, envying the explorers of ἡμέρας ἀληθινὴν ("true day").

Let's put this unfortunate regression in historical context: Into the early 20th century, caretakers of the public sanity scarcely recognized the mind at all. Doctors treated hysteria with oophorectomy, clitoridectomy, and "paroxysm" (orgasm); they treated depression with electrical stimulation, and psychosis with restraint or, under the best conditions, benevolent supervision. Before Freud, mental illness was incomprehensible, hopeless, and disgraceful. But his half-century of work, ending with his death in 1939, blazed a trail of understanding the culture could have profitably followed. As Geoffrey Gorer, an anthropologist, wrote in 1958:

> Because Freud lived and worked, the weak and unhappy are often treated with a gentleness and charity and attempts at understanding which constitute one of the few changes in the climate of opinion in this century of which one need not be ashamed.

Gorer's was a lonely voice, because the modern public, in the space of a half-century, rejected Freud. It even mocked his discoveries. Meanwhile, Melanie Klein and Wilfred Bion brilliantly deepened and extended Freud's work; but their insights too fell upon an impregnable cultural soil.

Envy of medicine and medicine's envy of Mindsight

Invidia, tamquam ignis, summa petit.
("Envy, like fire, seeks the highest." Livy)

For two summers in high school, I worked in a surgery, emergency room, morgue and medical wards. I watched doctors operating with meticulous care and, what was to me, amazing dexterity and skill.

I envied them.

But, I noticed, only partly to evade envy, that medical cure isn't mental cure. Mentally ill pre-operative patients, an impressive proportion of surgical and medical patients, as it seemed to me, left the hospitals physically healing, but just as mentally ill.

So, I thought of medicine as a necessary but insufficient response to human misery. And at college, I learned there were two paths to psychoanalysis: Medicine or clinical psychology. I took the second, continuing straight through to psychoanalytic training. For this decision, of course, I paid the price of yet more physician-envy. But the decade I added to my analytic career, the extra decade of helping people grow their minds, has, perhaps, repaid the psychological inconvenience.

When I began my practice, even in the 1970's, the world despised psychoanalysis. I've thought, for decades, about this self-defeating cultural rancor. Though it's a global phenomenon, its history in our own country reveals its inner nature.

Here, it was love at first sight, apparently. On American shores, in the early 1900's, a seemingly enlightened psychiatry celebrated a European science that for the first time in history, promised lasting psychological help for the mentally ill: Psychoanalysis.

But Americans were already sowing the seeds of its rejection. Janus-faced psychiatric leaders affected public acceptance but practiced private resistance. In the end they chose to ease the private and public anxieties raised by psychoanalysis, rather than use psychoanalysis to educate society about those anxieties.

To be fair, however, Europeans greased the American slide into perdition.

In June 1929 Sigmund Freud and his British friend Ernest Jones argued about the Americans. Their New World colleagues had insisted on restricting psychoanalytic training to medical doctors, asserting that only the medicalization of psychoanalysis could prevent quackery; only the credibility of physicians could legitimize the new profession in the United States.

Thus began the famous battle over so-called "lay analysis." This critical struggle in the history of psychoanalysis (Hale, 1971, 1995) publicly exhibited the universal anxiety over inclusion and exclusion. But more importantly, as I will show, it illustrated *envy of mindsight*. Mindsight's the ability to link conscious with preconscious thoughts, to discover the unconscious fantasy that has infiltrated consciousness. Mindsight respects the *psychoanalytic axiom*.

In today's idiom, "lay" means "not having professional qualifications or expertise." But among the early psychoanalysts, "lay analyst" (a term largely abandoned in the 1960's) meant merely "psychoanalyst who is not a medical physician." There was nothing unqualified about non-medical analysts, who underwent the same training in psychoanalysis as psychiatrists.

Nonetheless, Jones agreed with the Americans; but Freud was wary. He thought the Americans were rationalizing guild interests and also thought, presciently, that they were acting out an unconscious hatred of psychoanalysis itself. So, Freud insisted that psychoanalysis, instead of becoming a handmaiden of psychiatry, preserve its independence.

Many European analysts saw it Freud's way, but the deep-pocketed American membership was waving dollar bills in their indigent faces. In 1938, the Americans, whose numbers dominated the International Psychoanalytic Association (IPA), demanded "total internal autonomy" in setting training standards in the United States. The IPA trembled and obeyed. Before the contractual ink had dried, the American Psychoanalytic Association (APsaA) had outlawed lay analysis. Not until 1957 did the APsaA allow a few talented non-physicians into their institutes, and only after extorting from each and every one a signed promise never to do psychoanalysis except for research.

The policy was, of course, unenforceable. And it variously disgusted or amused many outside the medical circle and embarrassed some within it. It forever stained the integrity and credibility of official psychoanalysis.

And what the APsaA touted as a bulwark against incompetence actually propagated mediocrity, because the ranks of medicine were not necessarily rich in psychological acumen. Although several American physicians did become superb analysts, their exceptional skill had little to do with medical training. Many of their colleagues were unsuited to bear the burden of self-awareness. Owing mostly to psychological limitations, they ham-handled the delicate practice of psychoanalysis and their awkwardness fed public suspicions toward the new science. It turned out that medical talent was fundamentally different from, and often incompatible with psychoanalytic talent.

To explain this incompatibility, we will dissect the talents that help people succeed in physical science-based fields. This study digs deeper into the undervalued ability I have called *mindsight*. It helps explain the intelligencia's rejection of psychoanalysis. And above all, it illustrates envy's special hatred of that ability.

Mindsight is envy's highest target. Why? To begin with, mindsight insults a universal self-flattery: As Freud put it, because everybody has a mind, everybody thinks they're psychologists.

But most of us are middling or bad psychologists. If we're one of these, the mindsighted among us make us burn. To intellectuals accustomed to mastering everything intellectual, mindsighted people are especially galling. Mindsightedness enrages intellectuals close enough to mindsight to understand its incomparable value, without quite being able to access it. I'm thinking of several public Freud-bashers of the late 20th-early 21st centuries.

Earlier I said that mindsight is psychological-mindedness. Now I want to refine and deepen its meaning. Mindsight is sensitivity to the non-conscious wishes and defenses that determine thoughts, feelings and behavior. Mindsight encompasses and exceeds "emotional intelligence," the concept popularized by writer Daniel Goleman. Emotional intelligence is the relatively narrow ability to recognize and manage one's own feelings and to recognize the feelings of others. I've already distinguished it, too, from the attention-based "mindsight" of Daniel Siegal. Mindsight goes much deeper than both of these. It knows that feelings are deceiving, that apparent love can be actual hate, or pity, or disgust. It is not satisfied to identify and manage feelings; it seeks their true identities, origins and natural histories.

Mindsight is penetrating: It probes beneath the mental surface, it reads between the conversational, textual, or gestural lines, knowing that actors or speakers are rarely conscious of the motives driving their actions, speech, or emotions.

Mindsight is skeptical: It doubts the conclusions people come to about themselves, respecting, as it does, the evasive cunning of the mind. The person has mindsight who, having been reproached for habitual lateness, takes it to heart. He does not dismiss it with the platitude, "Well, nobody's perfect." He might, upon reflection, recognize in his lateness an impulse to put others into states of need and suspense, making them feel his own exclusion and abandonment fears. He respects psychoanalysis and, having undertaken it, might also discover cruelty behind his mask of carelessness. His education to the inner life will deepen, diversify and refine his life experience and even, as both a practical and *spiritual* matter, improve and enrich his relationships.

Mindsight is symbolic thinking: It understands the composite character of symbols, whether they appear in conversation, art, or dreams.

Mindsight is grateful: It feels awe for the unconscious mind and is willing, even determined to invest time, money and personal safety in its exploration.

Mindsight is uncommon: Most people misperceive psychological material and many are almost blind to it. Their blindness often breeds blindness in others. People like Hitler and Stalin, ignorant of, indifferent to, or complacent about their own inner lives, imbecilitated whole nations. Countless others do the same on the smaller stages of cities, villages and homes.

Now we can return to the American story. The APsaA psychiatrist-psychoanalysts, many of whom were deficient in mindsight, were not, of course, Hitlers or Stalins; cruelty didn't arouse them like it did history's black-hearted examples. Nonetheless, their propensity for *isolation* handicapped them in their pursuit of mindsight. Isolation is a plague upon all highly intelligent people who covet mindsight.

Isolation helps explain the brilliance of children who become scientists or—our focus group—medical students. Their enviable ability to retain and manipulate scientific and mathematical material is due in part to their precocious attainment of an intense focus. However, when the capacity for imperturbable concentration is acquired too early, it's over-used. Then other capacities languish, chiefly the intuitive openness—that is, the mindsight—essential for psychoanalytic work.

The dynamics of isolation are important, because in this country almost all of the early psychoanalysts were physicians, and they determined the trajectory of American psychoanalysis. It's also the cultural trait that fatefully elevated STEM educations over humanistic ones.

We are not born with the ability to concentrate intensely, and most of us acquire that capacity slowly. But the group of children from which emerge many of our future physicians, scientists, engineers, and mathematicians rapidly master this valuable skill. They owe their precocity partly to an early discovery of the rewards of isolation, a defense mechanism that severs links between feelings—like anxiety, sadness, shame or guilt—and the thoughts associated with those feelings. Isolation reduces thoughts into data. It strips the residual percepts, ideas and actions of their disturbing or confusing aspects. In this way isolation frees the mind to think.

Children who master isolation insensibly lose the ability to let their attention wander or pursue fugitive impressions or hunches. They seldom let themselves be "struck" by peripheral details. They don't let contradictory actions, attitudes and thoughts linger long unresolved in the mind. Brilliant, but tending toward detachment, narrowness and inflexibility, these children, as they age, lose the ability to experience ideas with their associated emotions and so lose access to psychological information critical to the understanding of inner reality. Many such children become medical students. And from this population, many early analysts emerged.

But what happens to isolators when they are thrown together with the mindsighted, as they were in the early decades of psychoanalysis? These two species, it turns out, are like oil and water.

A.A. Brill and Isolation

Isolation and its power of self-deception invigorated the psychoanalytic civil war referenced above, the battle over "lay analysis." The psychiatrists, once they'd realized how easily they had pinned this mischievously demeaning term on colleagues who were depleting their caseloads and practicing with such gratifying autonomy, were surely pleased. The psychiatrists realized that the phrase worked well: It lowered the status of the non-medical group; undermined the enviable autonomy of psychoanalysis as a science; and implied that their competitors were disabled or, in the language of the unconscious, castrated. So, the medical analyst is uncastrated, included, and enviable; the lay analyst is castrated, excluded, and envious.

In the final reckoning, however, it's hard to tell which side suffers, or provokes, the most envy. Medical analysts have enviable knowledge about bodily sickness and health and, at least in their pre-analytic career enjoyed, or suffered, all manner of physical privileges with their patients. They enjoy, moreover, unquestioned authority when peoples' lives are on the line. They have high cultural status. From all this, lay analysts were excluded.

On the other hand, medical analysts are conflicted by their dissonant professional obligations and chafe at their administrative straitjackets. Non-medical analysts enjoy professional coherence and the satisfaction of living out the fundamental autonomy of psychoanalysis.

With this background information on isolation, mindsight and status envy, we can better understand the deeper issues in this early psychoanalytic war, American psychiatrists on one side, Freud and most Europeans on the other.

We start by acknowledging that wisdom and folly attended both sides. It is true that Freud and his colleague Otto Rank created problems in the New World. They inadequately analyzed some visiting Americans—physicians and non-physicians—and let them prematurely end their treatments.[3] They returned to the US, and legitimized themselves by flaunting their European analysis. Many of them, predictably, practiced psychoanalysis badly. This hurt their patients and the reputations of both psychoanalysis and psychiatry in the U. S. So, medical analysts argued, correctly, that allowing untrained people to call themselves "psychoanalysts" was harmful all round.

However, American psychiatrists, many of whom were even more poorly trained to do analysis than the dabblers returning from Europe, argued wrongly that physicians would always practice the new treatment more responsibly.

Even though Freud was a poor judge of other people's trustworthiness outside of the consulting room, he was alert to subtle resistances. And having already navigated the hostility of European medicine, he understood that psychoanalysis would die an early death if it subordinated itself to psychiatry, an entirely different profession, activity, and mentality.

So, Freud argued for lay analysis until his death. We can summarize his

[3] A manifestation of Freud's and Rank's own ambivalence toward analysis.

case in this way: Medicine is grossly inexpedient training for someone who is about to work with relatively complex psychodynamic material, rather than relatively simple somatic material; and medicine calls upon, and inculcates habits of thought often inimical to symbolic and affective thinking.[4]

Psychoanalysts, unlike doctors, do not seek to bring the patient relief with medicines and surgical alteration, imposed from without. Instead, they "…. seek to enrich our patient from his own internal resources, by putting at the disposal of his ego those energies which, owing to repression, are inaccessibly confined in his unconscious, as well as those which his ego is obliged to squander in the fruitless task of maintaining those repressions."

Freud's claims notwithstanding, the battle raged. At its center stood Abraham Arden Brill (1874—1948), a New York psychiatrist, "one of the most influential American psychiatrists of the [20th] century," according to the *American Journal of Psychiatry.*

Brill had left his overbearing parents in Austria when he was fourteen years old and emigrated to America at sixteen, alone, in 1890, to seek his fortune. He earned his medical degree, and in 1907 returned to Europe, met Freud, and planned with him to translate Freud's writings into English.

Brill's translations were not universally admired, but they launched an outstandingly successful career. He founded the New York Psychoanalytic Society and helped establish the American Psychoanalytic Society. He was, no doubt, a champion of psychoanalysis in the U. S. He practiced, taught and wrote about psychoanalysis. But was he a mindsighted man?

I have read some of his work and found it lively, entertaining, clear-minded expositions of psychoanalytic ideas. He does, however, sometimes drift into pop birth-order psychology, and in his *Basic Principles of Psychoanalysis* (1948) hardly mentions transference, the core of analysis, the place where the deep waters lie. Brill was more comfortable in the shallows.

His behavior in the lay analysis controversy casts a lurid light on his character. More than once, as both friend and colleague, Brill visited Freud in Vienna, and when Freud made his only visit to America, in 1909, Brill hosted him in New York.[5] Between these visits, however, Brill was faithless.

---

[4] Habits of thought such as *isolation* and *intellectualization*. Mental science requires opposite habits, habits of symbolic, intuitive, and emotion-informed thinking.

[5] An older colleague once permitted me to relax in a chair he'd acquired from Brill's estate, a furnishing said to have occupied Brill's living room at the time of Freud's famous visit and accordingly advertised as "a chair Freud may have sat in."

According to Jones, "On his visits to Freud, to whom he was devoted, he would be genuinely persuaded that American recalcitrancy was deplorable and [pledged] to convince his colleagues on his return. Back in New York, however, he would soon [readopt] their attitude, which was really his own" (p. 298).

So, Brill would *volte-face* and, partly to please his peers, partly to please himself, partly—with how much awareness?—to defy Freud, led the fight against lay analysis. In 1925, for example, Brill wrote a New York newspaper article, expressing disapproval of lay analysis. Then, in the autumn of 1926, Brill led the charge for successful NY state legislation against lay analysis. Psychoanalyst A. A. Richards (2006) says Brill was "unalterably opposed to the practice of psychoanalysis and psychotherapy by nonphysicians."

Did Brill, in his solitary moments, reflect upon his apparent whipsaw changes of heart, his dissimulations, his gross inconsistencies in speech and action? If so, was he uneasy about this duplicity, if it was that, or incoherent behavior, if it was that? If he was indifferent or oblivious to these defects, how had he achieved such cluelessness? By *isolation* and *displacement*. We already know about isolation. *Displacement* is the instantaneous shifting of attention from troubling ideas or images to neutral, pleasant or at least less troubling ones.[6] In this way, displacement preconditions isolation, as it did in the following circumstance: In 1937, Brill reminisces on his visit with Freud's lapsed colleague Joseph Breuer in 1907.[7] During that meeting, he'd asked Breuer for permission to translate and publish his works. Breuer agreed. After the meeting, Brill fretted that he had not been "specific enough" in his request.

Then he writes, "… I was again and again annoyed by the visits of this *ghost*, which always made me feel somewhat guilty." He goes on to say that he went on with his life, "But the old *ghost* refused to remain buried … the thought that I had deliberately kept from Breuer the fact that I did not intend to translate any of his [other] works." He ends with, "Last, but not least, in paying my debt to the *shade* of Dr. Joseph Breuer, I am not just easing my conscience …." (all emphases are the author's).

---

[6] Displacement is also critical in *selective inattention*, taken up in Chapter 10.

[7] Breuer, Joseph and Freud, Sigmund. *Studies in Hysteria*, trans. A. A. Brill. New York: Nervous and Mental Disease Publishing Company, 1937.

Why did Brill scruple so painfully, for three decades, over this peccadillo? It substituted for a more malicious act—one worthier of three decades of remorse.

We can easily guess Brill's real victim: To Freud, Brill owed his career, success, reputation, social status, and maybe even psychological balance. Behind the figure of Freud stood the parents Brill hated enough to leave at 14, but to whom, of course, he owed his existence, his intelligence, and his resourcefulness. And so, to evade his guilt and remorse in relation to these three figures, he *isolated*, or detached those feelings from them, and then reattached them (*displaced* them) to a less important person, while displacing his guilt onto a less blameworthy action. To put it another way, Brill isolated his penitence toward Freud and his parents, and then displaced it onto a trifling impropriety with Joseph Breuer, someone to whom he owed so much less.

Brill's habit of isolation proved to be incapacitating, and stoked his envy of mindsight. Both were common among the self-enclosed doctors who dominated American psychoanalysis.

And so, as Freud had predicted, the APsaA policy spawned not an elite group of talented, ethical, and dedicated psychoanalysts, but a Master Race of psychiatrists, simulacra of psychoanalysts made so life-like by their jargon, credentials and gestures as to fool even themselves.

Their envy of mindsight only intensified over time, and targeted their gifted colleagues and everyone else upon whom nature had unequally bestowed this useful gift. And their secret resentment, expressed in policy, training curricula, and practice, undermined American psychoanalysis at its most critical stage of development.

So, the psychoanalytic institution never achieved the solidarity that would have sustained it against the public envy that the isolating doctors, *on behalf of the whole world,* had acted out. Sixty years later, a psychoanalysis more confident in itself, fortified by unanimity, might have survived its fear of the culture's envy. And a society that trusted psychoanalysis' courage in its own convictions might have matured, rather than regressed.

Now we examine a more straightforward enemy of psychoanalysis: A socially invaluable movement spoiled by envy: 20th century feminism.

The burden of mindsight-envy hung heavily on 20th century women intellectuals. The common feminist attack was to call psychoanalytic theories sexist, making those theories seem both invalid and repugnant.

The feminist anti-Freudian and, by implication, anti-psychoanalytic argument, promulgated by Betty Friedan, Kate Millet, Simone de Beauvoir and many others, was that Freud was out of date, culture-bound and phallocentric. They argued that Freud believed men were stronger, better, and more important than women. Society reckons Freud even today as anti-feminist, owing partly to his emphasis on penis envy—which outrages some women— partly to his occasional dismissal of the feminism of his own era, and partly to his specific idea that the female conscience is "weaker."

It is true that Freud never dealt with men's envy of women, and that he sometimes seemed not to fully appreciate women's frustrated ambitions to use their talent and political influence. He said, for example, "Anyway, women as a group do not profit from the modern woman's movement at all; at most a few." It is also true that, in 1925, Freud wrote "hesitantly" that the feminine superego "never becomes so inexorable, so impersonal, so independent of its emotional origins" as we demand in the male, and shows "less inclination to submission to the great exigencies of life, [and] is more often led in [its] decisions by tender or hostile feelings." He seemed to believe women have weak superegos.

So, Freud's feminist critics imply that he thought women the weaker sex. Freud biographer Peter Gay does regard Freud's assertion that men were the aggressors in sexuality, and other comments on supposed female idiosyncrasies, as proof of his belief in their "inferiority." Gay goes on to say, however, that "[Freud] did not want to spend all his energy on this limited though significant issue ... [he was] impatient to move on .... to grander riddles ..." (1988, p. 522). In Gay's opinion, more nuanced than other commentators', Freud doesn't fit the image of a woman-disdaining, oppressive, and chauvinistic Victorian white man. Early on, for example, Freud questioned platitudes, like the notion that "women were by nature sexually passive ...." Freud recognized that much of women's erotic passivity was not natural but imposed by society (Gay, p. 507-8). Möbius's contention, that women are "physiologically feeble-minded" (p. 512), Freud denounced as "dubious" and added that, even if intellectual atrophy could be demonstrated among women, it would be "the fault of society, which prevented them from occupying their minds with what interested them most—sexuality" (p. 512). These comments also refute Freud's supposed insensibility to cultural influences.

Concerning comparative vigor, Freud told Arnold Zweig in 1933, women were stronger than men and, in bearing the deteriorating political climate in Germany and Austria at that time, they "[stood] up better" (p. 512) than men. Freud also said that women, "are, after all, the more steadfast element; .... the male is biologically more likely to cave in" (p. 512). Here, though, Gay, no Freud hagiographer, discovers a "patronizing, if affectionate note" (p. 512). However, Freud's "conduct," Gay writes, "as the undisputed founder and leader of an international movement to which women made conspicuous and well-recognized contributions contradicted [Freud's] rhetoric."

When in 1910 Isidor Sadger opposed admission of women to the Vienna Psychoanalytic Society, Freud disagreed, saying he would "see it as a serious inconsistency." Freud never hesitated to suggest that female analysts might dig more deeply than could a male analyst into patients' earliest years, and that their intuition for early experience was stronger than men's. He said that psychoanalysis needed women and actively recruited them for the profession. Among the women who, very early in psychoanalytic history, attained the status of psychoanalyst, with no chauvinist opposition, were Lou Andreas-Salome; Helene Deutsch; Joan Riviere; Jeanne Lampl-de Groot; Ruth Mack Brunswick; Marie Bonaparte; and Anna Freud, all making substantial contributions to psychoanalysis, all welcomed by Freud. He even respected Melanie Klein, the "second genius" of psychoanalysis, though he resented her for challenging some of his daughter Anna's ideas.

Gay: Freud "never obstructed—on the contrary, he fostered—aspiring female psychoanalysts, and took their views seriously.... [he presided] over a profession in which women could rise to the top" (p. 508-509). "Making little of [their achievements], prominent woman analysts like Anna Freud and Melanie Klein were living embodiments of feminist aspiration, profiting from ... Freud's attitude" (p. 509).

So, Freud encouraged women analysts in the science's very beginnings, yet feminists heap opprobrium upon Freud. These include some of the 20th and 21st centuries' most highly educated women. Such considerations might inspire feminist soul-searching, and awe the rest of us with the envy-stimulating power of psychoanalysis.

Nor should any educated woman after 1960 have been misled by the claim that psychoanalysis ignores male envy of female identity, intelligence, creativity, genitalia and internal organs. Here is a brief vignette.

In 1957 Melanie Klein (1975, Vol. III, p. 210-211) reported a man in analysis with her. He understood his destructive impulses, but not yet his envious hatred toward Klein and her creativity. He reported a dream:

> *He was fishing. He wondered whether he should kill the fish he caught in order to eat it, but decided to put it into a basket and let it die. The basket in which he was carrying the fish was a woman's laundry basket. The fish suddenly turned into a beautiful baby and there was something green about the baby's clothes. Then he noticed—and became very concerned—that the baby's intestines were protruding because they had been damaged by the hook it had swallowed in its fish state.*

The analysand associated to the green cover of her books in the International Psycho-Analytical Library Series, and remarked that the fish in the basket stood for one of her books that he had stolen. Further associations showed that the fish stood not only for her work and her baby, but also for herself. Her (Klein's) swallowing the hook—"the bait"—expressed his feeling that he had fooled her into thinking better of him than he deserved and into not recognizing his pointedly destructive intentions toward her. .... She interpreted that the laundry basket in this connection expressed his desire to be a woman, to have babies, and to deprive his mother, and Klein, of them.

The patient was shocked and became depressed.

Men, if anything, abhor their women-envy even more than women detest their men-envy. It's too late now, but both genders had been better off had they learned long ago to live with and, by mutual generosity, soften the insults of these truths—perhaps especially women-envy, because that, as I believe, tunnels deeper into the bedrock of our doom.

So, humanity's envy of psychoanalysis, as so often, focused on Freud, and cast about for any and all weapons for his destruction: It recruited feminism, besotted the public intelligence, and diverted society from the inner world.

Thus did the intelligencia, on all fronts, erode public confidence in psychoanalysis, the confidence of analysts, and the confidence of psychoanalytic institutions. From the tempest of social envy, psychoanalysis tacked into the safe, but stagnant harbor of unconditional inclusion and social justice.

The twilight of psychoanalysis

For about four decades after Freud's death in 1939, psychoanalysis made invaluable discoveries. But society ignored them, and gradually relapsed into the shallowness from which psychoanalysis had briefly reclaimed it. Medicine, genetics, neuroscience and psychoanalysis itself all connived, as described in this chapter, to substitute a view of mental illness so simple, so disconnected from human relationships, so conceptually impoverished, and so politically inoffensive as to make its treatment by surgery, shock, transcranial stimulation, mushrooms and chemicals seem not ridiculous. Physicians performed, or promulgated, or ineffectively opposed an extended series of anti-psychoanalytic remedies: Insulin shock through the 1950's; lobotomy into the 1960's; and psychotropic medication and electroconvulsive shock to the present day. By 1990 society had restored the nihilistic psychiatry ("You have bipolar disorder; you'll be on lithium the rest of your life.") that before Freud had ruled the public view of mental illness. Now, once again untethered to depth psychology, people could dismiss or trivialize unconscious motivation and never understand war, prejudice, injustice and, above all, global denial of population-driven despoliation of the planet.[8] The erosion of mindsight allowed technological convenience and the social regression it encouraged to advance unquestioned and unimpeded.

In the last thirty years of the 20th century, public doubts about Freud resolved into certainty.[9] As time went on, psychoanalytic training attracted fewer psychiatric residents, and budgets of psychoanalytic institutes grew ever leaner. The resentment of the medical practitioners can only have been embittered, and their confidence undermined when, in the late 1960's and early 1970's, psychologists and social workers began to dismantle psychiatry's monopoly on psychotherapy. Faced with certain defeat, psychiatry retreated to its old redoubt, that fortress of nihilism—the medical model of mental illness—out from which its predecessors had cautiously ventured in a short-lived spirit of adventure and charity. Their flirtation with

[8] Psychology has addressed overpopulation, but only with principles of cognitive, not depth, psychology. See Wessendorff, (2010) Bridgeman, (2017) and Clayton et al (2017).

[9] Notwithstanding anti-analytic claims to the contrary, both the clinical effectiveness of psychoanalysis—or at least long-term psychoanalytic psychotherapy, a treatment grounded in psychoanalytic theory and technique—and basic psychoanalytic principles have accumulated empirical support. See Etkin et al., (2005), Glass, (2008), Leischsenring and Rabung, (2008), Leischsenring, (2009), Levy and Ablon, (2009), de Maat et al., (2009), Shedler, (2010), Green et al., (2012), Shevrin, (2012), and Bazan et al., (2013) among others.

depth psychology had come to its inevitable and painful end; so, psychiatry joined hands with the pharmaceutical industry, which became preposterously rich sedating an increasingly tension-averse culture. And, in the late 1980's, when psychologists sued the APsaA for admission to its institutes, the beleaguered medical gatekeepers laid down their arms.

Psychologists and social workers, having already filled the non-IPA, psychologist-run institutes created in the last half of the 20th century, began slowly to colonize the IPA institutes. They brought with them, perhaps, a better couchside manner. But by this time, they had imbibed, for their own protection, the culture's prevailing political sensibilities. They were further weakened, in this narrow case, by their punchless lack of medical hauteur, and grew more faint-hearted year by year. They sanitized psychoanalytic theory and technique according to modern tastes. They decided that the concept, or fact, of penis envy was improper; they discovered that the developmental theories of gender identity and sexual preference had unacceptable implications. In 1998, they even apologized, ceremoniously, for these insulting theories. Meanwhile, a number of analysts confessed that the couch was indeed a sinister tool of power over the patient.

Now, whatever in the theory or practice of psychoanalysis offended any vulnerable group, the new generation of psychoanalysts ejected from the canon. Psychoanalysis also retreated from its rigor, redefining psychoanalysis as four, then three and, among some analytic groups, two sessions weekly. This doesn't say that once or twice-weekly psychotherapy is worthless; careful listening is helpful in any dosage. This is only to say that psychoanalysis cosseted enviers of the courage, self-respect and mindsight implied in daily self-exploration.[10]

And its own custodians, like the university's, continue today to erode the rigor of a once magnificent educational system. Several years ago, a *Journal*

---

[10] "Who has the time and money?" some will ask. Motivated people find the time; impecunious motivated people find analysts willing to subsidize them. My own practice is typical: I give one-quarter of my schedule to analysands for hourly fees 1/2 those collected by plumbers, electricians, carpenters and mechanics and even, within the last decade, worked over 1000 hours at minimum wage.

More to the cultural point, any society that valued self-knowledge would subsidize psychoanalysis for its motivated poor citizens. It is remarkable, in this regard, that Medicare (though not Medicaid) still pays for "psychoanalysis." But that policy may be less for mental growth, than thrift: mental health care reduces medical expenses.

of the American Psychoanalytic Association issue included fanfaronades (Cherry et al., 2020; Fritz and Winer, 2020) from two psychoanalytic training centers. They'd both vanquished insolvency with the winning strategy of relaxing entrance and graduation requirements. The editors of an even more recent edition of the same journal (Vol. 69, No. 2, April, 2021) lapsed into social activism, dedicating its 8 articles and 148 pages to systemic racism. Then it repeated this envy-dispelling ritual in 2024 (Vol. 72, No. 3).

Throughout the world, envious revisionists continued to discredit—and, in the public mind, succeeded in discrediting—many useful truths like castration anxiety, penis envy, the Oedipus complex, and the psychogenic origins of schizophrenia, homosexuality, gender dysphoria and obsessive-compulsive neurosis.

By the beginning of the 21st century, official psychoanalysis had retreated so far from these and other disquieting ideas, that the editor of a top-tier psychoanalytic journal could shamelessly repudiate the unconscious mind itself, just as neuroscientists were beginning, after a hundred years of denial, to endorse it. Nobel Laureate Gerald Edelman had dedicated his neuroscientific book *Bright air, Brilliant Fire* (1992) to Freud and Darwin. Another Laureate, Eric Kandel (1999), had distinguished psychoanalysis as "still .... the most coherent and intellectually satisfying view of the mind." And yet, psychoanalysis had faded into a shadow of its former self.

Psychoanalysis, without which society's mental growth is unsustainable, had abandoned its scientific autonomy, not to another profession, like medicine, but more fatally, to public opinion, to guilt, shame, and fears of social exclusion. In the beginning, isolators infiltrated and fractured the community and unanimity of psychoanalysis. Then envious social attacks withered its confidence. Wobbled by envy-fear, psychoanalysis recanted ideas—however valuable experience had shown them to be—which offended the people.

These recantations helped society ignore its limitations. Does society today not smugly believe, more than ever, it can grow infinitely in a finite world? Ignore ecology? Trivialize self-deception? Belligerently believe it can flee biological endowments?

Group tension-evasion was, I concede, only one factor in the decline of psychoanalysis. Psychoanalysis, after all, promised access to secret parts of the mind and seemed to tap healing powers previously unknown. Wasn't it natural that this exciting science would attract, in addition to bright, creative, intuitive people, many inappropriate enthusiasts? And because psychoanalytic propositions refer to invisible structures and processes that elude verification, wasn't it natural too that public intellectuals would relentlessly challenge the profession?[11]

Natural to challenge, of course. But extermination, not verification, was the critics' mission, and appeasement was the analysts' response. It is therefore no accident that every innovation in psychoanalytic theory and practice nudged the institution toward more accessibility, more politeness, and more convenience. Over a century, psychoanalysis became easier, more palatable, less useful and, above all, less enviable to patient, analyst and culture.

Like the fading of Classical Humanism, the debasement of psychoanalysis served the great project of tension abolition. Psychoanalysis was uniquely positioned to teach humanity about the dangers of self-deception and reality-distortion, to puncture the world's complacency, to reacquaint humanity with its tragic dilemma, and, accordingly, to encourage mental growth.

But beset by cultural ignorance, hostility, and envy from within and without, the psychoanalytic worldview, capstone of Humanism, wasted away.[12]

Higher education, the other liberator of the mind, stumbled down a similar path. Their common fate suggests a kind of Second Law of Sociodynamics: When, against the odds, genius gives birth to something complex and beautiful, an insight that demands labor and care; when that insight generates tensions greater than those it relieves; then, having built it up, we will wear it down, just as nature ignites, then extinguishes, the stars.

[11] We recall the Grunbaun/Shevrin story above.
[12] See Moyn. (2016)

8.

The Envy of Humanist Education

Now that we understand some of the forces at play in the attack on psychoanalysis, we can start to understand the decline of the humanist university. We have already seen the destructive power of envy, and the antagonism between the scientific and Classical worldviews, that is, the omnipotent versus the tragic. We must see how these forces operate at a deeper level and analyze the particular fronts in the war against the university. Only then can I begin to tie the threads of my argument together—relating all the above to society's strange, prolonged blindness to overpopulation.

Let's recall, perhaps with some uneasiness, that whatever irritates our sensitivity to exclusion, inequality, or even trivial dissimilarities, awakens envy, the rabies of the heart.[1] Education's historical aristocratic associations and exclusionary ideals embittered social envy. The egalitarian sensibilities of a growing middle class aggravated it. Envy grew more bloody-minded in the late 19th century culture, as tension-tolerance fell. It sheared away even the remnants of the ideals of mental growth and tension-tolerance, leaving only *paideia's* ruins. Upon these society raised a gigantic apparatus of inclusion: A cultural purification program, an institution of prevocational training, entrepreneurship and technological innovation, a school of omnipotence, the panacea for tensions.

Conventional wisdom, however, explains the fall without the unpleasantness of envy-psychology. It says that the university abandoned the compulsory Greek and Latin curriculum simply because it no longer met the public's socioeconomic needs. This, the socioeconomic theory of educational change, is understandable, communicable, and socially acceptable.

And shallow. I've described the embarrassing abyss between my quaint notion of the university's ideals and true character. I explored my own blindness, wondering why the university's transformation had seemed obvious and natural to many people, but unnatural (and invisible) to me. Then,

---

[1] Melville's phrase.

moving on to the cultural problem, I wondered how academia, the institutional guardian of the public mind, could have forgotten the irreplaceable benefits, surveyed earlier, of Classical studies. Some deeper mischief, I thought, must be at play. In searching for that gremlin, I first asked: What, exactly, does modern society *think* it wants from higher education?

Writer and educator Louis Menand (2011) says that society asks three things of the university: To sort out citizens as to their intelligence and aptitude in the interest of optimizing national human resources; to enlighten and socialize its citizens; and to train them for vocations.

This seemed sound to me. And its logic implies that Greek and Latin studies at some point didn't meet those responsibilities, and that is why society devalued them. This is also the common understanding.

But when we look more closely, we see that Classical studies, even in its weakened modern form, meets every one of these responsibilities as well as, or better than studies in nearly every other field, fields such as pre-law, pre-medicine, mathematics, political science or business.

We established in chapter three the intellectual power of Classics students. It's clear that the Greek and Latin major is a reliable marker of intelligence.

We already know that Greek and Latin studies promote success in the professions. This remains true.[2] We can safely assume, I think, that Greek and Latin studies superbly serve the intellectual sorting responsibility of the university.

Classical studies also serve the vocational responsibility of the academy. Even if Greek and Latin do not specifically prepare students to become drug representatives, hospital administrators, bank branch managers or financial officers of eye clinics, the Classical curriculum wouldn't interfere with such preparation and might make them better at those jobs, not only by sharpening their memories and improving their logical and abstract thinking skills, but by sensitizing them to the wider social and historical contexts in which their jobs are embedded.

Finally, Greek and Latin students, from the beginning to the end of their training, are immersed in the core ethical and political values of a great world

[2] The Association of American Medical Colleges says that students who major or double-major in Classics have a better success rate getting into medical school than do students who concentrate solely in biology, microbiology, and other branches of science (Princeton Review, 2018).

culture, making Classical studies a beacon of cultural enlightenment, and solid preparation for useful citizenship and intelligent leadership.[3]

Therefore, the conventional reasons for the demotion of Classical knowledge in the university's hierarchy of values—that it doesn't optimize human resources, stoke the economic furnace, conduce to vocational preparation, and make good citizens—don't hold up. Yet the community has told itself that they do, because those specious reasons conceal the real reason for the demotion: Envy of the talent, the doggedness, the self-reflection necessary to pursue Classical education.

And so, few tears have fallen over this intellectual loss. The academy denies that anything meaningful has died, and reinforces this denial by continuing to drape itself in the robes, and to parade in the pomp, of the ancient tradition. Meanwhile, it panders, without a blush, to society's greed for ease and the delusive reassurance of growth (Pilling, 2017). And society, relieved thereby of the obligation for hard mental work, and satisfied with the convenience of prevocational training, has declined to point its finger at the university's humbuggery. If this behavior was self-destructive, as I think it was, the great academic shift became a psychopathological mystery to be solved.

The conventional forensics on the university's death arraigns economic expansion, scientific discovery, global exploration, religious doubt, and colonization. But these are merely accessories to the crime. The real culprit is envy.

We've already shown that the collective's decision to dismantle the humanist university was not entirely practical or rational. The collective was trying to solve an unconscious problem. And its solution discouraged young people from valuing their inner lives and maximizing their intelligence and talent. The collective's motive was apparently malicious.

Envy and Identification with the Aggressor

Society marginalized humanist education, as it did psychoanalysis. The institutions' respective leaders beat frightened retreats from envious critics. They abdicated their duty to manage tensions, envy in particular.

---

[3] It's delightful to know, in this regard, that our country's Covid war hero, Dr. Anthony Fauci, was a Classics major.

So, the resentment of elite education fits the pattern we saw in the previous chapter. But because the university, compared to psychoanalysis, exerts more extensive social influence, envy of education, and envy-fear in educators, also exert wider cultural force.

That far-reaching forces link population growth, advancing prosperity, and public scorn for scholarship on one side, to envy-dread in the learned, on the other. Envy-dread, or the urge to appease envy in others, is as destructive as envy itself. We looked at its roots in Chapter 2.

Among the psychosocial dynamics that supported academia's appeasement of agitators for universal inclusion is a defense strategy called *identification with the aggressor.* Anna Freud coined the phrase to describe a particular form of tension-evasion. She saw this strategy at work in a young boy treated by her colleague August Aichhorn (1878-1949). Aichhorn was a Viennese analyst, celebrated author of the well-known *Wayward Youth* (1935).

Aichhorn's little patient had been disrupting classrooms by making faces, provoking his classmates to loud laughter. In consultation with the unruly pupil and annoyed master, Aichhorn observed that, whenever the teacher criticized, the boy produced an exaggerated scowl or frown. Though he accurately recreated the teacher's angry expression, he wasn't mocking his teacher. Aichhorn determined instead that the boy's grimaces were involuntary, like tics, but better organized. Aichhorn realized that whenever the boy was reproved, he mimicked the reprover's face to manage his anxiety. The teacher's anger scared him.[4] The boy, to momentarily escape fear, was identifying himself with his feared master and his less vulnerable position (Freud, A., 1966, Vol. 2, p. 110).

A young girl had similarly eased her fear of ghosts in her home's dark hallway by making odd "magic gestures." She told her little brother: "You needn't be afraid in the hall. You just have to pretend that you're the ghost." Her strange gestures turned out to be the movements she imagined the ghost might make (Ibid., 110-111). She too was adopting the less vulnerable position, that is, identifying with the powerful ghosts.

In the same way, the learned and their institutions—such as Princeton, which has eliminated Greek and Latin requirements from its Classics major, and Howard University, which dumped its Classics major entirely—are

---

[4] We ignore here the boy's deeper purposes in angering his teacher.

identifying with the aggressors. The aggressors in their cases are politically correct incriminators. The institutions, by self-amputation, are enacting the malicious aspirations of their accusers. In this way they escape their own imaginary weakness and vulnerability, identify with the more powerful aggressors, and disarm their indignant fury.

Princeton, Howard, and other timorous academies illustrate the irresistible power, in the modern world, of righteous indignation, a symptom of humanity's dematuration.

There is an immature, preliminary phase in the development of the conscience, or superego, a stage in which growing numbers are trapped. In this stage, children become indignant at others' wrongdoing whenever threatened by awareness of their own guilt. Here again, the children are identifying with the aggressor; the aggressors being their own consciences, projected into others.

Here's an example of conscience-projection: Anna Freud had a young patient who, from time to time, would torment her analyst with personal questions, receive no answer, and bitterly reproach Miss Freud with "secretiveness." Freud could have placated her with answers; but this would have short-circuited the process of psychological discovery. Freud realized that the reproaches would eventually die down. Then, after a while, they would erupt again in a stereotyped way.

Here's what was happening: The patient, as she free-associated, would occasionally approach some very private material but then, because of inhibitions, keep it secret. She knew she was breaking the fundamental rule of analysis, and betraying her analyst. She hated herself for this, projected the self-criticism onto her analyst and, accordingly, expected Anna Freud to rebuke her. To escape being criticized or even expelled, and to seize the power of criticizing, the girl hurled the anticipated accusations of secrecy back at her analyst. The patient was projecting inner criticism of her own cowardice onto Freud. Her outbursts coincided exactly with each episode of secret-keeping.

In general, indignation at someone else's wrongdoing is a precursor of, and substitute for, guilty feelings of one's own. It shows an unreadiness to tolerate genuine feelings of guilt. It is only when people can turn their attention inward, and repine their own bad impulses or actions, that they can tolerate others perceived as not only less bad, but even admirable and enviable. Only those who endure progressively heavier tensions of self-criticism and guilt can mature.

But many children never confront their own badness and guilt, and remain arrested, for all their lives, at this intermediate, immature stage, in which they deflect their self-criticisms onto others. This makes them ceaselessly scan their environment for new evils and new perpetrators to criticize. Many of these children become social justice activists.

If, as it seems, politically-correct censoriousness has grown more strident in the last half of the 20th century, it is probably because inner fearfulness and the inability to tolerate guilt for one's own badness, already worsening over the previous century or so, has deepened since the 1960's. What global changes have made maturity more unattainable for children?

That's the next question to confront.

I blame the population explosion. It has imposed new stresses on society, raised realistic fears of chaos, evoked deeper anxieties, and awakened formerly more quiescent dynamics. I believe these gigantic strains mobilized a general cultural regression, a dematuration.

Humanity, progressively intolerant of tensions, progressively childish, tried to eradicate exclusion and envy by resisting reproductive and immigration limits, and dismissing its hatred of crowding. It has even sanctified these self-defeating positions. But the cure has worsened the disease: It's heightened inclusion/exclusion tensions.

These tensions, as I've argued, link to unconscious fantasies rooted in the primal scene. Crowding pushes those fantasies toward collective consciousness. As they verge upon awareness, they force us all to wrestle with the dread (paranoid anxiety) and anguished remorse (depressive anxiety) associated with these fantasies. This unrelieved struggle has wearied society, and depleted its collective willpower.[5] Withering willpower made mental growth (maturation) and envy-tolerance hopeless.

We are starting to fathom our plight, but have really only scratched the surface.

---

[5] Even straightforward research (Sinha & Sinha, 1991; Evans and Stecker, 2004) discussed below, shows the will-depleting effects of crowding.

9.

Linking and Omnipotence

To work out the connection between envy, self-deception and overpopulation-denial, we must understand four hard ideas: 1. Our entropic heritage is embedded in envy. 2. Envy's ultimate target is mental growth. 3. People have children to avoid private envy. 4. Humanity imagines itself omnipotent to avoid collective envy. Humanity's infatuation with omnipotence blinds the species to ecological limits.

So, behind envy's (and envy-fear's) sabotage of the two institutions of mental growth, lay a much deeper and more uncontrollable psychological impulse: Envy of linking. Linking, I might say, is the primal scene immanent in the webwork of nature.

Linking, and envy of linking, are the basic antagonists of our being, our Good and Evil. Their deathless contest breeds the tensions that we must evade or confront. By viewing the university as a function of linking more generally, we can understand the culture's hatred of that institution. Mental growth is, after all, the thickening expansion of linking networks.

Envy's ultimate target is mental growth, self-enrichment, the proliferation of internal links. This helps explain the denials of overpopulation and over-immigration. Our denial protects them. They are the weapons envy has deployed to destroy the natural world. But, most pointedly, envy conscripted reproductive linking to annihilate the human network that makes mental growth possible, just as multiple sclerosis deploys myelin antigens to destroy the central nervous system.

The psychoanalytic theory of linking illuminates how annihilating envy is, no matter how much we deny it.

The prototype of linking is the infant-breast connection.[1] When the mother feeds her baby with warmth and pleasure, the baby interprets this as

---

[1] The infant's relationship to the breast, even for bottle-fed children, is the psychophysiological template for the child's subsequent relationships (*object relations*). Melanie Klein wrote that throughout her work she focused on the child-

her desire for its survival, her invitation to life, the most basic inclusion. The lactating breast persuades the infant that it won't be refused what it needs: The mother's milk, love, and protection and, by association, the father's love too. This confidence, once established, mitigates envy for a lifetime. It's as though the confident child says to itself: "Yes, I envy her for breasts, babies and penises, but at least I have her love."

The child's attachments to the mother, father, and parental couple are forms of social, not intrapsychic linking, but those attachments support intrapsychic linking. For the purposes of description and analysis, however, we'll consider social and intrapsychic linking separately.

Linking of the social kind mitigates envy by enhancing the feelings of belonging and inclusion—antagonists, as we know, to envy. Our everyday social successes and failures convince us of this fact.

Linking of the intrapsychic kind, mental linking, the process Chapter 5 described as *structuralization*, mitigates envy in a more complicated way. The infant who can structuralize, we know, has already been gratified, and gratification soothes the feelings of persecutorial deprivation and envy. Structuralization, meanwhile, enhances the child's sense of wholeness, coherence and identity, its sense of inner wealth, and worthiness, and these fortify confidence of inclusion.

Linking, even as it soothes envy in these positive ways, has what we might call an inverse benefit: It provokes envy in others, that is, in those who in reality or imagination are excluded from the link. In other words, linking is invidious: It offloads one's envious tensions onto other sentient beings. This strategy too, for better and worse, eases the torments of one's own envy.

To complicate the matter, our own mental growth, our own structuralization, provokes our own envy, described in Chapter One, a deeper envy.

Deep (Primal) Envy

Depth psychology, now over 60 years ago, constructed an elegant and powerful theory of envy. If it had held the public's skittish attention even a

breast link, the first of all object relations, because the infant's successful interaction with the breast restores the lost prenatal unity with the mother and lays the foundational feeling of security on which all future mental growth depends.

few years longer, psychoanalysis might have modestly educated society about the dangers of unconscious, or *primal envy*.

But primal envy, in any case, would have been hard to teach. The concept imposes both intellectual and psychological barriers.

Primal envy is as wierd as the vast realm of light-years and the miniaturist kingdom of quarks and bosons; as time-bending speed, annihilating gravitation, massless masses, or the entanglement of subatomic particles: It cannot be seen, heard or felt. Ordinary envy, like ordinary gravity, we immediately recognize and understand. But envy that, in unconscious phantasy, exenterates loved ones, scoops out and eats their brains, mutilates their genitalia or *destroys the envier's own mind*, shocks our common sense. Primal envy takes a long time and many intellectual approaches, even by the most receptive student, to grasp.

Primal envy, moreover, unlike physical concepts, is inaccessible to scientific instruments and mathematical models, the physicists' tools of verification. Therefore, primal envy is difficult to measure, validate and demonstrate. And even when we can demonstrate primal envy's existence, its incorporeal manifestations defy ordinary language.

Primal envy's ethereality, however, might emerge from a concrete foundation, the material substance of complexity. Complexity's matrix is the atoms and molecules that link into progressively independent, self-sustaining systems.

Returning to the biophysics of Chapter One, we recall that complexities survive on a reliable stream of energy. Nature furnished them, moreover, with a metabolic appetite for energy, and a warning system (hunger, for example) to signal an imminent energy shortage, a deadly threat. Both appetite and apprehension, even the most rudimentary, entail awareness. All living things, even single-celled organisms, pay for this crude awareness, this *aesthesis*, with existential strain. The Law of Least Tension makes them try to reduce or evade that strain.

Many tension-evasions are life-preserving. For example, when excessive intracellular waste accumulates, the cell expels some to avoid poisoning. But other evasions stop complexification. How could photosynthesis have evolved, for example, had there never existed a cell able to endure photons long enough to adapt to them?

This is life's dilemma: To evade, or not to evade. Evasion of strain can redeem or ruin. But evasion by self-deception usually ruins.

Self-deception, even by infants, might arrest adaptation and structuralization. It can impair contact with reality. Here's an example: Babies seem to form two opposing images of the breast (and of the mother, by metonymy). One is fruitful, comforting, and Good; the other barren, tormenting, and Bad. A weak flow of milk, the breast's absence, or even maternal uneasiness with sucking evoke the sense of badness.

The infant must connect the love and gratitude associated with satisfaction with the envious hatred associated with deprivation. The result, a dichotomous breast, is both more complex and realistic. The infant finds this image hard to sustain because, strange to say, it stirs the psychotic anxieties. To avoid those anxieties, weaker infants split the image back into good and bad part-breasts, and cling to this Manichean fiction. The mental divide protects the good breast from the bad breast's contamination. But the false partition destroys a complex bond (a link) and, in that destruction, freezes maturation. Similarly, throughout life, most self-deceiving tension-evasions, even those necessary to preserve sanity, impair reality-testing.

Primal envy's nettles agitate our search for resources and, in this regard, support life. But envy-evasions more fundamentally impoverish life. Primal envy looks like a remnant of life's grievance against the strain of its existence, an existence that was, after all, coerced from inorganic substance by energy flow. Primal envy, so conceived, would naturally attack every new sensation of admiration, love, wonder and gratitude. That's because these sensations evoke the links that excite joy and lust for life, not for death.

This speculation, that primal envy is a relic of matter's resistance to the strain of complexity, implies that humanity's aspiration to cultivate the interior life was hopeless at its birth. But the interface between immaterial envy and complexity's materiality seems to offer no escape from this dismal conclusion: Under the shadow of primal envy, human life was unsustainable, and was perhaps too seldom worth living.

Primal Envy and Self-destructiveness

I'm tempted to blame Nature for our fate, because She saddled us with primal envy. But She also showered us with opportunities for rich lives. Her providence enthroned us atop the pantheon of all complexities.

What do I mean? We are the most complex of complexities.

Complexity is quantifiable as *energy density*. Eric Chaisson, an American astronomer, has written, that of all known complexities, humans have the highest energy density.

Energy density is the magnitude of energy flowing through a given unit of mass in a given unit of time. Chaisson estimates that the energy density for galaxies is 0.5 ergs per second per gram (ergs/s/g); for stars, 2 ergs/s/g; for planets, 75; for houseplants, 3-6,000; for animals, 20,000; and for human brains, 150,000 ergs/s/g. We may be justified in thinking of the appearance of progressively energy-dense complex systems as a measure of "progress" in the universe over time.[2]

Energy-dense systems are resourceful—that is, they excel at gathering and processing energy resources. Resourcefulness, then, is functionally equivalent to complexity, and complexity, as I explained, has a structural substrate. The substrate of a human brain consists of more *possible* synaptic links than all the protons in the universe. All our resourcefulness springs from this structural virtue.

We value resourcefulness more than resources (*knowing how* to fish, more than *having* fish) and as we more highly prize the object, or ability, we envy it more. Primal envy, accordingly, targets complexity, the human mind, and rich internal worlds.

The destruction of the enviable gratifies envy; this has made envy deadly to the highest aspirations of civilization. To avoid their pain, enviers try to disavow, devalue or eliminate praiseworthy advantages wherever they see them. They'd have done better to emulate those advantages. But sometimes envy fails to inspire emulation of superiorities; then it *aims its fury at their destruction.*

This book delivers the terrible message that primal envy makes an educable, sustainable, humane society impossible. This might seem implausible; day to day, we don't appear fundamentally evil. That's because our sociality conceals the relentlessness of malice. Certain crimes, like mass murder or fetal abduction, briefly unmask envy's horrific cruelty, but we dismiss the perpetrators as freaks. And we cannot see the ubiquity of envious destructiveness. That's because envy's profound impropriety, even among the social primates, has forced it to refine its disguises, possibly for millions of years. Primal envy may be the most deceptively camouflaged of all human

---

[2] Chorost, M. (2012) The ascent of life. *New Scientist*, 21 Jan 2012, p. 36.

emotions. What is most clandestine is not, however, envious behavior itself, examples of which everyday life can astound the careful observer. What's sneakiest is envy's connivance in self-defeating behavior—the catastrophic expression of which is this book's concern.

Psychoanalytic Profiles in Envy

It is hard to understand the ubiquity of envy without living demonstrations. These most freely emerge in the relative safety of the psychoanalytic setting. So, in this and the next three sections we'll look in on three people, doing three kinds of self-harm, beginning with a man whose spite begrudged his own mental growth.[3]

A young lawyer was in psychotherapy for eight years, the first five consisting of once-weekly sessions, the last three of twice-weekly sessions. The analyst had at the outset recommended psychoanalysis (five sessions weekly); but the patient told the analyst that he had better things to do with his time.

This man believed he was homosexual, having but once kissed a girl at a picnic when he was fifteen years old. This, he said, had more disturbed, than aroused him. His passion instead was fixed on athletic, smooth-skinned, light-haired men whom, in his masturbatory fantasies, he or someone else would beat and humiliate. This was his sexual life.

His mother was a lawyer. His father, a slight, socially awkward man, was a theoretical economist, arrogant about his intelligence, a habitual arguer who yielded to no one in controversy except his wife, toward whom he was alternately servile or petulant.

Throughout the treatment, which he used as an opportunity to verbally beat and humiliate the therapist, the patient discharged a stream of insults, calling the analyst too dark, too pudgy and, always, too bearded. He tirelessly reminded the therapist that psychoanalysis was groundless dogma. The therapist, he said, was gullible and worse: Cold.

The young lawyer dismissed interpretations that displeased him. Any comment on his negativity was repulsed with a storm of derision, defied with icy silence, or attacked as an utterance of which the therapist ought to be

[3] Case vignettes in this book are disguised descriptions of real people, drawn either from my practice, my students' practices or the psychoanalytic literature, and in the last case, so referenced.

ashamed, unless he didn't know any better, in which case, as the patient recommended, he "ought to take a good long look at himself."

It might seem strange that such a prideful person would continue so long in therapy. But his negativity was not pure. From time to time, through the gloom of his captiousness, rays of appreciation shone through. He conceded, for example, that he had become a better lawyer during his treatment; he agreed that he was more at ease with, and interested in his clients. But then he'd say: "To be *fair*, time itself would probably have made this stuff happen."

Time made other stuff happen too: He made two new friends, became less self-defeating in his work, and found a girlfriend with whom he even made a sexual experiment. The adventure miscarried, however, when the sight of her genitalia, as he said, "made my stomach turn."

Belligerence was his prevailing adaptation, so it was surprising when he agreed in the fifth year of treatment to a second-weekly session, an admission that he valued the therapy, a concession that forever stuck in his craw. "My greatest mistake," he would call it, and for two years threatened to reverse it. Finally, just before reporting the dream now to be discussed, he did.

"I dreamt I was back in Georgia. It was very warm and I was standing near a peach tree belonging to some big landowner. My girlfriend was with me and I climbed the tree to steal some fruit before the woman owner spotted us.[4] I was strong and hung from the branches while I tossed my girlfriend the fruit. I said to my girlfriend, 'This is like what I did to my brother.' The peaches were a weird luminescent green. I couldn't take my eyes off them."

After reporting the dream, the patient said: "Yesterday I was pruning a tall apple tree in my backyard. The brother comment reminds me that my brother and I used to get money from our Dad to buy Hershey's kisses—real treats, considering his stinginess. We were supposed to split them. But while my brother was at baseball practice [his younger brother was better at sports] I took some of his. I also ate some of mine to make it look like we were eating an equal number. He never realized."

Among the many meanings of this rich dream, the therapist (whose name rhymed with "Peach") focused—as the patient did—on the peaches, which the therapist noted, to himself, were "green" with envy. The therapist thought of the tall green plant in his office, rising behind ("backyard") the patient. The

---

[4] This dream evokes St. Augustine's story about he and his friend stealing pears from a neighbor's tree, a story meant to illustrate destructiveness for its own sake. Our patient's Catholic mother may have told her son this story.

therapist privately inferred that the patient, who lay before him, envied the therapist's presumed comfort with masculinity (the therapist's "tall" plant, rising in the patient's "backyard"); that the patient, to prop up his feeble sense of manhood, had "stolen" the therapist's masculine confidence (the father's "treat," enviously diminished into Hershey's [fecal-like] kisses) by secretly identifying with him; and that he had hidden this maneuver from both the therapist and himself.

The therapist knew that the patient couldn't acknowledge his envy because to do so, in the patient's personal calculus, would be to enlarge the therapist by implied admiration and, by comparison, diminish himself, making the rich insufferably richer. So, to avoid infuriating the patient, the therapist interpreted in such a way as to diminish himself. He suggested to his misogynist patient that the dream represented the therapist as both the *girl*friend to whom he talked about his life, and the *woman* owner who (this was the important clause) might discover a secret, that is, some deception, maybe a self-deception.

The patient sighed. "How much proof do you need that my dreams are not about you? Just let that go." He then added, as he had often before, that the therapist just wanted to feel special; he pitied the therapist's inability to come to terms with this fact.

This patient squandered the potential of his therapy. The defenses he used—devaluing the valuable, glorifying the worthless—emerge in earliest infancy: They are common in human life, maybe increasingly so. How could envy justify such costly choices? The answer lies in envy's origins.

Penis Envy is Only the Beginning

Almost everyone scorns Freud's theory that women feel castrated and envy the penis. The world has agreed to agree that Freud was wrong.

From my experience and perspective, he was right.

What seems to be wrong is the consensus that penis envy is a myth and an insult.

The consensus is that women feel, and are justified in feeling, aggrieved by the advantages men have enjoyed historically in global politics and economics, including absurd advantages like higher pay for equal work. But they attribute this grievance only to those external issues, arguing that any group (including men) similarly disadvantaged, would resent the advantaged group, and might focus that resentment on a trivial but ineradicable difference like the penis.

This explanation of penis envy exemplifies society's wish to superficialize the mind. The feminist argument dismisses the unconscious childhood basis of penis envy, and maybe the unconscious altogether. The argument implies that adult women (maybe men, too) transmit the sense of social inequality to girls of age two and three. The children then, oppressed by this cultural injustice, appear to envy the penis, a symbol of men's social, political and economic power. Little girls, they argue, do not actually wish they had a penis for reasons any deeper than these. Their annoying wish, penis-envy-deniers believe, is not a psychobiological, but a social phenomenon. So, in their play, for example, when they delight in cutting long things in two, or knocking down tall things, little girls are only giving voice to their mother's, and their mother's mothers' rational and justifiable social resentment.

Freud's error was to neglect, though he would likely have acknowledged, the other kinds of envy that prey upon humans: The tone-deaf envy those with perfect pitch; the stupid envy the smart; the weak and awkward envy the strong and graceful. The oblivious envy the alert. Men envy the potency of other men; women, the beauty of other women. Men envy women their vaginas; women envy men their penises. Indeed, we envy whatever instrument of gratification or ability another might have that we do not. It might be said that everyone enjoys some enviable attribute, talent, quality, knowledge, or life experience.

The natural history of envy begins in infantile helplessness: The infant craves reassuring sensations of warmth, satiety and safety. When these sensations occur, he responds with feelings of love and gratitude. These in turn stimulate a desire in the infant, as they will throughout life, to preserve, protect and, as a final solution, control and possess his provider and her provisions: That is, to actually usurp the mother's role.

However, every new hunger pang, chill or fear, sensation of pain, every new frustration—every new gratification too, as explained above—reminds the baby that mother and her functions exist independently of him. Every reminder insults his omnipotence and, according to Melanie Klein, stimulates his envy of the mother's abilities and resources.[5]

Children's analysts observe their young patients enviously attacking, in fantasy, not only the entire maternal (or paternal) person, but also parts and aspects of her person. They envy her devotedness, her intelligence, her loving kindness, her caretaking and her body, notably the parts which give special pleasure or relief, parts like her nipples and breasts. And as in the case to follow, they envy the stomach. This, the child suspects, is the origin and treasure-house of babies.

On Monday three-year-old Sally looked at her analyst's stomach and said, "You've got fatter this weekend." Then, after showing the analyst a purse of which she was very proud, the patient went to a drawer and removed a brown paper bag filled with toy animals. Looking at the bag, she said, in a sudden fury, "Your purses are always bigger than my purses!" The analyst told her that Sally thought the analyst's tummy was bigger too, and full of babies, and that's why it was fat. Sally then filled a basin with water, tore the bag into shreds and threw animals, paper scraps and purse into the water, saying angrily, "Anyway, they're not *your* toys, they're *my* toys!" She then added soap, which clouded the water. The analyst said Sally wanted to take the doctor's babies and put them inside her own tummy, and because she was so angry, tear them all into pieces inside her.

The little girl looked sad. She said that, on Sunday, she'd had a bad tummy ache. She then looked into the basin and said it was a "muddle." This made her cry because she couldn't find her purse. Resisting the impulse to comfort her small patient by extracting the purse from the murky water, the analyst explained her dilemma, saying that when she thought she had stolen the analyst's babies and tore them up inside her, it made her sad. And she became frightened because she thought she had ruined her own body. This was because her body seemed "muddled up" with the analyst's. Sally then successfully retrieved her purse from the soapy water.

In the next session Sally spoke freely of her fear that the analyst or her mother would go on making babies, and said she wanted to be a "mummy full of babies" herself (Segal, 1981, pp. 34-35).

The analyst represented the girl's mother. She provoked envy and envy, in turn, mortified and enraged the little girl, who turned against her precious

---

[5] Satan's basic evil, according to Thomas Aquinas, is to believe he can be Godlike without God's help.

purse the destructive urge to spoil (tear apart) the analyst's baby-making stomach (the bag) and drown the babies (animals).

We underestimate envy because maturation has gratefully spread a veil of oblivion over the agonies of infancy. Peace of mind entails the subordination of envious impulses to realistic remedies for the residual envy that remains conscious. Envious adults console themselves, for example, with the satisfying exercise of their own talents, developed over a lifetime. A woman tortured by her friend's sexual success soothes herself with professional victories. Or, when reality offers no succor, psychotropics can anesthetize the sufferer.

No such succor consoles infants. Their physical helplessness, their bondage to their mothers, and their inability to see beyond the crib, leave them few paths of escape. Babies, so far from always enjoying their mothers as faithful allies, often fear or hate them. Babies are like hostages in love with their captors, godlike beings that variously torture, reward, deprive, and reassure their captives. But, unlike adult hostages, young infants cannot envision future freedom.

Babies are not, however, entirely helpless. They can remodel reality in their fantasies, even to the point of hallucination, and substitute this remodeled reality—for example, an ever-flowing breast under the infant's omnipotent control—for the real world.

Or, if reality has gained middling influence in the infant's mind, the hungry or disappointed baby might instead substitute for the real breast a "sour grapes" delusion: A defective, diseased, or barren breast. This devalues the breast (or the mother's loving care or intelligence) and lessens its enviability. We call this defense "spoiling."

Spoiling is associated with another artifice, the confusion of crucial objects with expendable objects. A baby might confuse the breast with a bottle, rattle, or stuffed animal. An adult might confuse mental growth or intimacy with wealth, social status or political influence, muddling up the valuable (enviable) with the merely desirable.[6]

Using mental tricks like spoiling and confusion, babies can obliterate perceptions that excite envy. Conviction soon adheres to these remodelings of inner reality, remodelings designed to be less disturbing or infuriating.

---

[6] Anonymous: Envy has two favorite methods: to praise what is bad, or alternatively, remain silent about what is good.

Most adults confine such dreamlike reconstructions to their sleep, but admit them to waking consciousness when they are blended, as religion is, with social affirmation. It is underappreciated how commonly these two contortions of the mind—devaluation and confusion—ward off envy from cradle to grave.

We have seen how the young lawyer, unable to tolerate his envy of what he admired in the therapist, spoiled his therapy by devaluation and, by clinging to this defense, curtailed his development.

The pugnacious little girl tried to confuse herself, to muddle awe and admiration with spitefulness. Behind that defense lay sadness and envious dismay that she couldn't do what grown up women do .

Similarly, by spoiling or muddling its values in the service of envy, society undermined the psychological commonwealth. Envious devaluing spoiled the humanist university, the culture and the planet.

Paranoia, Persecution and Pregnancy

When we try to expel our envy, the savage impulse retorts upon ourselves. This happens because we embed our mental life in the endless back-and-forth transactions of human relationships, both real and imaginary. That is, the mind uses relationships as pressure relief valves for tensions. In particular, to relieve our envy, we make others envy us.

As a trivial example, a man might let it drop in a small gathering that he has just returned from Paris, having had a fabulous experience, the best of his life, truly indescribable, totally unforgettable. He pauses to let the irksome sensation steal into the minds of his audience. Through gritted teeth, they congratulate his good fortune and press him for details. But they cannot hide, from his searching eyes, the subtle distortions of voice, the slight asynchronies of posture and movement, the overcompensating cheerfulness. His satisfaction in their discomfort, a discomfort felt by all violated organisms, briefly relieves him of his own envious pain.

Had the process ended there, our invidious traveler might have gotten away with it. He would only have started a game of hot potato in which his victims pass envy from one to another down the social line.

But the instigator's mischief twists back upon himself. Having deposited his envy in others, he undergoes an unanticipated and unnoticed internal change: His relief changes into fear. This is because, in order to vicariously experience, so that he might enjoy, his victims' uneasiness, he was obliged to import the minds of his aggrieved victims. Said another way: To achieve his aim he had to sample the mental experience of those he was provoking. In sampling their experience, however, he allows them—that is, his internal representations of them—to colonize his mind. For his peace of mind, he pillaged theirs. So, having been trod upon, they will turn, and *persecute* their provocateur. In this internal drama, the persecutors model their menaces on his worst childhood fears: Castration, or bodily perforation, mutilation and extrusion of its precious contents. Exenterate not, lest you be exenterated.[7] His fear fulminates into terror, like when the solitary hiker meets a grizzly cub and feels the beady gaze of its nearby mother. His mental gambit has awakened the *paranoid process,* the origin of nightmares and night terrors. His only escape is to shrink his range of self-awareness.

The paranoid process lurks beneath consciousness and controls the behavior and judgment of individuals and groups alike. Where does it come from?

As above, and in the earlier case examples, paranoia is fear of retribution, often provoked by imaginary envious attacks. All infants, no matter how excellent their mothering, will suffer moments of frustration, fear, exclusion and the attendant feelings of rage, persecution and envy. When, for example, hunger awakens fear of starvation, babies sometimes believe that the mother, who actually does wield the power of life or death, is maliciously withholding milk for herself, or invidiously giving it to the father instead.

For these or other reasons, children attack their mothers. Then they anticipate equal and opposite attacks. Those imaginary reprisals are embittered by the ferocity of the child's projected envy. The imaginary avenger, in the baby's earliest months, assumes forms we can, of course, never perfectly envision, but is no doubt assembled, as they are in dreams, from the experiences of the baby's everyday life. By giving anxiety a *persecutory* form, one of the two *psychotic anxieties,* infants manufacture an enemy they can, at least, fight or flee. Choosing to fight, however, only heightens the child's anxiety; he imagines yet more furious counter-counterattacks, as in escalating feuds between people and nations.

---

[7] I've already mentioned Snow White's mother's desire to exenterate her daughter. Other literature, art and history seem to confirm the importance of this envious phantasy of plundering the bodily interior. Some medieval manuscripts, for example, represent Nero looking on, wide-eyed, his face contorted with a deranged smile, as his mother's abdomen is cut open and her uterus exposed (*TLS*, 8/19/16).

At about the fifth month of life, the character of persecution undergoes a momentous change. Children now begin to understand that the person they have imagined burning with their urine, tearing into bits with their (prospective) teeth, or poisoning with their excrements, is the same mother who, at other times, has fed, soothed or warmed them. They assume, with horror, that their rageful attacks have *spoiled* their cherished *object*.

This horrible realization, which comes and goes, floods the infant with despair. One can witness this torment in the shadows of sadness passing over the faces of infants of this age. This is *depressive anxiety*. Its anguished remorse strikes the baby as persecution of a different cast, and so is also hated and evacuated.

Only the rare adult—sometimes by the gift of mindsight, sometimes by the imposition (gift?) of mental illness—glimpses the internal persecutors. Most of us repress them by late childhood. But their sinister shapes haunt us forever.

Perhaps the most effective scheme for abolishing the paranoid nightmare, that is, the boomeranging attack provoked by the invidious forcing of envy into others, is pregnancy.

Pregnancy aspires to linking, both corporeal and psychological: Two bodies and minds uniting to create a third. But unacknowledged parental needs and fears undermine this noble aim. People misuse pregnancy to equalize or enhance status. They misuse it to shed painful memories, emotions, attitudes and conflicts. The three-year old patient described above, we recall, had already foreseen these opportunities: She was planning pregnancies to undo her mortification and envy. She already knew that pregnancy reduces the woman's envy of other women, women who have been copulating and procreating and reveling in this basic life-function.

Pregnancy is the great equalizer between the indigent and prosperous, the misfits and socialites. By impregnating, or being impregnated, the envious and the excluded can crash the party of life. As if by *omnipotence*—for few achievements are so autonomic for men as ejaculation, so effortless for both men and women as fertilization, and so automatic for women as fetation—the participants obliterate envy.[8] Parenting, subsequently, obscures these sensations for a lifetime. It reduces the urgency to project envy. In that way

[8] People use autonomic sexual functions to disavow reality (Adair, 1993).

pregnancy curbs the persecutory anxiety that projected envy would have provoked.

Pregnancy also wards off depressive anxiety. Pregnancy reassures the expectant mother of the unmutilated soundness of her body. It also attests her innocence of any past or present envious and hateful attacks on her mother's cavity and creative organs. Her care and love of her child constantly atones for her vicious attacks on her own mother. It staves off the stabbing remorse that threatens her sanity. Pregnancy's matchless power to evade the two terrors makes it almost irresistible.

I've now described the abuse and overuse of pregnancy as evasion, the evasion that ruined our world. From here we can we move on to the envy of mental growth.

Every new, or renewed mental link, analogizes copulation, and evokes parental copulation. We recall that infantile phantasy locates parental copulation in the mother's interior, the love-nest of linking. So, these faint evocations incite destructive envy toward the maternal cavity and, by association, the internal life.[9]

Envy's Destruction of the Mind

Primal envy of linking, like dark matter, is invisible in everyday life. And to expose that invisible violence, active in us all, was not for Freud or Klein, but for the third genius of psychoanalysis, Wilfred Bion, the English analyst introduced earlier. Bion discovered that some psychotic people, dominated by envy, had ruined their own minds.

One of his patients complained that he wasn't sleeping. With a trembling voice he said, "It can't go on like this." Bion made an interpretation, which the patient couldn't consider because he was "wet." This puzzling pronouncement reminded Bion, who was listening with free-floating attention, of enuresis. So, he told the patient he was afraid of sleep because sleep was like letting his mind ooze away, and added that the patient felt the initial interpretation (envied by the patient) was suddenly so finely fragmented (by the patient's attack) that it had become mental urine, seeping uncontrollably away, and that the patient's leaked-out mind couldn't be repaired. To all this the patient said, "I am dry now." Then Bion reflected that

[9] Julia Kristeva (2001) connected the historical devaluation of women to of the fecund maternal interior.

the patient now felt awake and able to think, but that this good state was fragile.

Another patient (maybe the same patient, disguised by Bion) mentioned a girl who'd been compassionate to him. He then convulsed, as though stabbed. When Bion tried to draw his attention to the convulsion, the patient ignored him, and then told Bion that the room had filled with a blue haze. Eventually the haze cleared, but now the patient felt depressed. This sequence meant, Bion said, that the patient felt understood, then violently attacked that good sensation and disintegrated it into hallucinated molecules of blueness, which changed over into sadness for having destroyed valuable understanding.

Half of another session passed in silence. Then, after hallucinating that a piece of iron had fallen onto the floor, the patient convulsed repeatedly, as if he were being attacked from inside his body. Bion finally said the patient could not make contact with him (Bion) because he feared what was happening inside him. The patient said he was being murdered, and then asked, "What would I do without the analysis? It makes me feel better." Bion told the patient he felt envious of himself and Bion for being able to work together to make him feel better. His envy made him devalue their link. He'd made one of them into a dead piece of iron and the other into a dead floor that came together (copulated) not to give him life, but to murder him. The patient felt frightened; he said he couldn't go on. Bion said this was because he felt he was dead, or alive and so envious that he had to stop good analysis.

Bion's patients destroy connections between themselves and their analyst, between their own thoughts, between their presents and pasts. A lifetime of such attacks had frayed the fabric of their minds.

"Understanding" represented a link between himself and Bion. The patient could not bear this life-giving link, and tried to degrade it into a bizarre copulation (the collision between iron and floor) between lifeless objects.

Linking, the University, and Omnipotence

We have now seen how envy attacks and destroys links, even when they support our equanimity or growth. But we have also seen, perhaps more disturbingly, how envy can destroy our own minds.

Envy naturally turned its hatred of mental growth against the institutions of mental growth. And to persevere at its destructive work, free of interference from our better angels, envy capitalized on the human proclivity for self-deception; it hid itself easily in both private and public pieties, like unconditional inclusion. We will presently describe the most capacious hiding place, the collective fantasy of omnipotence, a fantasy itself sacralized in the concept of limitless human expansion.

But the chief piety used in our culture is social justice. I consider social justice, the intolerance of exclusionary behavior, language or thoughts, to be on one hand, a sign of advancing group coherence, or linking, as defined above. Each group in today's society aims to extend its sympathy to other groups, especially those perceived as victims or excluded groups or individuals, variously perceived as African Americans, ethnic minorities, homosexuals, handicapped people, women, etc.

That this movement conduces to internal linking, however, is wishful thinking. Social justice, at best, only lays a foundation for internal linking. It's a cultural safety net, a support for potential mindsight. But those lacking mindsight, and accordingly more vulnerable to self-deception, can never be sure that their zeal to protect the oppressed is truly selfless.

Wishfully believing in its selflessness, modern society grew complacent toward both its mind and its habitat. I thought these two complacencies might be connected. What if the dissolution of humanist education enabled the behaviors crumbling our habitat: The world's uncontrolled reproduction and migration? Clarifying this connection could help explain the academy's dismissal of the Greek and Latin curriculum.

The Greek and Latin academy tried to build minds, enhance critical thinking, and teach the collective wisdom of a culture. At first it educated only the upper class; later much of the upper middle class; and finally, as its life was ending, a meaningful portion of the middle class.

The disappearance of the compulsory Greek and Latin curriculum, deprived our best minds of two essential nutrients. The first was the *tragic vision of life*, a vision of limits to human ability and satisfaction, a vision antagonistic to wishful thinking. The tragic vision remained robust in Shakespeare. It continued in 17th century drama by tragedians like Corneille and Racine. It was vividly depicted by Ibsen, Strindberg and Chekhov, and kept alive in America by post-World War II playwrights meditating on human loneliness and desolation. But by the late 20th century our society had habituated to the panaceas of modern life. We had submitted to a collective fantasy of omnipotence, and to our animus toward mental growth. Then, according to the late Richard Benson Sewall, author of *The Vision of Tragedy*, we let tragedy quietly fade away.

We lost the second nutrient when vocationalism hunted Classical Humanism out of higher education. By vocationalism I mean the pumping out not only of engineers, computer technicians, mechanics, electricians, and other breadwinners, but also middle-class professionals: Doctors, lawyers, and corporate executives. This momentous change deprived our best minds of *paideia*, a spur to self-knowledge and mental growth.

And in this condition of double starvation, the finest minds no longer grew to their natural height. The rest of society, gradually deprived and at length destitute of lofty models, withered too. Now, unwilling or unable to acknowledge or regret its losses, the culture distorted its value system and began to glorify its degradation. It devalued mental refinement and glorified technology, the engine of omnipotence.

Similarly, the culture, with growing resolve, refused to hate its swelling numbers and isolated (as described in Ch. 7) its dread from the disturbing fact of shrinking resources. Society was too frightened of the private, symbolic, paranoid implications of reproductive and immigration constraint. So, the group looked on in an eerie stupefaction as its life-sustaining climate deteriorated. Even the spectacle of the Atlantic Ocean rolling through lower Manhattan in 2012 could not make society understand the link between its growth and its ruined planet. Because now, deprived of institutional support for minds taught to recognize and mistrust the vanity of omnipotence—or its manifestations, that is, complacency and limitlessness—the collective more and more easily ignored omens like Greenwich Village under water.

The loss of the old curriculum was both a symptom and a cause of deteriorating intellectual discipline, endurance, and breadth. It was pathognomonic of the group's intolerance of frustration. Its members evade frustration with a kind of mutual mass gaslighting. They curry each other's illusion of an unconquerable species, caparisoned with visual reality headsets, beaming with artificial intelligence, swaggering across a conquered planet.

These symptoms—cultural complacency, learning disability, and self-inflicted cruelty—might also represent the atrophy of the group's executive ego. The executive ego inhibits impulses, restrains omnipotence, weighs prospective actions, selects the most prudent and efficiently executes it.

The executive ego, by a different name, was Plato's concern in the *Republic*. Princeton Professor of Politics Melissa Lane (2011) has shown how

Plato exalts self-discipline, a crucial function of the executive ego. The *Republic* concludes that self-discipline is the key to happiness, not happiness as maximum gratification, but, Lane writes, as the "fabric of flourishing." Plato's visionary society recognizes self-discipline as its ethical fabric and reinforces that ethos with its political structures. His society reposes upon the agreement to acknowledge the limits of reality, a pact that prevents overreaching, a symptom of omnipotence.

This kind of group happiness differs from American exceptionalism, a hopped-up happiness expressed in platitudes like "We're the greatest nation on Earth," a phrase abused for centuries. We reluctantly recall that our nation was born an impostor, yelping for liberty (as Dr. Johnson put it) while annihilating indigenous peoples and birching the backs of abducted blacks. Hypocrisy too is a kind of omnipotence, a manic belief that self-contradiction is psychologically harmless.

While thinking through the loss of humanist education and the wider social changes with which these losses were associated, I confronted again and again the group's refusal to abandon omnipotence, a refusal I myself adopted when I stubbornly idealized academia.

So, let's home in on the human infatuation with omnipotence. Omnipotence, in psychoanalytic theory, is the belief that thoughts alone are able to gratify wishes without the help of corresponding actions or help from another person. The omnipotence of defense mechanisms, particularly those associated with fantasies of taking in or expelling objects (loved persons), tend to dissolve the distinctions between self and others. These defensive fantasies *help us avoid experiences of separateness, exclusion and envy*.

Humanity's collective self-idealization, what we call human exceptionalism, is just as grandiose as private omnipotence. We think our technical genius will sweep aside all obstacles to our wishes and hopes and all threats to our safety. We think we matter more than our kindred creatures. We think our charity will bring justice and inclusion to every soul. We think we will vanquish all human tensions.

On a hypothetical scale of mental health, omnipotence is sicker than tension-tolerance. But sometimes omnipotence complies with physical laws (science and technology) and manipulates political realities (social justice) to legitimize its utopian ambitions. This makes omnipotence healthier—in the sense used here—than psychosis, which utterly rejects tension and substitutes hallucination for reality.

In early childhood, when the forces of maturation depose psychosis (hallucination) from the rule of the mind, psychosis only fakes its resignation, and furtively installs omnipotence as its vicegerent. We see omnipotence's normal sway in 10–18 month-old toddlers, elated by their new physical skills, scampering in glee from the very mother whose help, only months ago, they needed simply to be flipped from belly onto back. They collide uncomplaining with furniture, fall down and bounce up without a whimper. The world is their oyster.

Many children do not renounce omnipotence when this normal regime has ended; they adopt it as a permanent solution to pain and then, as adults, make it rival self-reflection and self-restraint as prerequisites for mental growth.

The social cost of replacing self-reflection with omnipotence is high: Because omnipotence is haughty, it is ineducable. Crowding, congestion, superstorms, environmental degradation—cannot educate us. The alarms sounded by depopulation activists, steady-state economists, and more recently, United Nations' scientists, are tinkling brass.

Because omnipotence is cruel, torture and murder have always been required to validate its false reality and gratify the malice that sustains it. Numberless ancient emperors, in whom their subjects collectively vested their private omnipotence, illustrate this connection. The 6th century B. C. tyrant of Acragas (Sicily), Phaleris, is alleged to have roasted his enemies alive inside a brazen bull, acoustically designed to turn his victims' shrieks into bellowing. As they died, Phaleris exulted in the omnipotent illusion of having imparted life to an inert metal beast.[10]

Omnipotent modern adults dream of inexhaustible human cleverness, or a protective hand of technology poised over civilization. We dignify this omnipotence as *rational optimism*: This notion feeds human complacency, obscures our hatred of limits, dread of death, sorrows and frustrations. It obliterates terrifying memories of infantile dependence, helplessness and envy.

Omnipotence discreetly imbeds its psychotic character in rational optimism: "We're safe because we're infinitely adaptable. Whatever's wrong,

---

[10] Phaleris—or his legend—demonstrates our fascination with—and dread of—pregnancy and immurement in the mother's body. The story reflects, again, the survival of early infantile phantasies of enormous cruelties perpetrated there by the child upon the mother or father, or by them upon the child in retaliation.

we can fix it." Rational optimism, made plausible by scientific and technological achievements and expanding global prosperity, calms our panic over the environmental disaster:[11] "Our innovative genius protects us."

Here is an American rejection of reality, even more destructive globally than the New World's bloody beginnings, even more harmful than many reckon its 2016 and 2024 presidential elections. This reality-denial exemplifies my subsidiary ecological theme:

In 1970, Congress chartered the Rockefeller Commission on Population and the American Future. After two years of study, the commission recommended that the nation stabilize its population, 204 million in 1972, a number thought by many scientists even then to be unsustainable. This alarmed business interests because wealth, and especially unlimited wealth, needs a perpetually expanding human market. Business linked arms with the people, who can't bear limits, with Catholic natalists, and with a majority afraid of being deprived of the envy-dispersing comforts of children. The total political weight of their collaboration smashed this extraordinary initiative.

So, President Nixon rejected the study he'd supported and Congress abandoned its own creation. So, the country's indiscipline and faintheartedness deepened the chaos Martin Luther King had condemned just six years earlier as the "plague of overpopulation."[12] Afterwards, we piled up fifty-five more years of environmental damage, resource depletion, infrastructure decay, crowding and encroaching squalor at the door of early 21st century America. We also broadcast the doctrine of self-indulgence to a copycat world and, above all, inflicted a terminal wound upon national self-respect.

Plato's collective self-discipline, then, could have supported group pride. It could have opened a spring of confidence from which dispirited citizens could have drawn refreshment again and again. It could have established a kind of happiness almost unimaginable to moderns, a happiness anchored in the knowledge that we as citizens, guided by realistic leaders, are confronting, not fleeing, reality. But omnipotence indulged the illusion that self-discipline and rigorous education are optional.

---

[11] The great Solon warned: Abundance leads to hubris, and hubris leads to ruin (Jaeger, 1945, I, p.252).

[12] Acceptance speech for Margaret Sanger Award for Human Rights, 1966.

So, we lost a valuable educational paradigm, enfeebled self-discipline and self-control, and ruined the planet. These misfortunes were predictable and preventable. Not to have prevented them was malicious and self-destructive.

I tried to understand how this cascade of group mental events transformed humanist education into prevocational training; how academia exchanged mental growth for economic growth; stopped questioning hubris in order to encourage it. This transition seemed to me an attack on the collective mind. The crucial steps in this sequence began in exclusion's envious rage.

Omnipotence nullifies exclusion and rageful envy. So, civilization binds its members to the pursuit of technological omnipotence. It binds our 8 billions to the credo that artificial intelligence will save us the labor and care of managing inner and outer reality. The God of *Genesis* watched men building a tower to Heaven and said, "Behold, they are one people .... ; and this is only the beginning; nothing… will be impossible for them" (11:1-9).

That human ambition lives on; we're resolved to raise a cybertechnological AI tower of Babel, determined to establish here on Earth a laborless, tensionless and—by dint of social justice—exclusion-less and envy-less Heaven.

Hallucination may have prevailed, after all.

10.

Selective Inattention: Overpopulation

Selective inattention is a well-known kind of tension-evasion. It's a crude defense, like inflammation, the body's most primitive defense against pathogenic invaders. Selective inattention (the basis of denial) is perhaps the mind's most primitive defense against disagreeable realities. Consciousness has somewhat more control of its attention-function than it has over other defenses we have discussed, defenses like reaction formation, repression, or isolation. This control, makes us, in a sense, more responsible for selective inattention.

In general, our ability to focus on or ignore various stimuli helps us improve or expedite our thinking; it allows us to ignore distracting or inessential stimuli. But we can also misuse attention to evade instructive tensions. And with habitual abuse, selective attention—as selective *inattention*—breeds habitual self-deception. It's addictive, spreads like wildfire, and guarantees the global denial of dangers.

Selective inattention is not a new discovery; it is, instead, a forgotten one, a truth that has itself been selectively ignored. Long ago, Plato understood that the best guide to attention is an awareness of reality, tested in the crucible of dialectic. He understood that humans, when presented with intolerable, or merely unpleasant realities, tend to misuse attention to corrupt that awareness. As he writes in the *Republic*, as part of his Allegory of the Cave:

> οὐκοῦν κἂν εἰ πρὸς αὐτὸ τὸ φῶς ἀναγκάζοι αὐτὸν βλέπειν, ἀλγεῖν τε ἂν τὰ ὄμματα καὶ φεύγειν ἀποστρεφόμενον πρὸς ἐκεῖνα ἃ δύναται καθορᾶν, καὶ νομίζειν ταῦτα τῷ ὄντι σαφέστερα τῶν δεικνυμένων;
>
> "And were he compelled to look straight at the light [reality], wouldn't the pain in his eyes make him flee and look toward those things [familiar misperceptions] he is able to see, and see more distinctly, than those now being presented to him?" Plato, *Republic*, VII, 514e (my translation).

Unpleasant realities, Plato knew, tempt us to avert our attention.

As a psychoanalyst, I see people abuse their power of attention—and memory, too, a function of attention—to evade awareness of tensions. Selective *attention* helps us focus, helps us evaluate the salient, relevant or novel fact. In selective *inattention*, we use that very same ability to ignore disturbing and unpleasant facts. In the service of private equanimity or public tranquility, we divert our attention from more to less disturbing realities. If consciousness is an inner theater, we, our own stage directors, can instantaneously strike distressing scenes and raise less distressing scenes in their place.[1] As the philosopher William James said in 1890, "My experience is what I agree to attend to."

Consider two short examples from psychoanalytic practice:

1) A woman repeatedly finds herself forming a mental image of her sick husband's corpse. But before her consciousness fully captures this image, she interposes a less painful—though still unpleasant—image drawn from her memory: The image of having dropped and shattered a vase her father had given to her.

2) A dermatology patient talks fretfully about a small facial cyst while her doctor eyes a grotesque year-old melanoma protruding ominously from the patient's back.

In these instances, selective inattention has reduced or obscured tensions: Grief and guilt in the first and terror in the second. At the same time, it has corrupted the consciousness of its victims, though not so much as to detach them entirely—psychotically, that is—from reality.

This kind of selective inattention has consumed society. How and why would a truth so old and today so important, be ignored by society and its leaders?

The fateful tug-of-war between the push for mental growth, and pull of regression seems to have begun in prehistory. Around nine thousand years ago, when the first agrarian communities arose, the species began to oscillate between two cultures with incompatible goals. Just as they do today, these two life-ways coexisted within single communities, even within individuals. One way of life, the culture of evasion, venerated the tool and weapon, despised tensions, and ignored limits. The second, the culture of education, of

---

[1] "It is a much-abused privilege of conscious activity to conceal every other activity from our eyes." (Freud, 1900, *5*, p. 614)

paideia, venerated the mind, tolerated tensions, and respected limits. Without the first, the second would perhaps have been impossible.[2] But there was a moment when evasion's progress had served its foundational purpose—that is, to construct a technological and political world that supported life—after which further advances were superfluous and, eventually, degrading to the species. It might have been the moment shortly after the scientific, industrial and cultural revolutions had enabled the masses to read and learn. Or maybe that moment came a century or so later, after we'd acquired penicillin and automatic washing machines. In any case, at one of these propitious moments—the pinpointing of which could forever exercise historians—we might have stopped growing. We might have spread adequate comforts throughout a much smaller population, cultivated the simple fruits of peace and justice, and forever after dedicated ourselves to the second way of life. This was the only sustainable option. Instead, the species, helpless to its propensity for self-blinding, embraced evasion even more. We did not resist the totalitarianism of the 2nd Law; we became its quislings.

Some will call this naïve, saying humans could never have stopped growing. It's our nature to keep exploring, investigating, expanding. It's who we are.

Yes, but it's also our nature to discern, foresee and restrain. One of the oldest stories in the world, the 1700 BCE Babylonian *Epic of Atrahasis* is an account, not only of discernment of overpopulation, but hatred of it. Plato, Aristotle and some Romans also described overpopulation's dangers. So, humans discerned and foresaw its dangers long before Malthus. But could they have reversed it?

Long before *Atrahasis,* some human groups did that very thing. *The Dawn of Everything* (Graeber and Wengrow, 2021) says that some Neolithic foragers, having become agriculturalists, thought better of it and resumed their former, numbers-limiting ways. If our species was ever capable, even once, of restraining itself, it could, in principle, have done it again with a larger, more complex group.

I'm grounding my hypothesis of an oscillation between the cultures of evasion and education on its suggestive correspondence with what in

[2] Or not. Paleontologist Marshall Sahlins (1972) suggested that our forager ancestors worked only 3-6 hours a day and the rest of the time perhaps sat around telling stories. Modernization might not have been essential for the leisure we think necessary for education.

psychoanalysis is called the individual's *crucial decision*. This is the infant's decision to evade or to manage tension. Bion (1962/1983, p. 29) said that every infant struggles to abandon hallucination as the strategy for need-gratification in favor of work. Every infant must choose one way or the other as its prevailing lifeway, and the decision is fateful.

Even after the crucial decision, however, the developing infant, child and adult must balance these two competing intentions. They must daily renegotiate their earlier decision on less momentous choices.

A similar deliberation on evasion and education, I suggest, proceeds within the human group. Some may judge these two psychological cultures, this dichotomy, dubious. But there are similar dichotomous tendencies that co-inhabit our individual or collective souls. I think of love and hate; progression and regression; impulsiveness and prudence; tension-discharge and tension-tolerance. So, the distinction is plausibly real. And if education teaches us to manage other dichotomies in life by finding realistic compromises, then humanist education was key to reconciling these two cultures—evasion and education—throughout history.

Education was meant to harmonize our values and goals with our actual achievements. This is humanistic congruence; it is hard to pursue, to attain and to sustain. The pursuit of private and public harmony—the progressive approximation of our ideals—is effortful and tension-filled.

So, we tilted toward incongruence. And the disharmony of unmatched ideals and efforts is everywhere visible today. We find it, for instance, in technology. Our efforts to master every new software tool excreted from the minds of Stanford graduates fail to match any meaningful goal of mental or spiritual growth. Similarly, the ideal of ecological responsibility makes a disgrace of economic growth. Surely such behavior belies indifference to goals and ideals, and a tension-evading refusal to connect current work with future reward.

Accordingly, the view of education I adopt in this book leaves less room for toolmaking than society has come to think is desirable, or reasonable. The tensions my education aims to relieve are not the tensions that tools eliminate. My education, by fostering congruence, is meant to relieve tensions arising from incongruence, the failure to fulfill one's mental potential and care for one's dignity. It's meant to manage, while mitigating, the tensions of deeper awareness.

The tensions that tools relieve are different. Tools relieve the tensions arising from vegetative needs for hunger, sleep and sex, or from anxious impulses to flee consciousness of oneself or one's fears of exclusion. Tool-eliminated tensions, moreover, can be relieved easily and instantaneously. Tools, in my educational vision, justify themselves only insofar as they liberate us from education-robbing exigencies of life.

So, the Classical university, at its core, opposed the deification of tools and the culture of tension-evasion. Yet we don't even talk about the deeper purpose of the university anymore; we don't even talk about its vocationalization. We talk about rising tuitions, student debt, falling application rates, unqualified students and cyber-schools, focusing the lens of public attention on issues of the day, economics, status or convenience. This is not to say that such discussions have *caused* our decline; it's to say that they *enable* it. People dwell on economic topics to avoid topics more tension-fraught. These topics might include inequality of ability, the kind of topic that mortifies the less able and (envy-) frightens the more able, topics whose examination destabilizes society.

Suppose the public mind began to think that replacing the hard traditional curriculum with an easy vocational curriculum had been irrational after all; that it was a self-defeating mistake. This concession would undermine the psychological status quo in a subversive, 7-step mental sequence: We'd admit to irrational and self-defeating policy; this would imply unconscious motivation; we'd acknowledge unconscious motivation; this would evoke shame, guilt, and anxiety; we'd acknowledge anxiety; this would demand self-examination; we'd do psychoanalysis and provoke new anxieties about where the mental turbulence would lead. In other words, group confession to irrational self-destructiveness would shatter its complacency and sense of exceptionalism.

So, the public's preoccupation with the university's socioeconomic issues diverts its attention from more disturbing problems: The self-destructive decay of higher education and atrophy of the public mind.

Society seemed to have created the university to protect, strengthen or restore our mental integrity by minimizing errors of short-sightedness, tunnel vision, ignorance, stupidity or, above all, sheer evasiveness. Higher education was meant to improve, and sometimes actually did improve, human contact with reality.

But, as I've pointed out, the university couldn't teach adequate methods of detecting unconscious self-deception. Even though knowledge and critical thinking—which the university could teach—can blow illusions apart, and expose their victories as fleeting. On those happy occasions when evidence and logic force error out into the open, the unconscious fantasy behind that error, like a snake in the grass, escapes detection; it slithers into its subterranean nest and spawns a new brood of errors.

The university was not enough to curb selective inattention and other non-conscious self-deceptions.

Inattention to Overpopulation and Crowding

The struggle against self-deception was to become the domain of psychoanalysis. And psychoanalysis was the consummation of *paideia. Paideia* urged care of the soul by progressively understanding, throughout life, both external and internal reality. It was a culture of mental growth.

Like Classical education, psychoanalysis was imperfect; but as I argued above, it was the only method powerful enough to so modify the mind as to make it more durably aware of its self-deceptions. That it could even occasionally succeed in this almost impossible task was, in my opinion, humanity's greatest achievement. But society cast off psychoanalysis even faster than it had Classical education. Then our species was destitute of both the self-discipline and the means to bring it back.

Accordingly, humanity was much freer, then, to evade unpleasant realities, and most catastrophically, the terrifying reality of overpopulation.

Human evil derives, as I have explained throughout the book, from innate biopsychological drives, working from deep within the unconscious mind. Population overgrowth, however, is one incarnation of that evil, deriving from what we call the death drive. Agricultural societies rapidly achieved overgrowth. This mobilized destructiveness and set spinning a vicious cycle: Uncontrolled growth fulfilled monocidal wishes; subsequent crowding, by its odiousness, heightened those wishes; and those heightened wishes fed uncontrolled crowding.

And how quickly we overcrowded! Just since 1970, we've lost half our living space.

Hatred of crowding might have compelled an attentive species, decades ago, to limit reproduction. But crowding, too, we selectively ignored. We would not understand the destructiveness of crowding.

Crowding itself seems to shrivel our minds. Studies in both the US and India show that crowding—irrespective of socioeconomic status—makes people less likely to persist on challenging puzzles, and to give up sooner. One of these studies (Sinha & Sinha, 1991) revealed that congestion and reduced personal space impairs complex task performance. Another (Evans and Stecker, 2004) showed that acute and chronic exposure to noise, crowding, traffic congestion, and pollution fosters helplessness and irresolution in adults and children facing challenge.

There's more: According to *IResearchnet.com.*, crowding reduces fertility, increases irritability and aggressiveness, and makes people withdraw from others even after crowding is alleviated, like a post-crowding stress disorder.[3] And crowding-stress increases over time.

So, crowding has deepened human self-destructiveness. This seems to have been a monstrous group plan, not to say conspiracy. Overpopulation is the culmination of a monocidal intrigue, first to evade envy, and then to exterminate envy by exterminating civilization. Selectively ignored overpopulation is the Final Solution to envy, the tension we learned to repress, but never to endure.

We recall the *primal scene*, that is, the vision of our mother rapturously copulating with our father, the two oblivious to the wretched infant looking on, consumed with envy. In the introduction I acknowledged the wholesome motives for coitus and even reproduction. But reproductive excess in a foresightful species is another matter. Unrestricted reproduction is an unconscious defense and rageful outburst against the primal scene.

Here's a more nuanced description: Humanity has enacted the primal fantasy by its population overgrowth. It's acted out both sides of that fantasy, the loving and destructive. We've mimicked the loving, copulating parents, absorbed in mutual sexual feeding, making swarms of new babies. And we've mimicked the rageful, attacking baby, by devastating Mother Earth. We've drained and poisoned her biosphere, extinguished her children-creatures and posterity's human babies.

We recognize this envious (and jealous) hatred more vividly in those unlucky people who discover their spouses in flagrante delicto. Its ferocity is

---

[3] This is the crucial concept of *density dependence*, the tendency of any overcrowded biological system to contract, often by reducing fertility. It's well-attested in humans today, expressed in dropping fertility rates around the globe. See, among many other investigators of this remarkable phenomenon, Rotella et al (2021).

so irrepressible, that France, until 1975, excused the murder of the cheater (s) as a crime of passion. And community sympathy for primal envy still sometimes mitigates judicial guilt.

So, we've raged, envied, and attacked. And we heard the vengeful footsteps of the Chimera. It's coming to inflict upon us, with equal and opposite force, the unspeakable mutilations we've wrought on our copulating parents. This Chimera is the *combined parent figure,* the rough beast, sleeping through the ages, awakened by crowding, slouching toward consciousness to be born.[4] Those who are intellectually voracious keenly felt the peril coming for them, because epistemophilia too is rooted in fantasies of plundering the maternal cavity.

So, the intelligencia sheltered their institutions in the moral citadel of social justice. There, some of them took up the realistic, noble, but distracting cause of climate change activism, the war against global warming.

Science has confirmed anthropogenic global warming. Its confirmation makes climate activism look sane, useless though that activism has been. But –here is a surprise— climate activism too serves selective inattention. Public cries over global warming and pleas for green energy and conservation have drowned out the murmurs about human over-reproduction—the real cause, after all, of anthropogenic global warming.[5]

"No," some may object, "the real cause is over-consumption. If we lived sparingly, global warming would stop." Further below, we'll document the problems with this popular, distracting claim.

The denial of overpopulation is deep and wide; it has demented both the dull and the bright. In June 2016 *The Atlantic* published "China's Twilight Years." The author, Howard W. French, writes that China's population is "aging and shrinking," even as its population was, at that time, growing at 18,000 per day. The *Guardian,* three years later, when China was growing at nearly the same rate, published an article by Lily Kuo and Xueying Wang, called, "Can China Recover from its Disastrous One Child Policy?" There we

---

[4] Please see Glossary.

[5] *Science Daily,* 4/20/09 (when global population was 6.84 billion, over one billion fewer than July, 2022): "Overpopulation is the world's top environmental issue." Charles Daly, a systems ecologist, put it in perspective: "If we had 100 million people on Earth—or better—10 million—no others [environmental issues] would be a problem." If Earth, that is, could be disburdened of 69/70 of its human population of seven billion (in 2009), there'd be no ecological crisis.

read that China is "Faced with a population that is *shrinking* and aging, policymakers …." (author's emphasis). This common mistake, at the highest level of journalism, arises from a preconscious wish, in the service of public tranquility and private comfort, to confuse population growth with population growth *rate* to deny overpopulation.[6]

Behind the Green Curtain of wind towers, solar panels and recycling, behind the public fantasy of a falling population, behind reassurances that average fertility has dropped to 2.25 children per woman (June, 2024), behind all the selective attention to this fantasy, over-reproduction is still out of control.[7] The world still grows at 200,000 every day, and the U. S. at 4,800 every day, most of our growth pouring through our porous borders.

The world's total numbers, because of *population momentum*, and despite falling fertility, will rise for another half-century. There's no birth dearth. This fact still eludes political sanction, popular dismay and governmental management. Instead, the world focuses on global warming—a weapon of mass distraction, to adapt political critic Dan Pletch's phrase. By selective inattention, humanity avoids confronting its unflattering reflection in the inner mirror of group consciousness: A clever but oblivious species, eating, drinking and crowding itself out of its planetary house and home. Society pushes that self-image from the center stage of public consciousness out to the wings. Only if the people had raised depopulation to the top of the public agenda; only if we had confessed that remedial action on overpopulation's derivative damage, like climate change, was futile; only *then* would the environment, quality of human life, and morale of humanity have improved. But society instead focused on climate change.

Climate Change Activism as Evasion

With the following remarks, I will explain how even climate change

---

[6] China's *National Bureau of Statistics* says that China's population was *still growing* in 2021, albeit with a record low increase. The media has been misusing sinking fertility to represent sinking population to alarm its readers, and encourage natalism. Bigger populations, perhaps incidentally, means a bigger readership, media's lifeblood.
However, today, the strain of crowding may finally be ending population growth in many countries. China's population has indeed started to decline, but only since 2023, 7 years after *The Atlantic* article.

[7] Replacement level is 2.1.

activists, by encouraging selective inattention, helped the world avoid the conclusion that depopulation was our only salvation. I also want to show that depopulation requires another difficult step: Stopping immigration. I want to show that climate change rhetoric, which doesn't prioritize curtailments of either births or immigration, is evading tensions.

Let's first consider a 2017 Canadian study by environmental scientists Seth Wynes and Kimberly Nicholas. *The Guardian,* under Damian Carrington's byline, summarized their work in "Want to fight climate change? Have fewer children" (7/12/17). Carrington writes, "By far the biggest impact of different actions [on global warming] is having one fewer child: 58 tonnes of CO_2 for each year of a parent's life." By comparison, eliminating a car saves only 2.4 tonnes per year.

Wynes and Nicholas had dropped a bombshell. But the world never heard the boom, felt the heat, or saw the light. The researchers had shown that, as far as climate change mitigation goes, we're thinking about it and doing it, all wrong. They showed that nothing we're doing to reduce atmospheric CO_2 is making much difference. All of our recycling, solar installations, wind turbines, electric cars, vegetarianism, etc. is inconsequential. There is only one difference-maker: Having fewer children.

The comparison, which the researchers themselves discretely understate, between having fewer children and every other strategy, is stark: The 2nd, 3rd and 4th most effective CO_2 mitigation strategies, altogether, add up to 4.8 tons/year. Not having a child saves over 12 times those other three combined.

This bears elaboration: When a couple has a child, they add over 58 tons CO_2/year to the atmosphere, for every year of the parents' lives. If the parents abandon their car for a bike, they'll save only 2 1/2 tons/year. Every other remedy, like changing online electricity with solar, saves even less. Let a climate change activist couple ditch five cars, decline five round-trip transatlantic airplane trips, install solar panels and windmills, stop eating meat, etc. and they won't come close to undoing ½ the damage their one child inflicts on the ecosphere. Looked at from another direction, if just 2.5% of the world's fertile couples had one fewer child, they would cancel out the CO_2 output of the global car industry and Internet together.

So, the Wynes/Nicholas study presented a formidable challenge to overpopulation denial. But it fell on resolutely deaf ears. The *Guardian* was an exception, but its report made no impression, even on climate change activists. Two years after the *Guardian* report, King's College researchers polled the English population (*The Conversation*, 9/15/19): They asked British citizens to rank nine actions (most of which were named in the *Guardian* report) in order of their effectiveness in mitigating greenhouse gases. The reader can guess the results: Respondents ranked recycling and hybrid cars 1st and 2nd, but having fewer children, 8th.

Though fertility has been falling since the late 1800's, it's fallen far too slowly to stave off catastrophic climate change. If fertility were reduced to zero today, it would take about 85 years, at current death rates, to depopulate to two billion, thought to be a survivable number (85 childless years would, however, leave zero humans young enough to reproduce). So, remediation is probably fifty years too late. If humanity had wanted to avoid, rather than sleepwalk into, extinction, every country, rich and poor alike, would have depopulated by 80% a half century ago, and to live well, a full century ago.[8] But our species couldn't contemplate, let alone pursue, that painful step. To relinquish reproduction was to abandon humanity's easiest strategy for envy-abatement, revenge, omnipotence and compensatory sense of goodness. Society felt this to be too high a psychological price, even for its own survival.

So is it unreasonable to say that any social energy spent upon remedies other than depopulation is based upon selective inattention?

I've deliberated upon the Wynes/Nicholas study and its reception to contextualize climate change activism (CCA), and to illustrate the subtlety of tension-evasion. I want to convince you that CCA, which seems to be a realistic reaction to global warming, is another social defense against tensions. I also want to convince you that the plethora of humans, much more than their fossil fuel usage, much more than their overconsumption in general, is by far the most powerful cause of global warming. Only then can we understand how CCA facilitates and conceals selective inattention.

This will help establish the root cause of global warming: Colonization of the New World, it is estimated, killed 55 million Native Americans after 1492 (Koch et al., 2019). These people had not burned oil, coal, or natural gas; they didn't drive cars, or take transcontinental plane trips. True, they burned wood and other vegetation, but not on an industrial scale. Yet their decimation, by reducing human land use and allowing reforestation (both reduce atmospheric CO_2) is thought to have globally lowered surface air temperatures by 0.15° C

---

[8] Poor countries must also depopulate: not only do their populations too need food, water and shelter. Their expansions into the habitats, and exposure to the diseases, of wild animals, will perpetually launch pandemics.

in the two centuries before the Industrial Revolution. Their appalling human losses possibly contributed to the coldest part of the Little Ice Age. Their everyday activities, pure Green by our standards—not the fossil-fueled, modern overconsumption CCA blames—had been warming the world.

Much more recently the ecologist William Rees (2023) dealt a fatal blow to Overconsumption Theory. He showed that, during the period 1961-2016, population growth accounted for 80% of the growth in humanity's ecological footprint, but excessive consumption, only 20%. It looks like those who overate overconsumption, and underate overpopulation, are deceiving themselves and their society.

CCA, in its current form, focuses our attention on how we spend our lives, not the lives themselves. It valorizes the very climate mitigation strategies that Wynes and Nicholas showed to be trivial. Drawing public attention to those hopeless strategies not only subtracts attention from the real problem, it confuses the trivial with the crucial, delaying still longer the convergence of public attention on the need to depopulate. CCA is well-intentioned, but directs public time and attention onto merely inconvenient remedies. It robs time and attention from the effective, but more disturbing remedy, depopulation. CCA doesn't consciously intend to discourage depopulation, but does so all the same.

To be sure, the CCA's backgrounding of human over-reproduction is a minor distortion of reality compared to that of climate change denial (CCD). CCD is more pathological. So, we can rate CCA a healthier compromise between tension-evasion and tension-tolerance. On the other hand, since CCA is more realistic than CCD, it might, paradoxically, divert more public attention from depopulation than does CCD, which is repulsively irrational. CCA can say, with justifiable pride, "I, unlike CCD's, can tell people to deprive themselves of certain discretionary comforts." But they should confess, "I can't tell my neighbors—black, white, or brown—to not have babies. I can't tell them, or my legislative representatives, or anyone who knows me, to outlaw immigration."

Immigration Activism as Evasion

Crowding, addiction to inclusion, and immigration justice have all increased global momentum toward the free migration of peoples. This may seem too strong, but because the world did not outlaw immigration a half-century ago, we can no longer depopulate Earth in time to save humanity.

I base this opinion on four points: First, emigration re-expands the sending country's living space, and relieves density stress. It fortifies national denial of hatred of crowding. Only insufferable crowding, it seems, could have awakened the claustrophobia, the terrible, but necessary, intimation of suffocation and starvation the species has deferred for ten thousand years. Unrestrained immigration has fatally postponed that day of reckoning.

Second, the exodus of discontented citizens emboldens the sending country's ruling power to persevere in its political, social and ecological injustice and corruption. Then, inadvertently, the emigrants bring corruption to their host country. Costermonger employers use cheap and plentiful immigrants to replace dissatisfied native workers, skirt labor laws, and bust unions. With impunity, these employers overwork and underpay illegal immigrant workers, and overuse them in hazardous industries like forestry, fishing and farming (Frum, 2019). When we overlook widespread institutional corruption, we impair collective reality-testing, and impaired reality-testing facilitates self-destructive behavior.

Third, immigration worsens crowding in the host nation. As I pointed out, the United States' growth rate, after a pandemic-related slowdown, has risen back to 4800 people a day. Immigrants and chain migration currently account *for over half* of this growth. In 2017, each new immigrant was sponsoring an average of 3.45 additional immigrants. The Census Bureau predicts that immigrants, asylees, chain migrants, and refugees will fuel two-thirds of the nation's future overgrowth.

Crowding, as documented above, damages the mind. It also erodes the country's material and political infrastructures. The United States no longer has enough roads, classrooms, emergency rooms or drinking water to serve its growing populace. For almost 60 years, the country neglected its highways, bridges, transmission lines, municipal water pipes and dams. Federal infrastructure spending totaled 11.2% of non-defense spending in 1960. By 2019, it was barely 3%. Predominantly, population growth and heavy spending on education and means-tested health and social programs caused this reduction. And a significant portion of these expenditures went to immigrants and their families.

But Biden's 2021 Bipartisan Infrastructure Bill seemingly reversed that trend, pouring $1.2 trillion into infrastructure projects over the subsequent five years 2022-2026. This will temporarily improve the nation's infrastructure. In 2024, however, even as we rebuild highways, bridges, and electrical grids, the pounding of our soaring numbers is grinding them back down faster than ever.

And, of course, we can't afford it: The Biden bill swells the national debt, adding over $39.5 billion to our already $1+ trillion annual interest payments on that debt. The program pushed our debt-to-GDP ratio, a measure of a country's default risk, to over 100%, 23 points higher than the "acceptable" 77%.[9] Creditors tolerate this risk by pretending their debtor country will eventually take corrective measures. The Penn Wharton Budget Model (10/3/23) predicted that make-believe will only restrain creditors for 20 more years, tops. But whenever they abjure self-deception, our economy will fall.

Trump's "Big Beautiful Bill" will raise the ratio to 125%, 48 points higher than acceptable. For those still dreaming of economic growth, this elevation will reduce investment and capital, leading to less productive workers being paid less and less.

An army of economists disagree. They beat the drum of infinite growth and immigration. This is music to the ears of the governments and corporate-affiliated research universities which employ most of them. But all their thunder cannot drown out the law of supply and demand. For example, this country cannot *supply*, for the 4800 daily new *demanders*, enough affordable housing. So, housing costs and the homeless increase together. Still, communities are frantically building multifamily housing units to shelter the exploding homeless numbers. The building blitz is, as always, futile and destructive. It belches imbedded carbon,[10] uses up farmland,[11] and sucks up scarce water.[12] The Economists' Immigration Lullaby doesn't sing these troubling verses.

Here is a more realistic economics: The Center for the Advancement of Steady State Economics (CASSE) counterweighs the airy fantasies of typical

---

[9] Several other countries have larger ratios. Japan's, for example, is over 200%. But the US economy is 2-1/2 times larger than Japan's, has much further to fall, and its collapse will pull down more of the global economy with it.

[10] Embedded carbon is the carbon footprint of a building before it is built, the building's "upfront carbon," the CO_2 outgassed during the construction process. A ten-unit apartment building embeds ~ 63 tons $C0_2$.

[11] The U. S. loses 175 acres/hr.

[12] At current consumption levels, the world may run out of water by 2040, says Bank of America Global Research (2023).

economists.[13] CASSE economists say open borders don't work; they make the host nation's rich richer, poor poorer, and its middle class immobile; and they destabilize the social order, while depleting state and urban economies. CASSE says we should help aspiring immigrants by helping their troubled homelands.

Ecology-free studies of the Federal economy are, unsurprisingly, more positive. These show national economic growth from immigration. But they discretely omit population-driven, future environmental stressors, like water shortages, which will sharply increase per capita costs. These omissions save economists the awkwardness of acknowledging how these stressors will kill the growth they adore, and irreversibly unravel the economy.

By indulging the outrage of immigration activists, the angry drumbeat of unconditional inclusion, and the pleonexia of corporate America, we enrage a different group: Those whom identity politics and bleeding borders have despoiled of their fragile personal and cultural identities. Theirs is the rage that not once, but twice elected Donald Trump. Self-inflicted national identity diffusion has detached millions of citizens from their government, its laws, and its experts. This may partly explain the dangerous anti-vaxxer movement and the hellish explosion of mass shootings in America.[14]

Fourth and finally, the migration of people from poorer to richer countries increases global CO_2 emissions, a fact that should exasperate climate change activists. Immigration raises global emissions by transforming low-consuming immigrants from poor countries into high-consuming residents of prosperous countries. Each immigrant to America, for example, increases global CO_2 output by an average of 4-10 cubic tons/year, depending on country of origin. On the whole, immigrants accelerate climate disaster and do nothing for their native country's problems.

It's hard for anyone steeped in our culture of limitless inclusion to confront immigration with cool objectivity. But if we don't, we'll never understand that immigrant activism is a self-defeating mistake. Envy-fear has

---

[13] Center for the Advancement of Steady State Economics, a group dedicated to the science of a non-growth global economy. It emerged from the Ecologic Economics of the late Herman Daly.

[14] The National Institute of Justice (Feb., 2022) reported that in the 59 years from 1960 to 2019, 20% of all mass shootings occurred in the 5 years 2014-2019. This horrible burst occurred *before* the yet more horrible Covid burst. Violent crime dropped rapidly from late 2023-24, but mass shootings in 2025 are on track to return to the levels of several years ago (Rockefeller Institute, 6/6/25).

mobilized the selective inattention necessary to make this mistake, and selective inattention, in turn, has damaged group reality-testing.

Some might dismiss my immigrant case as self-serving casuistry. But then I, the accused, might ask: How unselfish is it to comfort millions of unfortunate contemporaries, when that comfort ensures the greater misery of posterity, our most neglected underclass? In 2050, will the tens of millions fleeing their doomed coastal homes; the tens of millions of inland residents whom those refugees will already have overwhelmed; and the rest of the half-billion Americans whose social fabric has been torn apart and whose quality of life is plunging .... will they praise our charity? Will they thank us from their knees?

By selective inattention, humanity postponed until some unknown tomorrow the epiphany that, a century earlier, when we numbered only two billion, we could have saved ourselves.[15] We could have pruned our population with humane economic and social incentives for reproductive and immigration control. But we'd despoiled ourselves of psychoanalytic Humanism, the school of inner and outer reality. And we'd damned ourselves to eternal self-deception.

So, when darkness finally enfolds us, our lamentations, though we are so small, will fill the universe.

[15] World Counts predicts Earth systems will fail by 2050. But failure could come earlier. MIT scientists predicted, in 1972, that society would disintegrate by 2040. In 2014, Australian sustainability researcher Graham Turner reassessed MIT's prophesy, and found no reason to revise it. Then, just three years ago, Dutch econometrician and sustainability researcher Gaya Herrington (Helmore, 2021) called the prediction "on schedule."

Conclusion

[the boy] ...blew mimic hootings to the silent owls
That they might answer him...
And when it chanced
That pauses of deep silence mocked his skill,
Then sometimes in that silence, while he hung
Listening, a gentle shock of mild surprise
Has carried far into his heart the voice
Of mountain torrents ...[1]

When Abby applied to college, now so long ago, I never dreamt that higher education had forgotten the value of Greek and Latin learning. As far as I knew, Abby had the mother of all angles. She would tell Northwestern that she could sing the very songs its ancient founders had sung. She would touch the academy's heart and spring its ivied gates. She'd blow admissions away.

How happily we anticipated their answer in late winter 2002!

In the second and third weeks of that March, just ahead of the traditional April 1st deadline, three schools responded: Miami, Trinity, and Rochester, in order of rising selectivity, accepted her and, doubtless loving her Greek, offered her merit scholarships or honors programs. And then another week passed.

On March 30, Tufts rejected her.

Shocked, I grasped at straws: "Maybe Tufts competes with its Boston superiors, Harvard and MIT, for cultural purity. Northwestern, though, has midwestern spine; they'll want a scholar. They'll see what a prize they've got." By embarrassing mental strategies like these, I tried to keep hope alive, and we waited.

καὶ τότε δὴ χρύσεια πατὴρ ἐτίταινε τάλαντα...
and then Father poised his golden Scales...

---

[1] Wordsworth, William, "Prelude: Book Fifth, 'Books,'" lines 373-388. *Selected Poetry of William Wordsworth*, Ed. Mark van Doren. New York, Modern Library, 2001.

We didn't know it yet, but in that very hour, several thousand homes across the country—two or three, probably, even in New Hampshire—were celebrating. Families were chattering with delight, rhapsodizing on the curtained fog that drifts in off Lake Michigan, bedewing the campus on fine autumn mornings. There, at dinner, that happy, happy evening, they clinked their glasses, and sang the Wildcat fight song.

But our home was silent, stunned by the thin envelope from Evanston. Vanished was the vision of celebration and the jubilant call to my aging father.

I told my crying daughter she'd be fine; her options were excellent. I also told her, in deep understatement, that I was sorry I'd gotten it so wrong.

And, as the reader might have foreseen, I, for all my brave talk about tension-tolerance, did not gracefully accept this blow.

The next day I called Northwestern Admissions and asked for the Director. She was unavailable, her hands being full with the business of accepting Greekless candidates. So, Admissions Officer Mr. Smith got on the line. I told him who I was and asked: "What happened?"

He (cheerfully): "Oh, Abby was right in the mix."

"Why wasn't she at the top of the mix, making you all sing hosannas?"

(Laughing) "Well, her record at U-17 was very good, but it was .... subdued."

So, I said to Mr. Smith: "Yea, I'm sure you get a lot of shooting stars. But I still don't understand. You don't have room for a quiet scholar? Didn't you see the Greek?"

(There's a pause and I hear the shuffling of paper. The sunny voice has gone.) "Um, yes, we saw that." (Long pause)

"What was your reaction?"

(Pause) "We thought it was… well… unusual." (Pause)

"That's all you thought?"

Five awkward seconds passed, then, "Well… of course… remember, we consider every application as a whole."

I thanked him for his time.

Probing for life, I sent a letter to the Director. I wrote: "Tolstoy said

> I knew nothing before I knew Greek... without knowledge of Greek there is no education.

So, how does Northwestern, a place for education, answer?"

While we waited for that answer, I called the Chairman of the Northwestern Classics Department and told him the story. He offered to petition the Dean (I kick myself for not telling Abby to call him before she applied).

Meanwhile, I sent letters to the school's President and Chairs of pertinent departments, turning over every rock, searching for someone breathing the spirit of the university, making an ass of myself.

But my, and the kind professor's pleas, fell on deaf ears, if ears there ever were. Several days later, we received the Director's cordial reply, making it clear that she had ignored, thought irrelevant or, more likely, found unintelligible, the Tolstoy doctrine.

Several weeks later, calmer but still baffled, I interviewed all the schools to which Abby had applied, and several others besides. On came the aftershocks: Her Greek hadn't excited the admissions committees of one single school, even those that had accepted her. Nor, I learned, would it have interested the most elite schools, including Harvard.[2] This discovery laid bare my utter misjudgment, the childish idealism of my fantasy. And that's when I asked myself, "How was Greek, and the entire idea of Classical education, devalued and driven from the schools, so that now, knowledge of Greek, instead of being the basis of education, is not even considered a charming addition to a university community?"

At the end of the Introduction, I described an imaginary Republic of Mental Growth, a humanist psychoanalytic culture. Has my subsequent inquiry shown such a culture could have saved society? I'll answer with Aristotle's words:[3] "I have done. You have heard me. The facts are before you. I ask for your judgment."

We wistfully recall, as we end this meditation, the diapauses in history's march to dissolution, the cultures that cared for the communal mind. These include the 6th and 5th century BCE Greeks; the Indian (Buddhist) and Chinese (Confucian) societies of the same, so–called Axial Age; the short-lived Carolingian empire; the sodalities of Irish and Muslim scholars; and

---

[2] I spoke to the admissions Dean at Harvard, and admissions officers at six other elite schools. Only the University of Chicago was intrigued by Abby's Homer.
St. John's College in Annapolis, (and its branch in New Mexico) incidentally, is unique in requiring its students to learn a little Greek and Latin. 'Ως κύδος μικρὸς σφίσιν. ("therefore, a little honor on them").

[3] This is his peroration in *Rhetoric.*

Renaissance society. Although they were all encumbered by scientific ignorance and what we might call psychosocial immaturity, those societies nonetheless, on the strength of their ideals, culturally overachieved. Being inured to a wide range of frustrations, they could briefly sustain the rigors of mental cultivation, rational inquiry, or both. But humanity gradually weakened, and its hatred of limits, tensions, exclusion and reality, prevailed.

So, the network of mutual understanding that once united all educated people—the scholars of the Enlightenment, Renaissance, Middle and Dark Ages, of the Byzantine and ancient worlds—those bonds of reverence for human genius which the university once nurtured, are now disintegrated. The timeless bonds that enriched our lives, that consoled our mortality and final solitude, have vanished. The links to the ageless beauty that the Greeks, the pioneers of the human spirit, bequeathed to us, that gift which once redeemed the inescapable pain of human limits, have been severed. And the lapsed guardians of that gift of song have so far devalued and forgotten it that its rare singers cannot reawaken their institutional memory.

Reflections

Decades ago, on early summer evenings, my wife and I could hear the loveliest sound in the woods: The veeries, middle-size thrushes that warbled their falling scales of sixteenth-notes from the edges of the forest surrounding our house. We listened as the sun sank behind the Presidential Range.

Then they went silent. The crowded, fast-warming world drove them from our forest. Now, on the summer evening I write this, only gibbering bats flit here and there around our porch, engulfing the moths and mosquitoes that flutter in the stifling air.

The doomed insects remind me of the little voles which, on winter nights, would scoot along the forest floor beneath thirty inches of snow, invisible, but marked by the owl, perched in a towering ash. From seventy feet above, the owl targets the rustling below, swoops down in silence, thrusts its legs into the bursting snow and crushes the vole in its talons.

One cold October night in 1989, picking my way by moonlight up the steep forest path winding along our creek, I saw above me the silhouette of a wide-winged barred owl gliding through the gloom from one treetop to another. The next day I described the thrill to my five-year old daughter, and offered to take her some evening to summon Big Bird. She was afraid of the owl and the night and the woods. But a few days later, trusting, as I like to think, in her father's invincible strength, she asked to go call the owl.

So, we made plans to go "owling" beneath the Snow Moon. That's February's full moon, when Northerners used to visit the woods and hoot to the owls, that they might answer them.

In those days, still within living memory, two feet of snow reliably blanketed the frozen February forest floor. Those winters evoked stories of the old, but now melting arctic world, the Yukon. Its scenes quickened the imagination of my father as he versified to his small children sitting on the floor beside the crackling fire. He spellbound us with Robert Service's secret tales of the frozen trails winding through the land of the midnight sun. Thirty Februarys ago in New Hampshire too there were once clear, -20⁰ nights, moonbeams shimmering on snow, scattering into an unearthly luminous gray, brightening the darkness everywhere the grateful nighttime hiker looked.

ὡς δ᾽ ὅτ᾽ ἐν οὐρανῷ ἄστρα φαεινὴν ἀμφὶ σελήνην
φαίνετ᾽ ἀριπρεπέα, ὅτε τ᾽ ἔπλετο νήνεμος αἰθήρ:
ἔκ τ᾽ ἔφανεν πᾶσαι σκοπιαὶ καὶ πρώονες ἄκροι
καὶ νάπαι: οὐρανόθεν δ᾽ ἄρ᾽ ὑπερράγη ἄσπετος αἰθήρ,
πάντα δὲ εἴδεται ἄστρα, γέγηθε δέ τε φρένα ποιμήν.

As when in heaven the stars about the bright moon
Sparkle clear, when the aether is windless;
And into view all the peaks and beetling rocks
And valleys show forth; and unto utmost heaven breaks
open the infinite air
And all the stars appear, and the shepherd rejoices in his
heart.
(*Iliad*, VIII, 555-559, my translation)

Before the man-made climate arrived in the early 1990's, back when Northerners could still enjoy those bracing winters, Abby and I got one last Snow Moon. We drew a map of our expedition and practiced the raptor's hoot. We fortified ourselves with hot chocolate and then, wrapped in layers of socks, sweaters, and coats beyond counting, strode into the breathtaking -16⁰ night and plowed through deep powder into the glowing woods. We stood silent near the frozen creek, reluctant to shatter the crystalline stillness with our shouts. Then we hooted to the owl hidden somewhere in the leafless canopies above, and waited, unanswered, except by the muffled voice, beneath the ice, of the mountain torrent.

So, Abby went on to study Greek at the University of Rochester—she together with exactly seven others of that school's nearly four thousand undergraduate students. There would have been only four, had she gone elsewhere. One of her friends, Christie, began as an English major but, intrigued by Abby's scholarly fervor, switched to Greek and never looked back. A younger sorority sister also admired Abby's enthusiasm and joined the ancient masters. A third recruit was Mary, a biology and psychology major headed for a profitable career in medical research. Being a curious student, she decided in her junior year, with Abby's encouragement, to sample Ancient Greek and Latin. Two months later she canned biomedical science and applied to graduate school in Classics. "Just think," said Christie, "of all the time Mary wasted on chemistry."

There was almost a fourth. One day, as graduation approached, her friend Rachel, a senior English major, approached Abby and her classmate Audrey in the library when they were translating their Greek lesson. On being told what was happening, Rachel asked if they liked being Classics majors. They gave a heartfelt and reasoned answer. Rachel hesitated, then said, softly, "Maybe I should have been a Classics major."

Abby graduated with Honors in Classics and linguistics, concentrating in ancient Greek literature, and she single-handedly doubled the number of Classics majors in a university known for science and technology.

She's still waiting for the school to thank her.

Glossary

These definitions are adapted from, among other sources, English and English, 1958 (EE); Moore and Fine, eds., 1968 (MF); Eidelberg, ed., 1968 (ED); Hinshelwood, 1989 (HW); Laplanche and Pontalis, 1973 (LP); Spillius et al., 2011 (SP) and author (JJP). Definitions of terms from the physical sciences are drawn from standard sources. The Oxford English Dictionary (OED) and American Heritage Dictionary (AHD) supplied definitions for everyday usage. Italicized terms (example: *Internal reality*) are cross-referenced in Glossary.

Acting-out: The tendency of some persons to reproduce forgotten memories, attitudes, and conflicts by actions, rather than words, while lacking conscious awareness or recognition of the fact.

Adaptation: Involves the capacity to cope reasonably and advantageously with *external* and *internal reality*. Adaptation can also be seen as any change in behavior or internal dynamics in response to a reward or survival function.

Aesthesis: Rudimentary sensation.

Aggression: A drive oriented toward attack or hostile action. Aggression, however, is often fused with love toward oneself or another, and in these circumstances facilitates healthy self-protection, autonomy, generosity or curiosity.

Analysand: The patient in psychoanalysis.

Apaideusia: απαιδευσια>ἀπαιδευσία.

Argumentation: The study of reason-giving to justify acts or beliefs and influence the thoughts or actions of others.

Attention: The process of bringing some mental product (a percept of the external world, a memory, idea, fantasy, feeling etc.) up to the level of awareness by the observing function of the *ego*.

Basic Assumption groups: Collectives of humans that evade *psychotic anxieties* and panic by adopting one or more of these three *basic assumptions*: 1) There exists a leader (or deity) upon whom members can depend to save them ["dependent group"] 2) There exists some strategy of fighting or fleeing by which group members will be saved ["fight-flight group"] 3) There exists a pair of members who will give birth to a messiah who will save the rest ["pairing group"].

Basic assumption groups, in distinction to *work groups*, are not in contact with reality. Work groups use effort, contact with reality, and mental growth to solve group problems. If work groups do not eventually emerge from within basic assumption groups to correct or mitigate the wider group's errors, catastrophe results. The university, for example, was meant to be a work group within society, society being a blended basic assumption group.

Further exposition on basic assumption and work groups: *Group mentality* consists of the unanimous opinion, willpower, or desire of the group at any given moment. Group mentality may conflict with certain private desires; the interplay between private desires and group mentality is called *group culture*, the organization of the group. One may observe group culture in the behavior of its members, the roles they perform, the actions of the leaders and the behavior of the group as a whole. At any given moment, group culture emerges from the conflict between the unconscious collective willpower on one hand, and individuals' wishes and needs on the other.

If *group mentality* is the common, unanimous and anonymous opinion of the group at any given moment, serving as the container of all the members' psychological contributions, then the *basic assumption* describes the organizing principle of these contributions. We can also think of the basic assumption as an underlying emotional impulse that expresses a shared group fantasy of an omnipotent or magical way to preserve the group, achieve its goals and satisfy its desires.

The first basic assumption, *Dependence*, is a group conviction that someone on whom its members absolutely depend can satisfy their needs and desires; that there is a being, a protective deity whose goodness, potency and wisdom are unquestioned, whose function is to provide security for the group as an "immature organism."

The second basic assumption, *Fight-flight*, is a group conviction that there exists an enemy, a bad external object, and the only options for salvation are to destroy (fight) or avoid this enemy (flight).

The third basic assumption, *Pairing*, is the collective belief that, whatever the group's present problems or needs, something unborn will solve it. The group invests its hope in a couple, or something symbolizing a couple, whose unborn child—an idea or person—will be the Messiah. What matters to the pairing basic assumption group are future hopes, not present problems, usually the problems of hatred, destructiveness, or despair. To sustain belief in the Messiah, the group's hope must remain unfulfilled.

To summarize, *basic assumptions* are *omnipotent* group fantasies about the way group problems will be solved. The basic assumptions are group reactions to *psychotic anxieties* reactivated by the individual's dilemma in the group and the regression this stimulates in him. These salvational strategies, meant to protect the members from dangers implicit in the psychotic anxieties, are magical; they avoid the frustration entailed in learning from experience, which requires effort, pain, and contact with reality.

Another positive level of functioning exists within every group: The *work group* (WG). The WG requires cooperation and effort from its members. It results from maturity and training. It maintains a mental state in contact with reality, tolerant of frustrations and in control of emotions. Work groups use rational and scientific methods. Their leaders are those most efficient in this approach. The work task, often painful, promotes growth and maturity in both group and members. It tolerates new ideas, and does not, after a period of apparent acceptance, evacuate them. In WG, the individual, while committed to cooperation, nonetheless remembers his distinctiveness, even in the midst of a regressive pull to forget it. He still feels the loneliness, isolation and pain associated with growth and evolution.

Occasionally, the regressive appeal of a basic assumption supports the activity of the work group. For example, higher education offers the "pairing assumption" (the teacher and student will pair up to give birth to a better, brighter, more knowledgeable, more powerful and adaptable being) in the service of promoting contact with reality, growth and evolution. Such an institution, which panders to a basic assumption to support the WG, is called a *specialized work group*. (Wilfred Bion)

Benign circle: One of two kinds of drive cathexes (mental investments) of intrapsychic *objects* and forces (or their prototypes). The other kind is the *vicious circle*. The benign circle begins in love and gratitude toward satisfying objects, increasing the goodness of both object and subject, alleviating *envy*, facilitating yet more love and gratitude, further enhancing subject and object's goodness, reducing fear of vengeance. The benign circle supports mental health.

Binding: A term used by Freud in both a general way and on distinct levels (both biological and psychical) to denote an operation tending to restrict the free flow of excitations, to link ideas to one another and to constitute and maintain relatively stable forms or structures.

Castration anxiety: Fear of genital loss or injury, often experienced as feelings of defectiveness or inferiority.

Cathexis: The investment of the *psychic energy* of a *drive* in a mental representation (image, symbol, fantasy, idea or concept). This investment may be conscious or unconscious.

Classical Humanism: See *Humanism.*

Character (or personality) disorder: A pathological character disturbance. Character disorders exhibit a habitual inflexibility of behavior patterns without marked subjective discomfort. It is said: Neurotics make *themselves* suffer; character disorders make others suffer.

Combined parental figure: An early, terrifying phantasy of the parents, or their sexual organs, locked together in permanent intercourse. The phantasy is often represented in childhood nightmares, or even waking illusions, as a malicious, inhuman monster.

The fearsomeness of the combined parental figure derives from the infant's wish to penetrate his mother's body, not only in response to inchoate sexual impulses, but also from anger and frustration, and in this latter case to injure her organs and other internal objects, or to plunder them for himself. This penetration, raiding and robbing is the nuclear core of a terrifying phantasy of the mother's body containing the *father's* retaliatory penis. Cerberus, and the proverbial dragon guarding the treasure-filled cave, are symbolic examples of the father as sentinel, guard and retaliator. The combined parental figure, having been conceived in the infant's sadism, envy of parental intercourse, and painful feeling of exclusion and desolation, thus becomes an extremely cruel, malicious and dreaded persecutor, unified into a single monster (HW).

Complex adaptive system (complexity): A collection of adaptive (see *adaptation*), diverse, connected entities with interdependent actions. It is also defined as a relatively autonomous and stable cyclic network that degrades energy (Schneider and Sagan, 2005). Such a system is described as *complex*, and in this book, is called a *complexity.*

Complicated: Describes a system of connected, diverse, interdependent parts that are not adaptive. Not to be confused with *complex.*

Compromise formation: One of the most basic functions of the mind, a necessary operation being necessary for social and psychical survival.

Compromise formation (CF) is the tendency of the mind to balance the forces causing psychological phenomena. It tries to afford to *drive derivatives* the most satisfaction possible without generating intolerable anxiety or depressive affect (Charles Brenner).

CF's consist of: 1) a partial, substitute gratification of *drive derivatives* and the *unconscious* fantasy wishes associated with them; 2) the opposition to, or *defense* against such gratification by *repressing* and *adaptive* psychic agencies. In other words, CF is any product of the *intrapsychic conflict* between an unconscious wish ("repressed idea") and the demands of the defense ("repressing idea"). The CF aims, on one hand, for maximum satisfaction and, on the other, minimum unpleasure (the anxiety, sadness or regret that satisfaction or anticipated satisfaction might occasion), taking into account all external and internal constraints. This mechanism influences all human action, speech, and thought.

The drive tries to discharge tensions even as the defense tries to inhibit that discharge, because the consequences of discharge might cause tensions greater than those that the drive is trying to soothe. The mind's mediation between drive and defense results in a highly disguised, incomplete, and therefore unrecognizable form of drive expression.

All *symptom formation,* and most CF, incurs some degree of suffering. Suffering satisfies the unconscious demand for self-punishment made necessary by the gratification of drive derivatives achieved in the symptom or CF.

Pathological CF's—for example, *neurotic* symptoms and neurotic character traits—are those that too severely restrict gratification of drive derivatives, unduly impair functional capacity (to love, work, assert oneself, etc.), allow too much unpleasure (anxiety, depressive affect, or both) to develop, create too much conflict with people or engender too great a tendency to injure or destroy oneself or others.

Conception: The mating of an innate expectation, known as a *preconception*, with the corresponding real event. Babies' innate expectations, or "knowledge" of sucking become conceptions when their mouths first find the nipple. Conceptions are critical steps in the infant's construction of thoughts and theories.

Condensation: A function of the dream-work, carried out unconsciously. Condensation is the compression of the extensive network of dream thoughts into the meager, brief, symbolic narrative of the dream-content, or manifest dream. By distorting the underlying meaning of the dream, condensation helps the mind censor unwanted thoughts and feelings.

Condensation shortens the latent dream story, the written explication of which might, for example, fill ten pages, into a short dream report of perhaps only one-half page.

Conflict, intrapsychic: Conflict between opposing forces within the mind, as distinct from conflict between the individual and the outside world.

Confusion: The unconscious but deliberate perversion of values in order to avoid envious feelings stimulated by admirable qualities, attainments, or abilities.

Consciousness: A state of awareness of *perceptions* coming from the outside world and from within the body and mind; a subjective phenomenon whose data can be communicated to others only by means of language and behavior (MF).

Context starvation: The reduction or distortion of vocal, visual, tactile, olfactory and gustatory cues, all components of the rich phenomenal context of face-to-face human interactions. Deception and self-deception can deprive all parties of context, even those in face-to-face interactions. Modern life, moreover, has imposed context starvation on a global scale by substituting technology-mediated communication for face-to-face and even voice-to-voice interchanges (JJP).

Contingent envy: See *Envy, deep* (*or primal*)

Counterphobia: A compulsion to seek, and act out, a feared situation, to dispel the perception of anxiety. Examples are Russian roulette, cliff-diving and other extreme sports. In counterphobia, the subject finds pleasure in successfully negotiating the danger situation. The ego is trying to master anxiety by repeating, and surviving, the feared activity.

Counterphobia exemplifies the basic ego process of transforming what has been passively endured (extreme anxiety) into active mastery.

Crowding: The subjective sensation of being crammed in among others or too near others. It is also the perception, sometimes implicit, of scarcity, whether of water, food, natural space, or any other necessary or desirable physical or psychological means for satisfaction. It is virtually synonymous with *population density stress*, and correlates strongly with, but is not identical to population density. Crowding can be progressive and cumulative. It hurts task performance, personality development, interpersonal relationships, and physical and mental health in general.

Crucial decision: A hypothetical life-directing choice made by every infant: To evade, or not to evade frustration. The first option predisposes the infant to a lifetime denial of reality, sometimes to the point of psychosis. The second predisposes the infant to recognize and manage reality.

Culture: The collective conditioning of the mind, giving rise to a system of values that influence group behavior, morale, and mental health. An *educational* culture is a social environment supportive of personal development, such development driven by the pursuit, and progressive acquisition, of knowledge of *external* and *internal reality* (JJP).

Decompensation: The loss of an existing compensation (or *adaptation*) through the breakdown of certain ego *defenses*, and characterized by the appearance of anxiety, depression, thought disorder, or other symptom or disability not previously present (ED).

Deep education: The laborious achievement of psychophysiological links—that is, links both mental and physical—within the student's mind, between present and past cultural realities, realities both internal and external. This is done by learning the literature and language of past cultures, trying to approximate, as closely as scholarship allows and to the degree that the student's talent permits, the *embodied simulations* of ancient writers and readers, the actual sounds and rhythms, the psycholinguistic performance and experience, of that literature and language (JJP).

Defense mechanism: Any unconscious strategy by which the ego protects itself against danger. Danger can be defined as any change liable to threaten the integrity or stability of the bio-psychological individual or group. Both internal excitations and external situations unpleasureable to the *ego* (that is, phenomena adverse to individual or group equilibrium) can initiate these changes (LP). Dangers can include, among others: Unpleasantness, anxiety, shame, guilt, and the loss of self-esteem any of these feelings might cause. The primary dangers are the two *psychotic anxieties*.

1) Reaction formation (supports *repression*): A defense consisting of the replacement in conscious awareness of a painful idea or feeling by its opposite. Acts of apparent kindness and generosity, meant to replace in consciousness what is actually hatred or hostility (because awareness of these emotions would stimulate guilt) are often signs of reaction formation.

2) Projection: Attributing a painful internal impulse or idea to the external world.

3) Projective identification: Refers to the patient's forcing aspects of his internal world (part- and whole objects, anxieties, self, affects, defenses) into the analyst's mentation (Solomon, 1995).

4) Introjection: The process of internalizing a part-object, the mother's good, nourishing, idealized breast, the basis of ego strength. The infant absorbs her tolerance, acceptance, and capacity to reduce stress. A similar adult process is the taking in of a culture's ideals to support the individual's self-regard (Solomon, 1995).

5) Splitting: One of the earliest defenses, it exists to separate good from bad experiences, to safeguard the good primary internal *objects* (the parental figure or part-object breast, nipple or penis) from the danger of the infant's rage and hatred. Splitting also refers to the partitioning of both the ego and internal and external object (Solomon, 1995).

6) Isolation: Splitting ideas off from the feelings originally associated with them. Examples: The ideas of plunging a knife into someone, throwing a child out of a window, or shouting obscenities in public occur without the emotions appropriate to such thoughts. This deprives the thought of its motivational force, thwarts destructive or erotic action, and avoids guilt, because the thought seems alien.

7) Rationalization: Concocting plausible reasons to account for behavior or beliefs that are actually motivated by unconscious wishes or needs. Rationalizers often believe they are giving real grounds for their behaviors or beliefs.

8) Repression: Consists of the expulsion and withholding from conscious awareness of an idea or feeling.

9) Displacement: Consists of the investment of repressed feelings (or ideas) in a substitute object.

10) Denial: A primitive or early defense in which the *ego* avoids becoming aware of some painful aspect of *reality*. To bolster this effacement of reality, a fantasy is formed in the mind that contradicts the disagreeable and unwelcome fact. Thus, a helpless, frightened

child may comfort himself with a fantasy of being powerful or even *omnipotent* (MF).

11) Dissociation: Refers to a defensive state of organization, or activity, of the ego, a state in which patients manifest confused thought processes and disorganized behavior, as in psychosis or severe hysteria (multiple personality, fugue states, somnambulism, major amnesias) in order to avoid awareness of some painful aspect of *reality*.

12) Undoing: Eliminates the conscious or unconscious feeling of remorse by the use of a magical gesture that annuls the forbidden act (ED). Baptismal washing is a magical undoing of "original sin." Undoing preserves *omnipotence*.

13) Other defenses, here undefined: Ambivalence (or ambivalent oscillation); avoidance; conversion; derealization; exaggeration; fixation; negation; reversal into the opposite (of sadness into happiness, for example); turning round (of a drive derivative) upon the subject's own self (ED).

Degradation (physics): Destroying the quality of energy, that is, the capacity of energy to produce *gradients* that can accomplish work; degradation produces low-grade heat, that is, infrared radiation that can do little or no *work*.

Demographic fatigue: A term commonly used today to describe the depletion and degradation, by overpopulation, of non-renewable resources and the infrastructure needed to support modern civilization. This book expands its meaning to include the depletion or degradation, by overpopulation, of group and individual ego functions, that is, the psychosocial infrastructure. Demographic fatigue is a function of *crowding* (JJP).

Denial: See defense mechanism.

Density dependence: Change in the birth and death rate of a population as a result of changes in population density; usually in the form of increased mortality rate and decreased fecundity as density increases (Science Direct).

Density stress: The stress that occurs when a population is crowded, which can affect a person's immunity, stress hormones, and gut microbe composition.

Depressive anxiety: One of the two psychotic anxieties. Depressive anxiety is fear for the survival of the loved object. Depressive anxiety includes anguished guilt for having hatefully wished the object's destruction (HW). The appearance of depressive anxiety is a sign of maturation: It recognizes the value of the object, rouses fear of its loss, and stimulates deep remorse for hostile attacks on that object.

Dialectic: The art of investigating or studying the truth of opinions; the art of discussion or debate; inquiry into metaphysical problems and solutions (AHD). Similar to argumentation.

Originally, dialectic was the art of reasoning or disputation by question and answer, "invented," according to Aristotle, by Zeno of Elea, and scientifically developed by Plato, by whom the term διαλεκτική (dialectike) was used in two senses: (a) The art of definition or discrimination of "ideas," (b) the science which views the interrelation of the ideas in the light of a single principle, "the Good"; corresponding broadly to logic and metaphysics (OED).

Displacement: See *Defense mechanism*.

Dissipation (physics): The movement of energy through a system, to be distinguished from degradation.

Dissociation: See *Defense mechanism*.

Dream: A universal and normal regressive phenomenon occurring during sleep in which thought processes and affects are represented in predominantly visual and (less frequently) auditory form. Dreams are disguised (often by condensation and displacement) hallucinatory expressions of wishes, even when these are the superego's wishes.

Drive: A motivational force that initiates behavior and both generates and directs mental activity. The drive's aim is to eliminate a state of tension.

Drive derivative: The expression of a drive modified (by a *Defense mechanism*) in compliance with superego or social constraints. Kissing, for example, expresses the aggressive drive to bite and/or erotic drive to suck, modified by [superego] injunctions: One, against injuring the love object, to avoid sadness and guilt, and two, against regressive infantile sucking, both to avoid shame and destructive engulfment of the love object.

Education: Systematic learning that, by increasing students' knowledge of both inner and outer realities, helps them reach the true aims of their lives and optimize their humanity (Jaeger). Under this definition, psychoanalysis is education to inner reality.

Education transmits the values and accumulated knowledge of a society and socializes or enculturates its members. Education molds the young in the ways of adulthood and guides them toward useful roles in society.

On the psychodynamic level, education channels, and perhaps more importantly, legitimizes the epistemophilic drive (curiosity). This drive needs legitimization because curiosity was associated in infancy with forbidden interests and sadism; without social legitimacy, the drive will more often succumb to inhibition or proscription by the superego, or seek perverse pathways.

The concentration of learning in formal settings (schools and colleges) accelerates, extends and deepens cultural knowledge and intellectual rigor in the student far more than mere observation and imitation can do.

In all these ways education tends to inoculate the mind against wishful believing (omnipotence or magical thinking).

This definition comprises the strengthening of the mind, education's instrument, and the rational analysis and assessment of information. It neither includes nor explicitly excludes the generation of new information (research), but assigns research to post-baccalaureate, specialty training (JJP).

Ego: A group of functions with an early beginning and subsequent growth. They are susceptible to numerous disturbances and may improve in the course of psychoanalytic treatment.

The outstanding function of the ego is adaptation to reality, a function that sometimes takes strange forms.

Ego corrosion: A progressively expanding tolerance for self-deception (JJP) (adapted from Zerubavel's [2006] "moral corrosion").

Ego functions: The seven fundamental capacities of the ego:

1) Maintains relationship to reality by: a) adapting to reality b) reality-testing c) organizing a coherent sense of reality

2) Regulates and controls drives by supplying tolerance for anxiety, frustration, depression, disappointment, and the postponement of expected satisfactions.

3) Maintains object relations by forming affectionate ties to other individuals, especially those of the opposite sex, over long times with minimal hostility.

4) Generates and sustains rational thought processes

5) Selects and deploys *defense mechanisms*

6) Regulates: a) perception b) motility c) intention d) intelligence e) thinking f) speech g) language

7) Synthesizes, integrates and organizes information from both the internal and external world

Ego ideal: Part of the *superego*, an image of the self to which people aspire, consciously and unconsciously, and against which they measure themselves. It is based on identification with the parents and other environmental figures as they actually are, were in the past, or have been idealized as being. The ego ideal emerges from the omnipotent fantasies of infancy and childhood and illusory experiences of infantile magic. Like all mental constructions, it has a certain degree of unreality, depending on the personality's degree of pathology. To the extent that the actual self does not measure up to the ego ideal, the person's self-esteem suffers. We distinguish the ego ideal from the *ideal ego*.

Emergence: A higher (macro)-level phenomenon that arises from the micro-level interaction among the components of a complexity. "Strong" emergence, the usage in this book, cannot be predicted from knowledge about the components (agents) of a complexity, or about the agents' micro-level interactions. Examples: "Wetness" is an unpredictable macro-level phenomenon that emerges from the micro-level interaction of hydrogen and oxygen molecules; "consciousness" is an unpredictable macro-level phenomenon that emerges from the micro-level interaction of neurons and other somatic agents.

Embodied simulation: The sights, sounds, feelings and actions we inwardly experience when we hear, say or think a word (Benjamin Bergen).

Empathy: A special mode of perceiving the psychological state or experiences of another person. It does not contain the elements of condolence, agreement or pity essential to sympathy. It is not "vicarious" experience, imitation or mimicry. Empathy establishes close contact in terms of emotions and impulses; intuition does the same in the realm of ideas. Empathy is the experiencing, intuitive function of the observing ego.

Encapsulation: A very primitive form of obsessional splitting of the *self*- or *object*-representations into parts, and the psychological encasement of these parts in delusive shells, which block their contents from conscious and even preconscious perception. Encapsulation protects valued or treasured parts of the self or the object from internal attacks. Francis Tustin, British child psychoanalyst (died 1994) known for her successful psychoanalytic work with autistic children, distinguished between "encapsulated children," children who are wholly encased, and less disturbed children who are "encapsulated in segments." The second concept is intended in this book.

Encapsulation can be seen as a subtype of the more basic defense of splitting of the ego, a fracturing of the mind to cut off communication among various functions and pieces of knowledge, creating expanses of self-ignorance. The severance of communication between thoughts and functions is an attack on mental contents, therefore on mental linking and, generally, awareness.

We recall, in this connection, that thought is based on the bodily experienced memories or phantasies of sucking, and on preconceptions of sex and the copulating parental couple, all of which excite sensations of envy.

Energy: (physics) any phenomenon capable of conversion into *work.* There are many forms of energy. The word is derived from the Greek phrase ἐν ἔργῳ (en ergo), meaning "work within," or potential to perform work.

Energy density: (physics) a measure of complexity: The energy flow through a given unit of mass in a given unit of time.

Energy, psychic: A hypothetical force in mental functioning considered analogous, but not equivalent, to the concept of energy used in physics.

Enigmatic message: The French psychoanalyst Jean Laplanche (see Scarfone, 2013) described a universal parent-child communication in which the parent unconsciously seduces the child, that is, enchants the child, with the parent's deepest erotic yearnings, encoded in the nuances of the parent-child interactions. In these yearnings is imbedded the parent's most deeply personal, most intimate dream of self-cure. Laplanche calls this unconscious parental communication the "enigmatic message." For the rest of its life, the child, unaware, is enslaved to the pursuit of the enigma, fails in that pursuit, and transmits the deep riddle, autobiographically modified, to its own child.

Entelechy: That which directs organisms' activity as a whole (Aristotle).

Entropy: (physics) a measure of disorganization, simplicity, atomic chaos, or randomness. The 2nd Law of thermodynamics describes a tendency for disorganization to increase, for atomic chaos to be produced in any real process, as time passes.

Environmental tipping point: The part of the complex human-environment system to which any change will produce positive feedback loops propelling the system on a completely new course.

Envy (common usage): The feeling of mortification and ill will occasioned by the contemplation of superior advantages possessed by another (OED).

Envy, primal: An implacable malice whose fundamental aim is the destruction of life and its sources. It is to be distinguished from both ambivalence and frustration. It is innate and universal, although constitutional and environmental factors can exacerbate or moderate its intensity (HW).

We should distinguish primal envy from secondary, or *contingent envy*. Contingent envy is provoked by self-debasing choices. Indiscipline, or cowardly denial, or unrestrained destructiveness inflames envy of discipline, courage, or self-restraint, respectively. Contingent envy has the same effects as *primal envy*: Increased malice, and increased fear of retribution. Contingent envy is a phase of the vicious cycle.

Epistemophilic drive: The drive to know, a component instinct of the *libido* associated with scopophilia (voyeurism/exhibitionism). Klein showed how epistemophilia was a necessary, exploratory drive, but involved phantasies of penetrating mother's insides to take over and destroy the riches within her (babies and father's penis). This excites a fear of retaliation, (*paranoid anxiety*) which in turn inhibits learning.

External reality (external world): The outer world of the individual's environment, as distinguished from the reality of his psychic life.

Expectancy (biology): Another term for *set point,* that is, a physicochemical condition that makes the organism operate properly.

Preconceptions may be considered psychobiological expectancies or set points.

Experience of satisfaction: A type of primal experience postulated by Freud, consisting in the resolution—owing to an intervention, often by the mother—of an internal tension occasioned in the suckling by need. The hungry baby cries, and the mother suckles the baby. The unique image and qualities of the caretaking mother (the satisfying *object*) subsequently take on special value in the construction of the child's lifelong pattern of desire. The unique experience of satisfaction, in other words, will always guide the subject's later search for love. The very young infant may recathect (see *cathexis*) the maternal image in the absence of the real object. Recathexis of the image constitutes a hallucinatory satisfaction of the wish (LP).

Fantasy: A product of mental activity that usually exists in the form of images or ideas. It represents an attempt at the fulfillment of a wish, and it is this wish-fulfilling quality that distinguishes fantasy from other mental products such as ideas. Fantasies also have the quality of being *conscious* or *unconscious* depending upon their nature, origin, content, and ultimate fate (MF).

Fantasy inertia: The resistance of a false perception or belief to correction by real experience. Fantasy inertia is a measure of time, equivalent to the survival time of the false perception after its perceiver has been exposed to evidence patently contradictory (JJP). Example: "The consensus that cybertechnology has simplified and lightened, rather than complicated and encumbered human life, has sustained a fantasy inertia for four decades."

Father (Paternal role): This book underemphasizes the psychological importance of the father in the interest of foregrounding envy toward the mother and her representatives in the post-infantile social world. The following attempts to slightly redress this imbalance: The infant's earliest concept of the father probably arises during episodes of maternal absence or gross misunderstanding. The infant conceives of the associated pain as a "bad" object and theorizes that this object, the penis, has preoccupied the mother (or her breast). The mother, in the infant's phantasy, has joined with the penis; the binary organism is envisioned as a "combined parent," engaging in a kind of mutual feeding, to the neglect of the baby. The baby therefore, at least initially, hates both the penis and the coupling parents (penis and breast).

Father is at first this phallic fragment of himself, but nonetheless a redoubtable force of nature. He lives inside the maternal space as the penis, with which mother (or the breast) is often preoccupied, to the neglect of the baby. The penis owns the tormentingly enviable privilege of inhabiting the maternal cavity and accessing her mysteries. Here we think of the priest, the scholar, and the psychoanalyst.

Later, when the baby has matured enough to care about the mother's welfare and happiness, the father—though still a fragmentary, phallic image—becomes her protector. The maternal "inner penis" still opposes the infant, repelling, avenging, and punishing his imaginary raids on the maternal cavity, like a dragon guarding the golden hoard within the cave. But now, at least, the father has assumed a positive role, the role of mother's protector. This calms the child, who fears his attacks on the mother might, if unopposed, injure or destroy her.

Later yet, when infants conceive of their objects as unitary, instead of fragmentary, father becomes a whole person to whom they can turn when disappointed in mother (as during weaning), and then can be loved and identified with. In later childhood, the menacing badness of the early period takes the shape of a strict and repressive father.

Final maturity lets the father and mother pursue, enjoy and cultivate their private, creative, nurturing copulation, the very union that, after all, spawned the child in the first place.

Feedback, positive/negative: A situation in which an action creates more (positive)/ or less (negative) of the same action.

Fixation: An arrest of development, the tendency of an early phase to acquire and retain strong charges of *psychic energy* and to strongly affect later mental functioning.

Free association: A sequence of ideas (images, memories, fantasies, thoughts) usually expressed in words and non-conscious body language unconstrained by specific instruction (EE) or, to the extent avoidable, the auditor's *conscious* preferences. Free association is typical of thoughts while driving, shaving, or other semi-automatic tasks. Impediments to free association, like blocking, evasion and discontinuity, are *resistances* that reflect the unconscious defenses against awareness of disturbing material. The complimentary abilities to let one's thoughts roam freely, while retaining the objectivity necessary to observe them and reflect on their meanings constitute an important criterion for analyzability (ability to engage in long-term *psychoanalysis*) (LP). Free association, in its psychoanalytic sense, might be considered the supreme form of cooperative human freedom.

Fundamental rule: The rule which structures the analytic situation: The *analysand* is asked to say what he thinks and feels, selecting nothing and omitting nothing from what comes into his mind, even where this seems to him unpleasant to have to communicate, ridiculous, devoid of interest, or irrelevant (LP).

Gradient: (physics) a difference (for example, in temperature, pressure, or chemical concentration) across a distance. Nature's "abhorrence of gradients" (Schneider and Sagan, 2005) means that gradients will tend to be spontaneously eliminated, most spectacularly by *complex*, growing systems.

Gratitude: Gratitude is not gratification, the satisfaction of a bodily need. Gratitude is, however, evoked and enhanced by the gratification that the object gives; gratitude is more akin to *object*-love. In Melanie Klein's view, gratitude originates at birth; *envy* (*primary*) is an antagonist to gratitude.

Group mentality: Consists of the unanimous opinion, willpower, or desire of the group at any given moment. Group mentality may conflict with certain personal desires; the interplay between these desires and group mentality is called *group culture*, the organization of the group (Bion).

Group culture: The organization of the group, established to manage conflict between the unanimous will of the group and personal desires of its members. One may observe group culture in the behavior of its members, the roles they perform, the actions of the leaders and behavior of the group as a whole. The group's organization, at any given moment, emerges from the conflict between the unconscious collective willpower, and individuals' wishes and needs (Bion).

Homosexuality: The overt or latent disposition to sexual desires and excitement directed toward members of the same sex, with sexual indifference or even aversion to the opposite sex.

The pre-20th century view of homosexuality, an organic, pre-psychological view, asserted that innate hereditary factors lead to homosexuality. In the early 20th century, Classical psychoanalysis explained homosexuality as a disturbance of the total *psychosexual* development. But society reestablished the pre-psychological view in the late 20th century.

Hormesis: A biological phenomenon in which stressors, at non-lethal intensities, strengthen an organism. This is the "what doesn't kill you makes you stronger" principle at the cellular or organismal level. Hormesis is *adaptation* to stress, improving the adapting organism's resilience or function.

Humanism: A devotion to studies that promote human *culture* and mental growth, an education rooted in Classical letters, guided by an individualistic, secular, critical spirit of inquiry. Humanism is "*education* deliberately modeled on a certain ideal conception of human nature .... the intellectual search for the true nature of man" (Jaeger).

Humanism is older than the *liberal arts*. Humanism emerged directly from the Hellenic Greek preoccupation with the ideal human life. The liberal arts did not appear until the late 5th century AD.

In pursuit of the ideal concept of human nature, humanist scholarship, which comprises both the humanities and the natural sciences, was handicapped in its study of the internal world. Humanism depends on rationalist inquiry, on what is called in *psychoanalysis*, *secondary process* thinking, a predominantly logical, conscious, controlled mode of thought, as distinct from the fantastic, mostly *unconscious*, and massive discharges of unbound energy involved in *primary process* thinking, the mode of thinking prevalent in dreams and facilitated by *free-association*. Humanism was thus barred from a deeper understanding of the internal world.

It is true that, before psychoanalysis, humanist studies often identified, by literary or artistic intuition, the *defense mechanisms* (that is, unconscious modes of self-deception); but had no method by which to modify defenses, nor a safe venue in which to expose and deconstruct such phenomena. Psychoanalysis established an interpersonal context for *free-association*—a unique form of human liberty—and invented defense interpretation, both of which have vastly extended and deepened humanity's appreciation of its needs. This contribution to human knowledge and mental freedom places psychoanalysis in both the *liberal arts* and *Humanism*. We may consider it their highest expression.

Described in biophysical terms, Humanism offers society a path to higher complexity that regulates, instead of maximizes, gradient destruction.

Hypomania: An inexplicable elevation of mood marked by disinhibited behavior and irritability.

Hysteria: A psychoneurosis characterized by conversion symptoms and apparent indifference to the symptoms.

Id: A totally unconscious part of the mental apparatus, representing the sum total of wishes arising from the individual's needs, needs indicated by their "mental representations," that is, the *drives*.

Ideal Ego: An intrapsychic formation which some authors distinguish from the ego ideal and define as an ideal of narcissistic omnipotence constructed on the model of infantile narcissism (LP).

Idealization: A mental process by means of which the object's qualities and value are elevated to the point of perfection. Identification with the idealized object contributes to the formation and elaboration of the individual subject's so-called ideal agencies (ideal ego, ego ideal) (LP). Idealization is often a *manic defense* against one or both *psychotic anxieties*.

Identification with the aggressor: Defense mechanism identified and described by Anna Freud (1936): Faced with an external threat (typically represented by a criticism emanating from an authority), the subject identifies himself with his aggressor. He may do so either by appropriating the aggression itself, or else by physical or moral emulation of the aggressor, or again by adopting particular symbols of power by which the aggressor is designated (LP).

Impulse: The sudden, unpremeditated welling up of an instinctual drive toward some action, the action usually having the quality of hastiness and lack of deliberation.

Incongruity: A mental condition characterized by inconsistency, incoherence, incompatibility, or inappropriateness (EE). Incongruence afflicts everyone, in different degrees, but when excessive or long uncorrected, it passes into habitual dishonesty, which degrades the self-concept and provokes self-disgust. This injury to self-respect sets in motion a downward spiral of defenses that become more primitive over time. The ego mobilizes these defenses against remorse and contrition, which threaten the ego with decompensation, impulses to suicide or homicide, or preemptive attacks on people who might expose the deepening imposture; this work exhausts the ego and deprives it of discretionary energy for growth (JJP). *Tensions* of incongruity are easier to obliterate from consciousness than tensions of congruity, that is, tensions stimulated by *self-knowledge*.

Insight: The subjective experiential knowledge acquired during psychoanalysis of previously unconscious pathogenic content, conflict and defenses. Analytic insight differs from other cognitive understandings; insight is marked by antecedent dynamic changes that weaken resistances and release energy.

(Pseudo-insight: Apparent understanding that actually serves patients' libidinal or aggressive purposes with respect to their analysts, for example, to please, deceive, or defeat them.)

Instinct: A controversial English translation of the German "Trieb" used by Freud to represent an evolutionarily determined, innate, constant motivational force. Many psychoanalysts have instead translated "Trieb" as "*drive*."

Internalization: A progressive process by which external interactions between the organism and the outer world are replaced by inner representations of these interactions and their end results. In human development, the interactions with which we are chiefly concerned are those of infants with their parents and the parents' relationship. In an evolutionary sense, the mental apparatus and its psychical substrata (including the drives) are structural records (internalizations) of the experiences of the race, substituting inner for outer controls and thereby serving the purposes of self-preservation and propagation of the species (MF).

Intellectualization: The psychological binding of the *drives* in intellectual activities, especially as a means of control (example: Adolescent preoccupations with philosophy and religion).

Internal world (internal reality/psychic reality): The conviction of the reality of the psychic world that exists unconsciously and is felt inside the person. This world consists of *objects* (people, or parts of people, including the subject) experienced as concretely real, engaging in relations with each other. These internal objects and their relations can cause real external change in the subject. The analyst Karl Abraham described how, within several months after his father's death, his black hair turned as grey as his father's had been, and back to black again.

The internal world is the totality of a person's mental representation of his physical instinctual life and of his thoughts, feelings, dreams and fantasies, memories and perceptions—regardless of whether or not they accurately reflect or correspond to objective reality. This totality comprises both conscious and unconscious elements.

Much of what children perceive in their relations with external reality is assimilated into the ego, and these assimilations, or *internalizations*, structure their psychic reality.

Interpretation: A form of intervention by the analyst, whose aim is to achieve therapeutic results by adding to the patient's knowledge of himself. Interpretation makes patients aware of psychic conflict, consciousness of which they had warded off.

Isolation: (see *Defense mechanism*)

Liberal arts: Originally, those studies considered appropriate for a free (*liberated*, not enslaved) man. The liberal arts, codified in the medieval university as the trivium (grammar, rhetoric, and logic) and quadrivium (arithmetic, music, geometry, and astronomy) originated in the late 5th century AD work of Martianus Capella, who distilled the intellectual activities of the ancient Greeks into a curriculum suitable to the abilities and tastes of his age.

Renaissance scholars studied the liberal arts in the spirit of *Humanism*, the philosophical basis of Greek education and higher culture.

This book defines liberal (humanist) education as: A reading knowledge of ancient Greek and Latin, and the poetry, drama, philosophy, mathematics and natural sciences extant in those languages; mathematics through single variable calculus, and a year each of biology, physics, chemistry and astronomy; the reading and study of the canonical works of all major cultures, and their educational significance. The liberal arts student is encouraged to read all works in their original languages.

Libido: A quantitative concept, some quantity of sexual energy, conceived by Freud as one great dynamic force (the other considered to be destructive) which gives rise to internal conflict in the course of mental development.

Linking: A basic capacity of the mind, of life, and of all physical matter subject to energy flow, to bring independent agents into interdependent relationships.

The mind can link its own perceptions, ideas, images, and feelings; to other minds; or to *reality*. The mind can also, under the influence of envy, attack and disintegrate any such links, and by that attack, distort or fragment its awareness of *internal or external reality*.

This book uses the phrases “internal linking,” “psychological linking,” and “mental linking” all more or less synonymously.

Manic defense: The manic defense wards off *depressive anxiety*, an early and anguished form of guilt due to hateful destructiveness aimed at a loved *object* (HW). This defense supports the fantasy of *omnipotence*. It consists specifically of denial, disparagement (contempt), control and idealization. Psychoanalysts sometimes speak of the manic triad, by which they mean contempt, triumph, and control—respectively—for, over, and of, the *object*. All manic defenses protect the subject from experiencing the painful consequences of dependence on love objects. The manic triad, because it gratifies the subject’s sadistic wish to overcome and humiliate the object, changes the abused object into an injured, vengeful internal persecutor of the subject. This raises *persecutorial* anxiety and intensifies defensive manic behavior and ideation as an effort to defeat and control the inner persecutor thus created.

Masochism: A propensity to seek physical or mental suffering in order to achieve, consciously or not, sexual gratification and arousal in the widest sense.

1) Sexual masochism
2) *Masochistic perversion*
3) *Moral masochism*
4) Masochistic character

Masochistic perversion: A condition in which sexual gratification is contingent upon physical or mental pain, such as beating, threats, humiliation imagined or actually experienced at the hands of the partner. In men, it is based on passive homosexual tendencies; in both women and men, is based on the particular form and means of undoing childhood fears of castration, of rejection, and of abandonment by the parents.

Mental growth: A psychical transformation from incoherence to coherence, stimulated by exposure to truth. The mind cannot grow unless a person decides to recognize, tolerate and reflect on pain, rather than evade it. When we tolerate pain, thought emerges: We scan our memories; we perform a rational analysis of the meaning of the pain; and we make predictions. Thought is intended to manage the pain and understand it—its cause, quality, and course.

Mental growth consists of a discovery that certain events are constantly conjoined, that is, always happening together. The reflecting mind forms an idea, abstraction, or concept that explains that conjunction.

Mental growth is a movement from evasion, to acceptance, of realities; reality includes inner pain, regret, shame and guilt.

This conceptual innovation binds the conjoining phenomena and prevents their dispersal back into chaos. Binding generates an expanding penumbra of meanings. This expansion touches other perceived or remembered events, turning up additional potential conjunctions to be recognized and bound, and new penumbra of meanings to be radiated. We recognize this process when a scientific discovery is followed by an elaboration of the discovery into a whole system, with a cascade of new insights. Of course, internal discovery is more private and more subtle.

Mental growth occurs when a *preconception* mates with a realization; an unsaturated variable becomes saturated into a constant. The resulting new conception becomes in turn a new preconception looking for another realization.

Metapsychology: An orienting and systematizing framework around which clinical data and lower-level psychoanalytic propositions can be organized. Metapsychology has six viewpoints: Dynamic, economic, topographic, structural, genetic and adaptive.

Mindsight (psychological-mindedness): Sensitivity to the non-conscious wishes and defenses that determine behavior.

Moral masochism: An unconscious or conscious need for punishment leading to symptoms such as anxiety states or self-inflicted suffering. These symptoms can be consequences of situations that would normally lead to satisfaction, rise of self-esteem, or happiness. This condition may lead to negative therapeutic reaction, one kind of therapeutic failure.

Motive: A specific personal or organismic factor controlling behavior; any state or event within the organism that initiates or regulates behavior in relation to a goal (EE).

Narcissism: Love directed toward the image of oneself (LP). Narcissism is a concentration of psychological interest upon the self, ranging from healthy self-esteem and self-concern to pathological brooding and schizophrenia. Injuries to narcissism—insults to one's pride, for example—evoke severe degrees of anger, referred to as narcissistic rage (MF).

Narcissistic supplies: Emotional supports like reassurance, praise, reward, esteem, pride and self-esteem.

Natural law: A principle derived from nature and binding upon human society in the absence of (or in addition to) *positive law*.

Neurocharms: The "natural classical" genres of art, such as poetic meter, that are believed to be universally appealing and promote emergence. They are seen as cultural universals, suggesting that there are inherent human preferences for certain artistic structures (Frederick Turner).

Neurosis: (Psychoneurosis) a disturbance in thoughts, feelings, and behavior that have their primary origin in the mind and are only secondarily related to events and stimuli of the current external world. It retains reality relationships that are lost in *psychoses*, and drive inhibitions that are lost in *perversions* and *impulse* disorders.

Object: A loved person.

An "anaclitic object choice" is a choice of object based on the unconscious wish to receive passive gratification; in other words, the wish to be fed and protected like a child.

Object relations: Human relationships taken in their broadest sense.

Oedipus complex: A characteristic grouping of *drives*, aims, *object relations* and fears universally found at the height of the phallic phase (3-6 years old). During this period the child strives in a limited way for sexual union with the parent of the opposite sex and death or disappearance of the parent of the same sex.

Oedipal conflict: A conflict between the urge for sexual union and *castration anxiety*.

Omnipotence: The fantasy of unlimited power, especially by thoughts and wishes, a global fantasy sometimes described as magical thinking (JJP). Omnipotence, in psychoanalytic theory, is the belief that thoughts alone are able to gratify wishes without the help of corresponding actions or an available external *object* (ED). The omnipotence of primitive *defense mechanisms*, particularly those associated with fantasies of taking in, expelling and annihilating *objects*, external or internal, tend to dissolve the real distinctions between self and others; these defensive fantasies are used to avoid experiences of separateness and of [*deep*] *envy* (HW). The frustration of omnipotence often excites negativism, stubbornness and, in extreme cases, catatonia (mutism, stupor, waxy flexibility, catalepsy).

Overdetermination: The causation or production of a specific symptom, item of behavior, or any element of psychic life by a variable number of intersecting causal paths.

***Paideia*:** (Greek: παιδεία) the title of a scholarly work by Werner Jaeger, early 20th century German Classicist. *Paideia*, loosely translated, is the educational and cultural spirit of the ancient Greeks, embodied in their literature. *Paideia* is an unswervable resolve to learn more and more about both the inner and outer worlds. This movement, preserved in *Humanism*, was revolutionary. It initially contradicted the prevailing aristocratic ethos; it asserted that character and virtue could be earned with effort, not just passed through bloodlines.

Paracrousis: (Greek: παράκουσις) a "false striking," as of a wrong note during a musical passage; psychologically, it refers to any stimulus that suggests an incongruence or inconsistency between what one actually knows and what one only senses.

Paranoia: A psychopathological condition characterized by strongly held ideas or delusions of persecution, jealousy and grandeur.

Paranoid process: An inherent potentiality, even in well-organized and healthy personalities, to shift, under appropriate eliciting conditions, in the direction of *paranoia*. The paranoid process shapes many aspects of human experience and personality functioning. It influences psychological development and the formation and consolidation of personal structure. This is as true of developmental paths ending in a mature and positive sense of personal identity as of those ending in personalities essentially pathological and defective. The theory of the paranoid process is an extension of the process of *internalization*. Core internalizations serve as the basis for the organization of the self and the source of externalizations (or *projections;* see *defense mechanism*) that influence and shape the individual's object relations (From W. W. Meissner, 1986).

Paraphilia: A distortion or anomaly of sexuality. Paraphilia includes both biologically-endowed and psychologically imposed (perverse) anomalies.

Penis envy: A mental attitude and feeling of discontent with one's own genital equipment, together with an aggressive urge to take for oneself, and dispossess the man of, not only male genitalia, but also the identity and imagined superior achievements and potency of the male.

Perceptions: The psychological equivalent to sensations generated by stimuli from the outer world, the body or the mind (MF).

Persecution (Persecutory anxiety): The sense of impending retaliation, violently powerful in young children, eventually appearing as nightmares and night terrors (pavores nocturnus) and persisting in less conscious forms throughout life. Greed, rage and envy stimulate persecution, from which the sufferer seeks relief by doing charitable and altruistic acts (*reaction formation*) or, to appease the persecutors, acts of self-destruction. Persecution is overt in paranoid states but plays an equally powerful, if less visible role in everyone's internal life and external behavior (HW and JP).

Perversion: A habitual and persistent sexual practice that deviates in aim or object choice from heterosexual genital union. It represents the persistence into adult life of infantile sexual activity. This is a psychoanalytic and scientific, not a moral or social concept.

Personality Disorder: See *Character disorder*.

Pleasure principle: A regulatory principle of mental functioning, a principle that regulates the need to recreate by action or fantasy any situation that had created the *experience of satisfaction* through the elimination of drive tension.

Fechner's constancy principle assumes that the organism seeks to avoid tension that disturbs its equilibrium, tension felt as unpleasure (see related entries *Principle of Least Effort* [Zipf] and *Principle of Least Expenditure of Innervation* [Freud]). This is also true of psychological tensions, tensions arising from either inadequately satisfied needs or wishes, or from external or internal dangers, which that satisfaction might incur.

Pleonexia (Greek: πλεονεξία): Mindless morbid greed; the degrading compulsion for wealth and status.

Pluralistic self-ignorance: Refers to the social phenomenon in which individuals guess wrongly about a group's beliefs and values.

Population density stress: (synonymous with *crowding, density stress, and density dependence*) the stress that occurs when a population is crowded, which can affect a person's immunity, stress hormones, and gut microbe composition.

Population momentum: The continuation of population growth after its growth *rate* has begun to decline.

Positive law: Law established or recognized by governmental authority, as distinguished from *natural law*.

Preconception: A psychological entity waiting for a realization that will "mate" with it (HW). Bion (1963) suggested that people have preconceptions for which experience more or less provides realizations. When we touch a baby's face, it turns its head and sucks; this reflects the innate knowledge—a preconception, a psychological form of *expectancy*—of sucking before sucking has ever occurred. The first act of sucking mates this preconception with the actual sensory and perceptual experience, producing a *conception*, an elementary mental structure from which complex thoughts and thinking can develop.

Boris (1994, p. 6) summarizes earlier contributions to the idea of preconception: "Kant (1781) suggested that people have what he called 'empty thoughts' to which experiences with real events are more or less approximate. .... Such so-called 'structuralists' as Levi-Strauss, the anthropologist, and Chomsky, the linguist, also found it logically necessary to infer that people have inherent ideas about experience. These ideas they call 'deep' or 'metastructures', and they view these structures as giving a shape to experience prior to, sometimes independent of, the influences of actual private or cultural experiences." Boris cites all the following as having recognized varieties of preconception: Chomsky, 1972; Gardner, 1973; Leach, 1970; Levi-Strauss, 1966, 1973; Lyons, 1970; Piaget, 1973; and Piers, 1972.

Preconscious: Mental content or process which is more or less logically organized into thought processes, memories, ideas, images and their verbal symbols as well as motor habits. All these mental phenomena are capable of achieving consciousness by the act of focusing *attention*.

Primal scene: A universal childhood recollection, or fantasy, of a couple, usually father and mother, engaging in sexual intercourse. The primal scene is a *preconception*. Both the fantasy and the actual event (see *conception*) provoke, and bring into consciousness, envious rage.

Primary process: Refers both to 1) a mode of psychic energy discharge and 2) a type of thought process.

1) This mode is characterized by the mobility of *cathexis* (the immediate discharge of energy and its facile shifts in attachment) as contrasted with delayed discharge (the *secondary process*).

2) A primitive, irrational type of wishful thought characterized by condensation, displacement and extensive use of symbols, the kind of thought characteristic of dreams. The primary process strives to hallucinate the *experience of satisfaction* (that is, achieve a "perceptual identity" with that experience), whereas the *secondary process* seeks conceptual similarities to that experience.

Principle of least effort: The principle of the least average rate of expectable (predictable) work rules every human thought and act. Whatever we think or do attempts to solve a problem, internal or external, with the least effort anticipated over time (proposed by G. K. Zipf, 1949).

Principle of least expenditure of innervation: The effortless and regular avoidance by the psychical process of anything distressing. This principle implies that consciousness of an idea, image or emotion will only occur if the mind is in a position to limit any development of unpleasure that may proceed from that consciousness.

Traumatic memories seem to contradict this principle. But the contradiction, as Freud explained, is only apparent, because traumatic memories actually do limit unpleasure. The evocation of such memories either satisfies demands of the conscience for suffering, thus appeasing or even pleasing the conscience; or their repetitive occurrence tends, by review and reassessment, to help the mind master and limit the unpleasure associated with those memories (proposed by Freud, 1900, *Int. Dreams*, 601b).

Principle of least tension (in expanded form: "Principle of least average rate of expectable perceptible tension"): We calculate the desirability of every thought and action by the magnitude of the tension (a stimulus for work) that the thought or action is expected to reduce. "Expectable" refers to foresight: How much future tension do we anticipate each of the current options will occasion? "Perceptible" refers to the susceptibility of the expected tension to obliteration from consciousness (JP).

Projective identification: Projective identification, originally the infant's method of evacuating painful feelings into the mother's mind, is eventually brought into service as a component of empathy. From our prenatal beginnings we have a sense of what others feel when they want what they don't have. But empathy's sister is paranoia, and paranoia's principle is the law of the talion (eye for an eye). Most people are entirely unaware of the *paranoid process,* though it is universal. To those who are free of conscious suspiciousness the concept seems fanciful or absurd. But in the unconscious world paranoia is chillingly real and tyrannizes the unsuspecting sufferer's life.

Psychic determinism: Theory that all psychic events and processes follow certain strict laws (though we may not understand these fully) and form a lawful universe similar to that of the universe of physical events and processes.

Psychoanalysis: 1) a branch of science developed by Sigmund Freud and his followers, devoted to the study of the *conscious*, *preconscious* and *unconscious* minds. 2) A method of psychotherapeutic treatment lasting many years, consisting of at least five weekly sessions, encouraging a *regression* in which derivatives of forbidden wishes and repressed memories find expression in the relationship between the analyst and patient. These derivatives often occasion anxiety, and evoke defenses against their raw expression. *Interpretation*, over time, draws wishes, defenses, and their conflicts into the patient's consciousness and gradually gives the patient's ego more control over them. It was to this process Freud referred when he wrote, "Where id was, there ego shall be."

In his paper "Psychoanalysis as a scientific theory" (1959), Heinz Hartmann called psychoanalysis "a systematic investigation of self-deception and its motivations" (Hartmann, 1964, p. 335).

Psychoanalytic function: A universal human *drive*, posited by Wilfred Bion, to understand the mind.

Psychodynamics: A body of knowledge and theory of human behavior which attempts to explain normal and pathological behavior as a result of interacting and opposing goal-directed or motivational forces.

Psychologist's fallacy: Attributing to the individual or group mind under examination what is actually true of the psychologist's own mind.

Psychosexual development: A regular sequence of libidinal manifestations beginning in early infancy and continuing to adulthood.

The early phases, described under infantile sexuality, are centered on and organized around the oral, anal and, later, phallic (penile and clitoral) zones. Psychosexual development undergoes a typical and (ideally) temporary arrest with the development of the castration complex in connection with Oedipal fantasies.

Psychosis: A disturbance in thoughts, feelings and behavior associated with severe personality disorganization and characterized by marked *ego* and *libidinal regression*, regression to the point of losing contact with *reality*.

Psychotic anxiety: The *persecutory* (sometimes called paranoid-schizoid) or *depressive anxieties* of infancy that live on in adults, usually only visible in psychotic states. "Psychotic" refers both to the extravagantly unrealistic nature—relative to *external reality*—and to the terrifying quality of the phantasies associated with these anxieties.

What causes psychotic anxiety? Babies make desperate attempts to contact their mothers for help. Some of these attempts, driven by greed or envy, infants interpret as attacks on their mother's body; they fear that they have damaged her insides (*depressive anxiety*). At other times they fear that the mother, or prized parts of the mother, or even the father—who is preconceived to inhabit the mother's body and, like the fabled dragon that inhabits and defends the treasure-filled cave will avenge the plundering and attack the baby's insides (*persecutory anxiety*). We think here of our inborn infantile terror of being seized by a predator, mutilated and devoured.

Bion believed that each individual approaches his or her group(s), as infants approach their mother's bodies—with passion and envy, and fear of doing damage or of being retaliated upon. Group members try to suppress these psychotic anxieties by collaborating in collective fantasies of salvation, known as "basic assumptions."

One of these fantasy-assumptions, for example, Bion called the "pairing assumption" (see *Basic assumption groups*). In this variation, two (or more) members of the group are imagined to pair up and give birth, or to have already paired up and given birth, to a new member, an omnipotent Messiah, who will solve the group's problems. The Messiah can be a person or ideology, such as a system of utopian expectations. For example, *rational optimism* exemplifies the pairing assumption, promulgating the messianic illusion that technology and science, offspring of innumerable "pairings of human genius," will solve our problems.

Rationalization: See *Defense mechanism*

Rational optimism: The plausible Enlightenment belief, apparently prefigured in Francis Bacon's unfinished novel *The New Atlantis*, in which the head of his ideal college, Salomon's House declares that the scientific (Baconian) method can enlarge "the bounds of the human empire, to the effecting of all things possible." Rational optimism believes that humans can progressively ease their lives with technical and scientific ingenuity.

Reality: Refers to both internal (psychic) and external reality.

1) Internal (psychic) reality designates the totality of a person's mental representation of his psychical/instinctual life and of his thoughts, feelings, dreams and fantasies. This comprises both conscious and unconscious elements. Psychic reality is reality experienced in evolving stages of development in the emotional and intellectual life of the individual.

2) External reality is reality as it appears to an objective adult observer brought up in a scientific tradition.

Reality principle: Modes of action and thought that take into account, and are shaped by, the exigencies and conditions of real life. Under the influence of the reality principle, the logical and rational appraisal of cause-effect relations in the outside world, in coordination with a growing awareness and understanding of oneself and of the needs, feelings, demands, actions and thoughts of other people, shape behavior and tame the drives.

The early infantile mode of uninhibited and unmodified searching for the satisfaction of needs and wishes and avoidance of pain (pleasure principle) is gradually replaced, in the course of normal development, by reality-adaptive modes of thought and action. This maturational process is conceptualized as the substitution of the reality principle for the pleasure principle. Maturation involves delays, postponements, renunciations and other more complex inhibitions and transformations of drive discharge and need satisfaction.

Reality-testing: An ego function consisting of the capacity for assessing the authenticity of elements of the internal and external worlds.

Reaction formation: (see *Defense mechanism*)

Regression: A psychological retreat or reversion, either 1) to an earlier phase of instinctual organization, usually of the infantile period, a retreat called *libidinal regression*, or 2) to earlier modes of mental functioning, a retreat called *ego regression*.

The concept of regression is related to the hypothesis that in the course of attaining adulthood, an individual passes through a series of maturational phases, each with a phase-appropriate mental organization.

Repetition compulsion: The general tendency in all human behavior to repeat painful experiences, this tendency is often attributed to "bad luck" or "destiny." Its varied manifestations include children's repetition of play that attempts to master the experience of loss; recurrent nightmares after trauma; reenactment of childhood conflicts during psychoanalysis, and character disorders with a persistent need for self-defeating behavior.

Repression: (see *Defense mechanism*)

Resistance: The automatic opposition of the mind to anything that disturbs the balance of inner psychic forces, that is, to anything that disturbs psychic equilibrium.

Ressentiment: French term for resentment. Suppressed feelings of envy and hatred that cannot be acted upon, frequently resulting in some form of self-abasement.

Secondary process: Predominantly logical, controlled thinking characterized economically by the use of minimal amounts of neutralized psychic energy. This is compared with, and in practice often opposed to, the free fantasies and massive discharges of unbound energy involved in the *primary process*.

Secondary process introduces the concept of delay, or postponement, of immediate discharge—a necessary precondition for logical thought—as distinguished from primary process, which strives for immediate discharge.

Self: A common sense concept, referring to the total person of an individual in reality, including both body and psychic organization, one's "own person" as contrasted with "other persons" and *objects* outside one's self.

Self-knowledge: A cultivated habit of searching for signs of self-deception; a habitual striving to recognize and remember one's characteristic strategies (*defense mechanisms*) of avoiding consciousness of tensions or emotional pain. Self-knowledge, as defined in this book, is not seeking to know *why* we do what we do, that is, our hidden motives, so much as seeking to know *how* we typically keep those motives hidden from ourselves.

Self-organized criticality: (physics and complexity science; first proposed by Bak et al. in 1987) a phenomenon in which interaction agents *self-organize* into states that can produce large events.

Self-organization: A form of *emergence* in which collected entities create a pattern or structure from the bottom up, the kinds of patterns or structures seen, for example, in sand piles, ant colonies or schools of fish.

Social defense system: A psychological system formed through unconscious cooperation among the members of institutions, associations, or societies to reinforce the internal defenses of the members against anxiety and guilt (Eliot Jaques).

Social propinquity: A socio-anthropological concept describing the degree of familiar interaction, socioeconomic equality, formal equality (equality under the law), and in this book, closeness in geometric space, characteristic of the members of a social group as a whole. Social propinquity is proportional to envy's inhibition of everyday life in a society: The more social propinquity, the more severe the inhibition.

Specialized work group: Those members (or aspects of members) of any group in contact with reality and reconciled to the demands of mental growth, who cooperate to secure the group's long-term survival (Wilfred Bion).

Spiritual: Here, referring not to religious experience, but to the nonmaterial transcendent or sublime intellectual, psychological, emotional and cultural activities, faculties and experiences of the human mind.

Spoiling: The inner devaluation of anything that enhances or deepens human experience; essentially an envious attack on life. It first appears in the infant's attacks on the mother and her life-giving aspects. Spoiling can take the form of disdain, contempt, cynicism or (I bring the reader's attention to this variation in particular) pessimism.

Structure: Any enduring arrangement, grouping, pattern or articulation of parts to form a relatively stable system or whole (EE). Structure is contrasted with function, or process. Mental structures are systems of mental elements that achieve a relative constancy of objective and consistency in mode of operation (MF).

Structuralization: The process of imposing form or structure upon formless or heterogeneous phenomena; or the result of the process (EE). Neuroscientist Gerald Edelman (1989) wrote of synaptic linkages forming local or global "maps," exemplifying structuralization on a neurological level. Psychological structuralization is the imposition of form and organization upon previously disparate mental elements, giving these newly united elements a relative constancy of objective and a consistency in mode of operation (MF). Thus the mind forms memories, analogies, predictive theories, an ego or superego, or even a global paranoid-schizoid frame of understanding.

Sublimation: The deflection of *drive* energies into aims more acceptable to the ego and superego, energies especially related to oral and anal wishes. Traditionally, artistic and intellectual creativity illustrate sublimation, but any activity that promotes the synthesis of the total personality is sublimation.

Superego: The group of psychic functions that, in their manifest expression, appear as moral attitudes, conscience, and a sense of guilt or shame.

The superego consists of both: 1) Critical and punishing functions that evoke feelings of guilt and shame and 2) protective and rewarding functions which set up ideals and values grouped under the term ego ideal

Superego anxiety: The dread arising from preconscious anticipation of severe guilt, shame, remorse or contrition provoked by actions, wishes, fantasies or impulses unacceptable to the conscience.

Symptom formation: The process by which symptomatic behaviors, affect states, or mental conditions are generated. See also *compromise formation*.

Symptoms arise from unconscious psychic conflict arising from contending forces within the individual. These forces consist of repressed derivatives (unconscious fantasies, impulses, wishes) of childhood drives (both sexual and aggressive) and the active energy of psychic structures (*ego*, *superego*) that oppose the entrance of such derivatives into conscious thought or behavior for moral or adaptive reasons.

When the strengthening of the former (drive derivatives) or weakening of the latter (ego or superego) disturbs the equilibrium between the drives and repressive forces, the derivatives threaten to emerge into consciousness, giving rise to anxiety, guilt, or shame. If these affects exceed their mild signal magnitude or value, then symptoms arise.

Symptom formation is a subset of *compromise formation*, the basis of every human behavior or thought.

Systems approach: A search for universal laws, models, or principles that hold for a broad class of systems irrespective of their particular kind, a science of *emergent* properties that tries to integrate holistic and reductionist observations within the framework of *complex systems* (Schneider and Sagan, 2005).

Tension: (see "tolerance of tension" in ED, "principle of constancy" in LP, and so on) a condition in body or mind of being stretched or strained, or a sensation suggesting this condition, caused by any force, internal or external, which disturbs physical or emotional equilibrium. Tension is a condition of strain produced by anxiety, need, or any sense of mental, emotional or physical disequilibrium (OED).

Tension-evasion: A tendency toward immediate and (mentally) unmediated obliteration of the perception of tension.

Transference: The displacement of patterns of feelings and behavior originally experienced with significant figures of one's childhood, onto individuals in one's current relationships, people such as a spouse or psychoanalyst.

Unconscious: Either the quality of being outside mental awareness or the dynamic state of exclusion from mental awareness. The unconscious may be described from three different viewpoints:

1) Descriptive unconscious: The aggregate of all mental contents and processes that at any given moment are outside conscious awareness (or are "unnoticed"). This includes contents that are "*preconscious*."

2) Dynamic unconscious: The mental contents and processes of the "system unconscious" (see below) which are incapable of achieving consciousness because of the operation of a counterforce known as *repression* (or censorship). This force manifests itself during psychoanalysis as a resistance to knowing. Unconscious mental contents are irrationally, rather than logically, organized around wishes and *drives*, and strive for immediate discharge regardless of reality conditions. In the dynamic unconscious, the *primary process* and the *pleasure principle* regulate wishes and drives.

3) System unconscious: A region of the mental apparatus, topographically considered, within which memory traces are organized by primitive modes of associations (i.e.: *Primary process*).

Vicious circle: A psychological pattern expressing one of the two kinds of drive *cathexes* (mental investments) of *intrapsychic* objects and forces (or their prototypes). The other kind is the *benign circle*. The vicious circle is a sadistic and anxiogenic (fear-inducing) experience. It begins in a sadistic or envious attack on internal objects; this provokes a fear of vengeance by the objects that have been attacked, provoking a more ferocious defensive attack on the avenging objects, in turn inflaming the counter-ferocity of the avengers. This sequence leads to mental illness, a failed solution to paranoid terror (one of the "*psychotic anxieties*").

Work (physics): A means of transforming energy into coherent action.

Work group: A general term for a collective of humans who, in distinction to *basic assumption groups*, cooperate to adapt their larger group to reality for the common good. Work groups use rational and scientific methods, are tolerant of frustrations, and control their emotions. "Work group" also refers to the mental activity of any group carrying out its tasks by rational and scientific methods.

Bibliography

Adair, M. (1993) A speculation on perversion and hallucination. *International Journal of Psychoanalysis*, *Vol. 74*, Part 1, pp. 81-92.

Aichhorn, August. *Wayward youth*. New York: Viking Press, 1954.

Albertson, Alicia. (2014) Study by assoc. prof. Derek Muller, Pepperdine School of Law. *NationalJurist.com*.

Alexander, F. (1921) Metapsychologische Betrachtungen. *Internationale Zeitschrift fur Psychoanalyze*, 6:270-65.

Alexander, R. D. (1975) The search for a general theory of behavior. *Behavioral Science*, 10, pp. 77-100.

------------------ (1987) *The Biology of Moral Systems*. New York: Aldine de Gruyter.

Alter, Adam. *Irresistible: The Rise of addiction technology and the business of keeping us hooked.* New York: Penguin Books, 2017.

Altman, L. L. *The dream in psychoanalysis*. New York: International Universities Press, Inc., 1969.

Andersen, Kurt. (2017) How America lost its mind. *The Atlantic*, September, 2017.

------------------*Fantasyland: How america went haywire—A 500 year history*. New York: Random House, 2017.

Apter, Emily. (2008) Untranslatables: A world system. *New literary history*: Vol. 39, No. 3, pp. 581-598.

------------------*Against world literature: On the politics of untranslatability*. London: Verso, 2013.

Ariely, D. *The honest truth about dishonesty*. New York: Harper, 2012.

Arum, R. and Roksa, J. *Academically adrift: Limited learning on college campuses*. Chicago: U. of Chicago Press, 2011.

Austerberry, Charles. (1997) (on Pre-Health careers) https://classics.artsandsciences.baylor.edu/careers/pre-health

Badcock, C. *Psychodarwinism: The new synthesis of Darwin and Freud*. London: Flamingo, 1994.

Bainbridge, C. M., Bertolo, m., Youngers, J., Atwood, S., Yurdum, L., Simson, J., Lopez, K., Xing, F., Martin, A., Mehr, S. A. (2020) Infants relax in response to unfamiliar foreign lullabies. *Nature Human Behavior*.

Balter, Leon. (2018) Spatial Translation and regression in dreams: The Nicholas Young Phenomenon. *Journal of the American psychoanalytic association, Vol. 66*, 4, pp. 619-645. DOI: 10.1177/0003065118797137

Bak, P. *How nature works: The science of self-organized criticality*. New York: Copernicus, (Springer-Verlag) 1996.

Baumeister, R. F. (2003) Ego depletion and self-regulation failure: A resource model of self-control. *Epidemiology and prevention. Alcoholism. Clinical & experimental research*. 27 (2) 281-284.

Baumeister, R. F. and Vohs, K. Willpower, choice, and self-control. In Lowenstein, G. Read, D. and Baumeister, R. R., eds, *Time and decision*. New York: Russell Sage Foundation, 2003.

Baumeister, R. F. and Vohs, K. and Bice, D. M. (2007) The strength model of self-control. *Current direction in Psychological Science*. Vo. 16, no. 6, pp. 351-355.

Baumeister, R. F., Gailliot, M., Dewall, C. N., and Oaten, M. (2006) Self-Regulation and personality: How interventions increase regulatory success, and how depletion moderates the effects of traits on behavior. *J. Personality*, 74, 1773-1801.

Baumeister, R. F. and Tierney, J. *Willpower: Rediscovering the Greatest Human Strength*. New York: Penguin. 2011.

Barber, Charles. *Comfortably numb: How psychiatry is medicating a nation*. New York: Pantheon Books, 2008.

Barnett, Ronald. *The idea of higher education*. Buckingham: Society for Research into Higher Education and Open University Press, 1990.

Bazan, A., de Kock, L., Geerardyn, F., van Draege, K., Brakel, A. W., Shevrin, H. (2012) Empirical evidence for Freud's theory of primary process mentation in acute psychosis. *Psychoanalytic Psychology*, 2013, Vol. 30, No. 1, 57-74.

Benatar, David. (2017) Kids? Just say no. *Aeon.com.* Essays/ Having-children – is-not-life-affirming-It's-immoral. 19 October 2017.

Benson, Etienne. Making sense of chords and conversations. *Monitor on Psychology*, July/August 2003, pp. 32-35.

Bernfeld, Siegfried and Feitelberg, Sergei (1931) The principle of entropy and the Death Instinct. *J. of psycho-anal., XII*, 1, pp. 61-81.

Bergen, Benjamin. *Louder than words: The new science of how the mind makes meaning*. New York: Basic Books, 2012.

Berry, T. (2000). *The great work: Our way into the future.* New York: Harmony/Bell Tower.

Bion, Wilfred. *Elements of psychoanalysis*. New York: Jason Aronson, 1979.

------------------*Attention and interpretation*. London: Karnac Books, 1984.

------------------*Learning from experience*. New York: Jason Aronson, 1962/1983.

Bloom, Allan. *The closing of the American mind: How higher education has failed democracy and impoverished the souls of today's students*. New York: Simon and Schuster, 1978.

Boardman, J., Griffin, J. and Murray, O., eds. *The oxford history of the classical world*, Oxford & New York: Oxford University Press, 1986.

Boris, Harold. *Envy*. Northvale, N. J. and London: Jason Aronson, Inc., 1994.

Boswell, J. *Life of Johnson*. London: Macmillan and Co., 1894.

Brenner, Charles. *The mind in conflict*. N. Y.: International Universities Press, 1982.

Bridgeman, Bruce (2017) Population Growth Underlies Most Other Environmental Problems: Comment on Clayton et al. (2016) *American psychologist*, *72*, 4, 386-387.

Brigham, N. L., Kelso, K. A., Jackson, M. A., & Smith, R. H. (1997). The roles of invidious comparisons and deservingness in sympathy and schadenfreude. *Basic and Applied Social Psychology*, 19(3), 363–380.

Broome, E. C. A historical and critical discussion of college entrance requirements. New York: College Entrance Examination Board, 1963 (reprint of original 1902 article).

Brown, David K. *Degrees of control: a sociology of educational expansion and occupational credentialism*. New York: Teachers College Press, 1995.

Brown, Dennis and Zinkin, Louis. (Eds.) *Developments in group-analytic theory*. London: Routledge, 1994.

Brown, Sarah. (2015) Global warming pushes maple trees, syrup to the brink. December, 2, 2015 edition of http://the plate.*nationalgreographic*.com/

Burkle, F. M., Jr. (2019) Character disorders among autocratic world leaders and the impact on health security, human rights, and humanitarian care. *Prehosp Disaster Med.* 2019: 34(1):2–7. Published online by *Cambridge University Press*: 15 January 2019.

Burrell R. W. J. (1963) The possible bearing of curse death and other factors in Bantu culture on the etiology of myocardial infarction, In T. N. James and J. W. Keyes (Eds.) *The Etiology of Myocardial Infarction*. Boston: Little, Brown and Company. 1963, pp. 95-97.

Butler, Shane. *The ancient phonograph*. Brooklyn: Zone Books, 2015.

Cahill, T. *How the Irish saved civilization.* New York: Anchor Books/Doubleday, 1995.

------------------ *Sailing the wine dark sea: why the greeks matter*. New York: Nan A. Talese/Doubleday, 2003.

Cannadine, David. *Victorious century: The United Kingdom, 1800-1906*. London: Allen Lane, 2016.

Cannon, W. B. (1942) "Voodoo death." *American Anthropologist*, 44, 2, 169-181.

Carhart-Harris R. L., Friston K. J. (2010). The default-mode, ego-functions and free-energy: A neurobiological account of Freudian ideas. *Brain* 133, 1265–1283 10.1093/brain/awq010

Carlat, R. *Unhinged: the trouble with psychiatry—a doctor's revelations about a profession in crisis*. New York: Free Press, 2010

Carsky, Monica. (2020) How treatment arrangements enhance transference analysis in transference-focused psychotherapy. *Psychoanalytic Psychology*, 37, 4, pp. 334-343.

Cass, Hilary. (2024) The Cass review, final report: independent review of gender identity services for children and young people, April 2024, at *https://cass.independent-review.uk/wp* content/uploads/2024/04/CassReview

Chapman, John W. The Western University on trial. In *The Western University on Trial*, ed. John W. Chapman. Berkeley: U. of California Press, 1983, pp.1-23.

Chappell, Richard. (2015) Is it ok to have kids? *Aeon.co*/essays/do-people-have-a-moral-duty-to-have-children-if-they-can. 24 December 2015

Cherry, S., Meyer, J. Mann, and Meersand, P. Professional and personal development after psychoanalytic training: Interviews with early career analysts. *J. Am. Psychoanal. Association*, 68, 2, 217-240. DOI: 10.1177/000306512 0921563

Chomsky, N. (1972) *Language and mind*. New York: Harcourt Brace.

Clayton, S., Steg, L., Bonnes, M., Carrico, A., Swim, J. K., Devine-Wright, P. (2017) Psychologists and the problem of population growth: reply to Bridgeman (2017) *American Psychologist, 72*, 4, 388-389.

Cohen-Charash, Y., & Mueller, J. S. (2007). Does perceived unfairness exacerbate or mitigate interpersonal counterproductive work behaviors related to envy? *Journal of Applied Psychology*, 92, 666–680.

Cribiore, R. *Gymnastics of the mind: greek education in hellenistic and roman egypt*. Princeton, NJ: Princeton University Press, 2005.

Crisp, P. A., Ganguly, D., Eichten, S. R., Borevits, J. O., and Pogson, B. J. (2016) Reconsidering plant memory: Intersections between stress recovery, RNA turnovers, and epigenetics. *Science Advances*. 19Feb2016: Vol. 2, no.2, e1501340. DOI:10.1126/sciadv.1501340.

Crabtree. Gerald. (2013) Our fragile intellect. *Trends in Genetics, Vol. 29*, 1. Part I, pp. 1-3; Part II, pp. 3-5.

Crawford, C. (1998) Environments and adaptations: Then and now. In C. Crawford and D. L. Krebs, (eds.) *Handbook of Evolutionary Psychology: Ideas, Issues and applications*. Mahwah, NJ: Lawrence Erlbaum Associates, pp, 275-302.

Cross, Gary. *Men to boys: the making of modern immaturity.* New York: Columbia University Press, 2010.

Crusius, Jan, Manuel F. Gonzalez, Jens Lange, Yochi Cohen-Charash, Envy: An adversarial review and comparison of two competing views, *Emotion review,* 10.1177/1754073919873131, 12, 1, (3-21), (2019).

Daniels, Marvin. (1964-64) The dynamics of morbid envy in the etiology and treatment of chronic learning disability. *Psychoanal. Rev.*, 51D (4):45-56.

Darwin, Charles. *The descent of man and selection in relation to sex.* Princeton: Princeton University Press, 1981. (Facsimile of [London: John Murray, 1871.])

de Maat, S., de Jonghe, F., Schoevers, R. and Dekker, J. (2009). The effectiveness of long-term psychoanalytic therapy: A systematic review of empirical studies. *Harvard Review of Psychiatry*, 17 (1): 1-23. Doi: 10.1080/10673220902742476. National Center for Biotechnology Information

de Mare, Patrick, Piper, Robin, and Thompson, Sheila. *Koinonia: From hate, through dialogue, to culture in the large group*. London: Karnac, 1991

den Nieuwenboer, Niki A. and Jennifer J. Kish-Gephart, Linda K. Treviño, Ann C. Peng, Iris Reychav. (2022) The dark side of status at work: perceived status importance, envy, and interpersonal deviance. *Business Ethics Quarterly,* 10.1017/beq.2022.2, (1-35).

Disalvo, D. *Our tricky brains*. New York: Prometheus Books, 2011.

DeAngelis, T. (2009) Unmasking 'racial microaggressions.' *Monitor on Psychology, Vol. 40,* No.2, 42-46.]

Dornes, M. and von Lupke, H. (1995) Psychodynamische aspekte des plötzlichen kindstodes. (Psychodynamic aspect of sudden infant death) *Kinderanalyse,* Heft 4, Dezember, 1995, pp. 315-332.

Duffy, M. K., & Shaw, J. D. (2000). The Salieri syndrome: Consequences of envy in groups. *Small Group Research*, 31(1), 3–23.

Dunbar, Robin. (1991) Functional significance of social grooming in primates. *Folia Primatologica,* 51, pp. 121-131.

------------------*Grooming, Gossip and the evolution of Language*. Cambridge, MA: Harvard University Press, 1996.

Dunn, J., & Schweitzer, M. (2006). Green and mean: Unfavorable comparisons, envy and social undermining in organizations. In A. Tenbrunsel (ed.), *Ethics in groups: Research on managing groups and teams* (Vol. 8, pp. 177–197). Oxford: Elsevier JAI.

Edelman, Gerald M. *The Remembered Present: A Biological Theory of Consciousness*. New York: Basic Books, 1989.

Edelman, Gerald M. *Bright Air, Brilliant Fire: On the Matter of the mind*. New York: Basic Books, 1992.

Elias, Norbert. *The Germans*. Trans. E. Dunning and Stephen Mennell. New York: Columbia U. Press, 1996.

Ellwood, Chas. (1910) Has crime increased in the United States since 1880? Journal of Criminal Law and Criminology, Vol. I, 3,3.

Engell, J. and A. Dangerfield. (1998) The market-model university: Humanities in the Age of Money. *Harvard Magazine*, May-June, pp.48-55.

English, H. B. and English, A. C. *A Comprehensive Dictionary of Psychological and Psychoanalytical Terms: A Guide to Usage*. New York: Longmans, Green and Co., 1958.

Entralgo, P. L. 1970. *The Therapy of the Word in Classical Antiquity*. New Haven: Yale University Press.

Erwin, Douglas H. Extinction: *How life on Earth Nearly Ended 250 Million Years Ago*. Princeton, N. J.: Princeton University Press. 2006.

Evans, Gary W. and Stecker, Rachel. (2004) Motivational consequences of environmental stress. *Journal of Environmental Psychology, Vol. 24*, Issue 2, pp. 143-165.

Etkin, A., Pittenger, C., Polan, H. J., Kandel, E. R. (2005) Toward a neurobiology of psychotherapy: Basic science and clinical applications. *Journal of Neuropsychiatry and Clinical Neurosciences* 17(2), 145-158.

Farber, Leslie. (1961) Faces of Envy. *Review of existential psychology and psychiatry*, Vol. I, pp. 131-139.

Feather, N. T. (1989). Attitudes towards the high achiever: The fall of the tall poppy. *Australian Journal of Psychology*, 41(3), 239–267.

Feather, N. T., & Sherman, R. (2002). Envy, resentment, schadenfreude, and sympathy: Reactions to deserved and undeserved achievement and subsequent failure. *Personality and Social Psychology Bulletin*, 28(7), 953–961.

Fenichel, Otto. *The psychoanalytic theory of neurosis*. New York: W. W. Norton, 1945.

Finley, Barbara. (2015) It hurts to be human: why pain is fundamentally different for us. *New Scientist. The Big Idea.* May 6, 2015.

Firor, John and Jacobsen, Judith. *The crowded green house: population, climate change, and creating a sustainable world.* New Haven: Yale University Press, 2002.

This article exemplifies the general unwillingness, into the early 21st century, to acknowledge the population disaster: These authors, in 2002, assure us that the world will grow, sustainably, to 8 billion. They wrote: "...population and environmental deterioration are *not* a car speeding toward a brick wall." [p. 208] (emphasis theirs) They advised, "... get back to work, with joy" [p. 213].

Since their publication, scientists have concluded that Earth can only sustain 2 billion people. In July, 2025 we are over 8.2 billion.

Foster, G. (1972). The anatomy of envy. *Current Anthropology*, 13, 165–202.

Foulkes, S. H. *Introduction to Group-Analytic Psychotherapy*. London: Karnac, 1948/1983.

Freeman, J. *Gifted Lives: What happens when gifted children grow up*. London: Routledge, 2010.

Fritsch, Richard and Winer, Robert (2020) Combined training of candidates, scholars, and psychotherapists: A model of psychoanalytic education for the twenty-first century. *J. Am. Psychoanal. Association*, 68, 2, 175-200. DOI: 10.1177/0003065120922846

Freud, Anna. The Writings of Anna Freud in 8 volumes. New York: International Universities Press, Inc., 1966.

------------------The Ego and the Mechanisms of Defense. New York: International Universities Press, Inc. 1966. (First published in German in 1936)

Freud, S. *The Standard Edition of the Complete Psychological Works of Sigmund Freud.* (*S. E.*) Trans. James Strachey. London: Hogarth Press, 1953.

------------------ (1905) Fragment of an analysis of a case of hysteria. *S. E, Vol. 7.*

------------------ (1911) Two fundamental principles of mental functioning. *S. E.* 12.

------------------ (1916) Some character types met with in psycho-analysis. *S. E.* 14

Gailliot, M. T., Baumeister, R. F., Dewall, C. N., Maner, J. K., Plant, E. A., Tice, D. M., Brewer Le E., & Schmeichel, B. J. (2007) Self-control relies on glucose as a limited energy source: Willpower is more than a metaphor. *Journal of Personality and Social Psychology*, 92, 325-336.

Gardner, H. (1973) *The Quest for Mind: Piaget, Levi-Strauss, and the Structuralist Movement.* New York: Knopf.

Garrett. N., Lassaro, S. C., Ariely, D., Sharot, T. The brain adapts to dishonesty. *Nature Neuroscience*, 2016; DOI : 10.1038/nn.4426.

Garvin, David A. *The Economics of University Behavior.* New York: Academic Press, 1980.

Geiger, Roger L. *The History of American Higher Education: Learning and Culture from the Founding to World War II.* Princeton and Oxford: Princeton University Press, 2015.

Glass, R. M. (2008) Psychodynamic psychotherapy and research evidence: Bambi survives Godzilla? *Journal of the American Medical association*, 300(13), 1587-1589.

Gleeson, T., Befus, K. M., Jascechko, S., Lsijendijk, E., Cardenas, M. B. The global volume and distribution of modern groundwater. *Nature Geoscience*, November 16, 2015.

Goldhill, Simon. *Love, Sex and Tragedy: How the Ancient World Shapes Our Lives.* Chicago: University of Chicago Press, 2004.

Goffman, Erving. *Behavior in Public Places: Notes on the Social Organization of Gatherings.* New York: Free Press, 1963.

Gorer, G. (1958) Freud's influence. *The Encounter*, November, 1958

Gorokhovskaia, Yana and Grothe, Cathryn. (2024) "Freedom in the World 2024: The Mounting Damage of Flawed Elections and Armed Conflict." *Freedom House*

Graeber, D. and Wengrow, D., *The Dawn of Everything: A New History of Humanity*. London: Allen Lane, 2021.

Green, S., Lambon, R., Moll, J., Deakin, J. W., Zahn, R. Guilt-selective disconnection of anterior temporal and subgenual cortices in major depressive disorder. *Archives of General Psychiatry* online 4 June 2012/ *Archives of General Psychiatry*, 2012, 135.

Gruen, A. *Der frühe Abschied: Eine Deutung des Plötzlichen Kinstodes* (*The Early Farewell*: *An interpretation of the Sudden Infant Death.*) Munchen: Deutscher Taschenbuch Verlag, 1988/1993.

------------------(1987) The relationship of Sudden Infant Death and parental unconscious Conflicts. *Pre- and Peri-natal Psychology*, 2(1), Fall, 1987.

Gupta, Tanvi and Preeti Krishnan Lyndem, Dual envy influences online shoppers' intention to purchase luxury counterfeits. *International Journal of Consumer Studies,* 10.1111/ijcs.13036, 48, 2, (2024).

Hale, Nathan G. Freud and the Americans: *The Origin and Foundation of the Psychoanalytic Movement in America, 1876-1918.* Oxford: Oxford University Press. 1971.

............*The Rise and Crisis of Psychoanalysis in the United States: Freud and the Americans, 1917-1985*. Oxford: Oxford University Press, 1995.

Hanson, Victor Davis and Heath, John. *Who Killed Homer: The Demise of Classical Education and the Recovery of Greek Wisdom*. San Francisco: Encounter Books, 2001.

Hanson, Victor Davis; Heath, John; and Thornton, Bruce S. *Bonfire of the Humanities: Rescuing the Classics in an Impoverished Age*. 2001.

Harris, Malcolm. *Kids these days*: *human capital and the making of millennials.* New York: Little, Brown, 2017.

Harrison, Mark and Wolf, Nikolaus. (2011) The frequency of wars. *Economic History Review.*

Hartmann, Heinz (1959) Psychoanalysis as a scientific theory. In *Essays on Ego Psychology: Selected Problems in Psychoanalytic theory.* New York: International Universities Press, 1964, pp. 318-350.

Haskins, Charles Homer. *The Rise of Universities*. Ithaca, N. Y.: Great Seal Books, 1957 (first published 1923)

Hay, Denis. *The Italian Renaissance in its Historical Background.* Cambridge University Press, 1976.

Hedges, Chris. *Empire of Illusion: The End of Literacy and the Triumph of Spectacle Paperback.* New York: Nation Books, 2010.

He, Jiali and Hanshu Liu. (2024) How does interpersonal curiosity impact peer rejection? The mediating effect of relative deprivation and malicious envy. *Frontiers in Developmental Psychology*, 10.3389/fdpys.2024.1375009, **2**.

Heider, Fritz. *The Psychology of Interpersonal Relations*. New York: John Wiley and Sons, 1958.

Heller, Nathan. (2016) The big uneasy: What's roiling the liberal-arts campus? *The New Yorker*, May 30, 2016, pp. 48-57.

Helmore, Edward. (2021) "Yep, it's bleak, says expert." *Guardian*, July 25, 2021.

Hinshelwood, R. D. *A Dictionary of Kleinian Thought*. (2nd edition) Northvale, N. J.: Jason Aronson, 1991.

Hoyt, M. F. (1979). An experimental study of the thematic structure of primal-scene imagery. *Journal of Abnormal Psychology, 88*(1), 96–100. https://doi.org/10.1037/0021-843X.88.1.96

Hofstadter, Richard. *Anti-intellectualism in American Life*. New York: Knopf.

Humphrey, N. (1976) The social function of intellect. In P. P. G. Bateson and R. A. Hinde (eds.), *Growing Pains in Ethology*. Cambridge: Cambridge University Press, pp. 303-317.

Hussain, Azhar; Ali, Syed; Ahmed, Madiha and Hussain, Sheharyar. The anti-vaccination movement: A regression in modern medicine. Cureus. 2018 July; 10(7): e2919. Doi:10.7759/cureus.2919

Hutchinson, Sharla and Brown, Rebecca (Eds.), *Monsters and monstrosities from the fin de siecle to the millennium*, Jefferson, N. C: McFarland, 2014.

Iqra, Muhammad Ali, Amber Baseer, Mahnoor Ali. (2024) Schadenfreude in working women of lahore: a phenomenological study. *Journal of Professional & Applied Psychology,* 10.52053/jpap.v5i2.278, **5**, 2, (342-360).

Jacobs, Jane. *Dark age ahead.* New York: Random House, 2004.

Jaques, Eliot. (1955) Social systems as a defense against persecutory and depressive anxiety. In *New Directions in Psycho-analysis*, ed. Klein et al. London: Tavistock.

Jaeger, W. *Paideia: The ideals of Greek culture.* (Trans. G. Highet) New York: Oxford U. Press, 1945.

James, William. *Principles of psychology*. New York: Henry Holt & Co., 1890.

Johnson, Samuel. *The yale edition of the works of samuel johnson.* (various eds.) New Haven and London: Yale University Press, 1958—.

Judt, Tony. *Ill fares the land.* New York: Penguin Press, 2010.

Jung, C. G. *The undiscovered self.* Boston: Little, Brown and Co., 1957

Kaada, B. (1987) SIDS induced by "the fear paralysis reflex." *Med. Hypotheses*, 22:347-356.

Kahn, R. (2012) Classicists are smart! *Discover magazine* website, January 2012. http://blogs.discovermagazine.com/gnxp/2012/01/classicists-are-smart/

Kandel E. R. (1998). A new intellectual framework for psychiatry. *Am. J. Psychiatry* 155, 457–469.

Kandel, Eric R. (1999) Biology and the future of psychoanalysis: A new intellectual framework for psychiatry revisited. *American Journal of Psychiatry, 156*: 4, p. 505.

Kapp, Reginald O. (1931) Comments on Bernfeld and Feitelberg's "The principle of entropy and the death instinct." *International Journal of Psycho-analysis, XII*, I, pp. 81-86.

Kateb, G. *Human dignity.* Cambridge: Belknap Press, an imprint of Harvard University Press, 2014.

Kern, Stephen. *Culture of time and space, 1880-1918.* Massachusetts and London: Harvard University Press, 1983.

Kernin, Alvin. *What's happened to the humanities?* Princeton, N. J.: Princeton University Press, 1997.

Klein, Melanie. *The writings of Melanie Klein.* New York: The Free Press, 1975.

Klein, M., Heimann., P. and Money-Kyrle, R. E. *New Directions in psycho-analysis: the significance of infant conflict in the pattern of adult behavior.* New York: Basic Books, Inc.

Knight, R. Unpublished lectures to nonpsychiatrist physicians: *Postgraduate Course in Psychiatry for Physicians,* Menninger Clinic, 1935

Knoll, James L., Stephen G. White, J. Reid Meloy, Envy and extreme violence, *International Journal of Applied Psychoanalytic Studies,* 10.1002/aps.1744, **19**, 4, (462-482), (2022).

Kopff, E. Christian. *The devil knows Latin: why America needs the classical tradition.* Wilmington, Delaware: ISI Books, 2001.

Koch, Alexander; Brierly, Chris; Maslim, Mark and Lewis, Simon. (2019) Earth system impacts of the european arrival and great dying in the Americas after 1492. *Quaternary Science Reviews,* Vol. 207, 1 March 2019, Pages 13-36.

Kramer, Thomas, Ozge Yucel-Aybat, Loraine Lau-Gesk, The effect of schadenfreude on choice of conventional versus unconventional options, *Organizational Behavior and Human Decision Processes,* 10.1016/j.obhdp.2010.11.010, 116, 1, (140-147), (2011).

Kristeva, Julia. *Melanie Klein.* New York: Columbia University Press, 2001.

LaFleur, Richard A. (1993) Foreign languages, the classics and college admissions. *ADFL Bulletin,* 24 (Spring) pp. 29-35.

----------------- (1997) Latina resurgens: Classical language enrollments in American schools and colleges. *The Classical Outlook,* (Summer) pp. 125-130.

----------------- (2000) Latin and Greek in American schools and colleges: An enrollment update. *The Classical Outlook,* 77, 3, (Spring) pp. 101-103.

Lane, M. *Eco-republic: ancient thinking for a green age.* Princeton, N. J.: Princeton University Press, 2011.

Lange, Jens and Jan Crusius, Dispositional Envy Revisited, *Personality and social psychology bulletin,* 10.1177/0146167214564959, 41, 2, (284-294), (2014).

Lange, Jens and Sara Protasi, An Interdisciplinary perspective on the value of envy, *Review of Philosophy and Psychology*, 10.1007/s13164-021-00548-3, **15**, 2, (403-422), (2021).

Lange, Jens, Delroy L. Paulhus, Jan Crusius, Elucidating the dark side of envy: distinctive links of benign and malicious envy with dark personalities, *Personality and Social Psychology Bulletin*, 10.1177/0146167217746340, **44**, 4, (601-614), (2017).

Langer, Susan. *Philosophy in a New Key*. Cambridge, MA: Harvard University Press, 1951; first published, 1942.

Laplanche, J. and Pontalis, J. B. *The Language of Psycho-analysis* (Trans. Donald Nicholson-Smith) New York: W. W. Norton and Co. 1973.

Leach, E. *Claude Levi-Strauss*. New York: Viking, (1970)

Lee, KiYoung and Michelle K. Duffy. A Functional Model of Workplace Envy and Job Performance: When do Employees Capitalize on Envy by Learning from Envied Targets? *Academy of Management Journal*, 10.5465/amj.2016.1202, **62**, 4, (1085-1110), (2019).

Leffert, Mark. (2011) The psychoanalysis and death of George Gershwin: An American Tragedy. *Journal of the American Academy of psychoanalysis and Dynamic Psychiatry, 39(3)*, 421-452.

Leischsenring, F. and Rabung, S. (2008) Effectiveness of long-term psychodynamic psychotherapy: A meta-analysis. *Journal of the American Medical Association*, 300(13), 1551-1565.

Leischsenring, F. (2009) Applications of Psychodynamic psychotherapy to Specific disorders: Efficacy and indications. In G. O. Gabbard (Ed.) *Textbook of Psychotherapeutic Treatment* (pp. 97-132)

Lejarraga, Tomas; Frey, Renato; Schnitlein and Hertwig, Ralph. No effect of birth order on adult risk taking. *Proceeding of the National Academy of Sciences*, March 11, 2019 https//doi.org/10.1073/pnas.1814153116, formed the same conclusion.

Levi-Strauss, C. (1966) *The Savage mind.* Chicago: University of Chicago Press.

----------------- (1973) *From honey to ash.* New York: Harper and Row.

Levy, R. A. and Ablon, J. S. (Eds.) *Handbook of evidence-based psychodynamic psychotherapy: bridging the gap between science and practice*. New York: Humana Press, 2009.

Lewis, Lionel S., and Altbach, Philip G. (1996) Faculty versus administration: A universal problem. *Higher Education Policy*, 9:255-258.

Lothane, H. Z. (1981) Review of F. Solloway's *Freud: biologist of the mind: beyond the psychoanalytic legend. psychoanalytic review* 68:348-361.

-----------------*In Defense of schreber: soul murder and psychiatry*. Hillsdale, NJ: Analytic Press, 1992.

----------------- (1994) Review of M. Macmillan's Freud evaluated: The Completed arc. *Journal of the American Academy of Psychoanalysis* 22:560-562.

----------------- (1996) In defense of Sabina Spielrein. *International forum of psychoanalysis* 5:203-217.

----------------- (1997) Review of J. Farrell's Freud's paranoid quest. *Journal of the American Psychoanalytic Association* 45:1319-1323.

----------------- (2001a) Freud's alleged repudiation of the seduction theory revisited: Facts and fallacies. *Psychoanalytic Review* 88:673-723.

----------------- (2001b) A response to Grunbaum's "A century of psychoanalysis: Critical retrospect and prospect (and other texts): Requiem or reveille?" *International Forum of psychoanalys*is 10:113-132.

----------------- (2006) Freud's legacy—is it still with us? *Psychoanalytic Psychology* 23:285-301.

-----------------The Sigmund Freud/Minna Bernays romance: Fact or fiction. *The American Imago*, 64: 129-133.

----------------- (2007) Response to Professor Adolf Grunbaum. *Psychoanalytic Psychology,* 24(3):577-585.

----------------- (2009) Dramatology in life, disorder, and psychoanalytic therapy. A further contribution to interpersonal psychoanalysis. *International Forum of Psychoanalysis* 18:135-148.

----------------- (2010) The analysand and analyst team practicing reciprocal free association: Defenders and deniers. *International Forum of Psychoanalysis* 19:55-164.

----------------- (2016) Freud and Minna: Facts and fictions. *Journal of the American Psychoanalytic Association* 64:1137-1154.

----------------- (2017) Freud's friends and foes: Bashers versus critics. *Swiss Archives of Neurology, Psychiatry and Psychotherapy* 168(4): 115-120.

----------------- (2018a) Free association as the foundation of the psychoanalytic method and psychoanalysis as a historical science. *Psychoanalytic Inquiry* 38:416-434.

-----------------(2018b) History. In *Textbook of Applied Psychoanalysis*, ed. S. Akhtar and S. W. Twemlow. London: Routledge, pp.13-26, 417-419.

Lyons, J. (1970) *Noam Chomsky*. New York: Viking.

Macaulay, Thomas Babington. "An essay on Francis Bacon" in *Lord Macaulay's Essays*. London: Longmans, Green and Co., 1895.

Mackay, Charles. *Extraordinary popular delusions and the madness of crowds*. New York: Metro Books, 2002. Originally publ. London: Richard Bentley, 1841.

Mackinnon, Catherine. Sexuality, pornography and method: "pleasure under patriarchy." (1989) *Ethics*, Vol. 99, No. 2, pp. 314-346.

Makari, George. (2011) He's back: Freddy Crews claws Freud. *Psychology Today*, Oct. 12.

Malcolm, Janet. *In the Freud archives*. New York: Vintage Books. 1985.

Marmot, Michael. *The health gap: the challenge of an unequal world*. London: Bloomsbury, 2015.

Masson, Jeffrey. *Assault on truth: freud's suppression of the seduction theory*. New York: Farrar, Strauss and Giroux, 1984.

-----------------*Final analysis: the making and unmaking of a psychoanalyst*. Reading, Mass.: Addison-Wesley Publishing Company, 1990.

-----------------*My father's guru: a journey through spirituality and disillusion*. Reading, Mass.: Addison-Wesley, 1993.

Mathis, J. L. (1964) A sophisticated version of voodoo death: Report of a case. *Psychosomatic Medicine*, 26, 104-107.

Meissner, W.W. *Psychotherapy and the paranoid process*. Northvale, N. J.: Jason Aronson, 1986.

Menand, L. The critics: why we have college. *The New Yorker*, June 6, 2011

Milgram, Stanley. *The individual in a social world: essays and experiments.* (3rd expanded Edition) London: Pinter & Martin, 2010, p. 12.

Miller, A. (2012) Children today are more imaginative than in the 1980's, study suggests. *Monitor on Psychology*, Sept. 2012, p. 12.

Mishra, Pankaj. Age of anger, a history of the present. New York: Farrar, Straus and Giroux, 2017.

Mokyr, Joel. *The lever of riches: technological creativity and economic progress.* Oxford U. Press, 1990.

Moore, B.E. and Fine, B.D. (eds.) *A Glossary of Psychoanalytic terms and Concepts*. New York: American Psychoanalytic Association, Inc., 1968.

Moore, Christopher. (2015) Self-knowledge in xenophon's *memorabilia. The Classical Journal*, 110, 4, pp. 397-417.

-----------------*Socrates and self-knowledge*. Cambridge, U. K.: Cambridge University Press, 2016.

Moran, Simone and Maurice E. Schweitzer. (2008) When better is worse: envy and the use of deception. *Negotiation and Conflict Management Research, Vol. 1,* 1, pp. 3-29.

Mouly, V. S., & Sankaran, J. K. (2002). The enactment of envy within organizations: Insights from a New Zealand academic department. *Journal of Applied Behavioral Sciences*, 38(1), 36–56.

Moyal, Adiel, Marina Motsenok, Ilana Ritov, Arbitrary social comparison, malicious envy, and generosity, *Journal of Behavioral Decision Making*, 10.1002/bdm.2172, 33, 4, (444-462), (2020).

Moyn, Samuel. (2016) A whole climate. *The Nation*, November 21, 2016.

Muraven, M., Baumeister, R. F., & Tice, D. M. (1999) Longitudinal improvement of self-regulation through practice: Building self-control strength through repeated exercise. *Journal of Social psychology*, 139, 446-457.

Nicholson, Adam. *Why Homer matters*. New York: Henry Holt and Co., 2014.

Nitsun, Morris. *The anti-group: destructive forces in the group and their creative potential.* London: Routledge, 1996.

Norris, Mary. *Greek to me: adventures of the comma queen.* New York: W. W. Norton, 2019.

Oaten, M. and Chen, K. Longitudinal gains in self-regulation from regular physical exercise. *British Journal of Health Psychology*, 11, pp. 717-733.

Osborn, Fairfield. *Our plundered planet.* Boston: Little, Brown and Co., 1948.

Parks, C. D., Rumble, A. C., & Posey, D. C. (2002). Effects of envy on reciprocation in a social dilemma. *Personality and Social Psychology Bulletin,* **28**(4), 509–520.

Parrott, W. G., & Smith, R. H. (1993). Distinguishing the experiences of envy and jealousy. *Journal of Personality and Social Psychology*, **64**(6), 906–920.

Pascarella, E. T. and Terenzini, P. T. *How college affects students: a 3rd decade of research.* San Francisco: Josey-Bass (Wiley), 2005.

Penrose, L. S. (1931) Freud's theory of instinct and other psycho-biological theories. *International Journal of Psycho-analysis*, XII, 1, pp. 87-97.

Petot, Jean-Michel. (1990) [1979] *Melanie Klein: Vol. I. First discoveries and first system, 1919-1932*. Trans. Christine Trollope. Madison, Conn., International Universities Press.

------------------ (1991) [1982] *Melanie Klein: Vol. II. The ego and the good object, 1932-1960.* Trans. Christine Trollope. Madison, Conn., International Universities Press.

Piaget, J. (1973) *The child and reality: problems of genetic psychology*. New York: Grossman.

Piers, M., ed. (1972) Some aspects of operations. In *Play and Development: A Symposium*, pp. 15-27. New York: Norton.

Pilling, David. *The growth delusion.* London: Bloomsbury, 2017.

Pinker, Stephen. *Better angels of our nature*: *Why Violence Has Declined.* New York: Viking, 2011.

------------------*Enlightenment now: the case for reason, science humanism and progress*. London: Allen Lane, 2018.

Polman, Evan and Rachel L. Ruttan. Effects of anger, guilt, and envy on moral hypocrisy, *Personality and Social Psychology Bulletin*, 10.1177/014616721142 2365, **38**, 1, (129-139), (2011).

Popper, Karl. (1959) *The logic of scientific discovery*. London: Hutchinson. English translation of *Logik der Forschung*, Vienna: Springer (1935)

Post, Jerrold M. *Narcissism and politics: dreams of glory*. New York: Cambridge University Press, 2015.

Postman, Neil. *Building a bridge to the 18th century*. New York: Vintage Books, 2000.

------------------*The end of education*. New York: Alfred A. Knopf, 1995.

Pridmore, J. *Northwestern university: celebrating 150 years*. Evanston, Ill.: Northwestern University Press, 2001.

Princeton Review (2018) (on medical school candidacy) Princeton Review.com.

Protasi, Sara. *The philosophy of envy*. Cambridge University Press, 2021.

Przybylski, A. K. and Weinstein, N. (2012) Can you connect with me now? How the presence of mobile communication technology influences face-to-face conversation quality. *Journal of Social and Personal Relationships*. Sagepub.co.uk/journalsPermissions.nav DOI:10.1177/0265407512453827

Real, Daisy del and Menjivar, Cecilia. (2024) The tools of autocracy worldwide: authoritarian networks, the façade of democracy, and neo-repression. *American Behavioral Scientist, Vol. 68*, 12. https://doi.org/ 10.1177/00027642241267926

Rees, E. William. (2023) The human eco-predicament: overshoot and the population conundrum. *Vienna Yearbook of Population Research*: Vol. 21, December, pp. 1-19.

Reisman, David. *The lonely crowd*. New Haven, Conn.: Yale University Press, 1950.

Ren, Menghao and Shengqi Zou, Siying Zhu, Mengjie Shi, Weiwei Li, Daoqun Ding, The effects of scarcity mindset on envy: The mediating role of the sense of control, *Current Psychology*, 10.1007/s12144-023-04872-y, **43**, 8, (7612-7627), (2023).

Rengifo, Manuel and Simon M. Laham, Careful what you wish for: The primary role of malicious envy in predicting moral disengagement, *Motivation and Emotion,* 10.1007/s11031-022-09973-y, **46**, 5, (674-688), (2022).

Richard, Carl. *The founders and the Classics: Greece, Rome and the American enlightenment*. Cambridge, Mass.: Harvard Universety Press.

Richards, A. A. Abraham Arden Brill, 1874-1948. *American journal of psychiatry*, 163:3, March, 2006.

Rohrer, Julia M.; Egloff, Boris; Schmukle, Stefan C.; (2015-11-17) Examining the effects of birth order on personality. *Proceeding of the National Academy of Sciences*, 112 (46):14224-14229doi:10.1073/pnas.1506451112.

Roszak, T. *The cult of information: The folklore of computers and the true art of thinking*. New York: Pantheon Books, 1986.

Rotella, A., Varnum, M. E. W., Sng, O., & Grossmann, I. (2021). Increasing population densities predict decreasing fertility rates over time: A 174-nation investigation. *American Psychologist, 76*(6), 933 946. https://doi.org/10.1037/amp0000862

Roudinesco, Elisabeth. *In his time and ours* (Transl. Catherine Porter). Cambridge: Harvard University Press, 2016.

Safit, Ilan. (2013) The ethics of survival: responsibility and sacrifice in environmental ethics. *Phenomenology & Practice*, Volume 7, No. 2, pp. 78-99.

Sahlins, Marshall. *Stone age economics*. London: Tavistock, 1972.

Salovey, P., & Rodin, J. (1984). Some antecedents and consequences of social-comparison jealousy. *Journal of Personality and Social Psychology, 47*(4), 780–792. https://doi.org/10.1037/0022-3514.47.4.780

Saul, L. J. (1958) Freud's death instinct and the second law of thermodynamics. *Int. J. Psycho-anal*. 39:323-25.

Sax, Leonard. (2002) How common is intersex? A response to Anne Fausto-Sterling. *J. of Sexual Research*, Aug; 39(3): 174-8. doi: 10.1080/00224490209552139.

Schaubroeck, John and Simon S.K Lam. (2004) Comparing lots before and after: Promotion rejectees' invidious reactions to promotees. *Organizational Behavior and Human Decision Processes. Vol. 94*, 1, May, 2004, pp. 33-47.

Schlaug, G. and Winner, E. (2008) …. (Online journal) *PLos ONE*, Oct. 29, 2008.

Schneider, E. D. and Sagan, D. *Into the Cool: Energy Flow, Thermodynamics and Life*. Chicago: U. of Chicago Press, 2005.

Schoeck, Helmut. *Envy: A Theory of social behaviour*. Indianapolis: Liberty Fund, 1987. (Originally published in German, 1966.) Trans. Martin Secker.

Schwartz, Katarina; Allain, Jean; and Nicholson, Andrea. Slavery is not a crime in almost half the countries of the world—new research. *The Conversation*, 2/13, 2020.

Segal, Hanna, *The work of hanna segal: a kleinian approach to clinical practice*. New York: Jason Aronson, 1981.

Siegel, Daniel J., *Mindsight: The new science of personal transformation*. New York: Bantam Books, 2010.

Selye, Hans. *The stress of life*. New York: McGraw-Hill, 1956.

Shedler, J. (2010) The efficacy of psychodynamic psychotherapy. *American Psychologist*, 65(2): pp. 98-109.

Shevrin, H. (2012) Links between unconscious conflicts and conscious anxiety disorder symptoms. 101st *Annual Meeting of the American Psychoanalytic Association*. June 16, 2012. Reported in *Science Daily*, 6 June 2012.

Shevrin H, Snodgrass M, Brakel LA, Kushwaha R, Kalaida NL, et al. (2013). Subliminal unconscious conflict alpha power inhibits supraliminal conscious symptom experience. *Front Hum Neurosci* 7:544.

Siedentop, Larry. *Inventing the individual: The origins of western liberalism*. London: Allen Lane, 2014. (also Cambridge, MA: Belknap Press of Harvard University Press, 2014)

Simmons, Tracy Lee. *Climbing parnassus: A new apologia for Greek and Latin*. Wilmington, Delaware: ISI Books, 2002.

Sinha, Sahab and Sinha, Surat. (1991) Volume personal space and density as factors in task performance and feeling of crowding. *Journal of Social Psychology, 131, 6.*

Slade, Giles. *The big disconnect: The story of technology and loneliness*. Amherst, N. Y.: Prometheus Books, 2012.

Smallets, Stephanie, Lindsey Streamer, Cheryl L. Kondrak, Mark D. Seery, Bringing you down versus bringing me up: Discrepant versus congruent high explicit self-esteem differentially predict malicious and benign envy, *Personality and Individual Differences*, 10.1016/j.paid.2016.01.007, **94**, (173-179), (2016). (incongruence exacerbates malicious envy)

Smith, David. (2002) The evolution of the unconscious. *Psychoanalytic Perspectives*, 20, 4: 525-548.

Smith, R. H. (1991). Envy and the sense of injustice. In P. Salovey (ed.), *Psychological perspectives on jealousy and envy* (pp. 79–99). New York: Guilford.

Smith, R. H. (2004). Envy and its transmutations. In L. Z. Tiedens & C. W. Leach (eds.), *The social life of emotions* (pp. 43–63). Cambridge, U.K: Cambridge University Press.

Smith, R. H., Parrott, W. G., Diener, E. F., Hoyle, R. H., & Kim, S. H. (1999). Dispositional envy. *Personality and Social Psychology Bulletin*, 25(8), 1007–1020.

Smith, R. H., Parrott, W. G., Ozer, D., & Moniz, A. (1994). Subjective injustice and inferiority as predictors of hostile and depressive feelings in envy. *Personality and Social Psychology Bulletin*, 20(6), 705–711

Smith, R. H., Turner, T. J., Garoznik, R., Leach, C. W., Urch-Druskat, V., & Weston, C. M. (1996). Envy and schadenfreude. *Personality and Social Psychology Bulletin*, 22(2), 158–168.

Soga, Mashima and Gaston, Kevin J. (2018) Shifting baseline syndrome: Causes, consequences, and implications. *Frontiers in Ecology and the Environment, Vol. 16*, 4, pp. 222-230.

Solomon, Irving. *A primer of Kleinian therapy*. Northvale, N. J.: Jason Aronson, Inc., 1995.

Spengler, Oswald. *The decline of the West* (two vols.). New York: Alfred Knopf, 1926/28 (originally published in German 1918/22)

Spillius, Elizabeth B., Milton, J., Garvey, P. Couve, Cyril and Steiner, D. *The new dictionary of Kleinian thought*. London: Routledge, 2011.

Spitz, Rene. (1945) Hospitalism: An inquiry into the genesis of psychiatric conditions in early childhood. *The Psychoanalytic Study of the Child*, I.

-----------------(1946) Hospitalism: A follow-up report. *The Psychoanalytic Study of the Child*, 2.

Stacey, Ralph. *Complexity and group processes: A radically social understanding of individuals*. New York: Brunner-Routledge.

Stork, J. (1989) The phenomenon of "cot death" from a psychological point of view. *Int. J. Prenatal and Perinatal Studies*, pp. 287-294.

-----------------(1994) Zwischen Leben und Tod—Aus der Behandlung eines Säuglings—ein Beitrag zum plötzlichen Kindstod (Between life and death—the treatment of a child--A contribution to Sudden Infant Death). *Kinderanalyse*, Jan., 1994, pp. 60-94.

Stray, Christopher. *Schools, universities and society in England, 1830-1960.* London: Clarendon Press, 1998.

Sue, D. W. et al. (2007) Racial microaggressions in everyday life: Implications for clinical practice. *American Psychologist, Vol. 2*, No. 4: 271-286. See also DeAngelis (2009) above.

Sullivan, Harry S. (1956) Envy and jealousy as precipitating factors in the major mental disorders. In H. S. Perry et al (Eds.) *Clinical Studies in Psychiatry*. New York: W. W. Norton, pp.128-144.

Sulloway, F. *Freud: Biologist of the mind.* New York: Basic Books, 1979.

-----------------*Born to rebel: Birth order, family dynamics, and creative lives. New York: Vintage, 1997.*

Tai, Kenneth, Jayanth Narayanan, Daniel J. McAllister, Envy as pain: Rethinking the nature of envy and its implications for employees and organizations, *Academy of Management Review*, 10.5465/amr.2009.0484, **37**, 1, (107-129), (2012).

Tesser, A., & Collins, J. E. (1988). Emotion in social reflection and comparison situations: Intuitive, systematic, and exploratory approaches. *Journal of Personality and Social Psychology, 55*(5), 695–709. https://doi.org/10.1037/0022-3514.55.5.695

Thornton, Bruce S. *Plagues of the mind: The new epidemic of false knowledge.* Wilmington, Delaware: ISI Books, 1999.

Traub, James. (1997) Drive-Thru U. *The New Yorker* (20/27 October): pp.115-123.

Trivers, R. (1971) The evolution of reciprocal altruism. *Quarterly Review of Biology*, 46, pp. 35-56.

----------------- (1981) Sociology and politics, in E. White (ed.), *Sociobiology and Human Politics*, Lexington, Mass. : Lexington Books, p. 1-43.

----------------- (1985a) Interview. *Omni*, July, pp. 415-416

-----------------(1985b) *Social evolution.* Menlo Park, CA: Benjamin/Cummings, 1985.

-----------------(1991) Deceit and self-deception: The relationship between communication and consciousness, in M. H. Robinson and L. Tiger (eds.), *Man and Beast Revisited.* Washington: Smithsonian Institution Press, pp. ; 171-195.

-----------------(2000) The elements of a scientific theory of self-deception. *Annals of the New York Academy of Sciences*, no. 907, pp. 114-131.

Trump, Mary. *Too much and not enough: How my family created the world's most dangerous man.* New York: Simon & Schuster, 2020.

Turner, F. (1996) Commentary: An evolutionary/chaotic theory of beauty and meaning. *Journal of Social and Evolutionary Systems*, 19, 2, pp. 103-124

Turner, Frederick and Ernst Poppel. Metered Poetry, the brain and time. *Poetry*, January, 1983.

Turner, Graham (2014) Is global collapse imminent? An updated comparison of *the limits to growth* with historical data. *Melbourne Sustainable Society Institute*, Report number: 4.

Twenge, J. and Kasser, T. (2013) Generational changes in materialism and work centrality, 1976-2007: Associations with temporal changes in societal insecurity and materialistic role modeling. *Personality and Social Psychology Bulletin*. Vol., no., pp.

Twenge, J. M. et al. (2017) Declines in sexual frequency among American adults, 1989-2014. *Archives of Sexual Behavior*, Vol. 46 (8), 2389-2401.

Rachman, Gideon. *The age of the strongman: how the cult of the leader threatens democracy around the world.* Bodley Head, 2022.

Readings, Bill. *The university in ruins*. Cambridge, Mass.: Harvard University Press, 1996.

Vecchio, R. P. (1995). It's not easy being green: Jealousy and envy in the workplace. In G. R. Ferris(ed.), *Research in personnel and human resources management* (Vol. 13, pp. 201–244). Greenwich, CT: JAI Press.

Vecchio, R. P. (2000). Negative emotion in the workplace: Employee jealousy and envy. *International Journal of Stress Management*, 7(3), 161–179.

Veith, Gene Edward. Jr. and Kern, Andrew. *Classical education: The movement sweeping America*. Washington, D. C.: Capital Research Center, 2001.

Waelder, Robert. Basic theory of psychoanalysis. New York: International Universities Press, 1960.

Wang, Pengcheng, Xingchao Wang, Jia Nie, Pan Zeng, Ke Liu, Jiayi Wang, Jinjin Guo, Li Lei, Envy and problematic smartphone use: The mediating role of FOMO and the moderating role of student-student relationship, *Personality and Individual Differences*. 10.1016/j.paid.2019.04.013, **146**, (136-142), (2019).

Weisman, Alan. *Countdown: Our last, best hope for a future on earth?* New York: Little, Brown and Company, 2013.

Weisman, J. (2015) "Study: Campus rape reaches 'epidemic levels.'" *New England Psychologist*, August/September.

Williamson, Harold and Wild, Payson, *Northwestern university: A history. 1850-1975*. Evanston, Ill., Northwestern University Press, 1976.

Wilson, Emily. *The death of Socrates*. Cambridge, Massachusetts and London: Harvard University Press, 2007.

Whitaker, R. *Anatomy of an epidemic*. New York: Crown Publishing [Division of Random House], 2010

Wood, D. and Rogers, K. Regional differences in personality exist, but how do we get to them? The case of conscientiousness. *American psychologist*, December, 2011, p. 917.

Wright, Ronald. *A short history of progress*. New York: Carroll and Graf Publishers, 2004.

Wynes, Seth and Nicholas, Kimberly A. (2017) The climate mitigation gap: Education and government miss the most effective individual actions. *Environmental Research Letters*, 12 (2017) 074024.

Xiang, Yanhui and Xia Dong, Jiaxu Zhao, Effects of envy on depression: The Mediating roles of psychological resilience and social support, *Psychiatry Investigation*, 10.30773/pi.2019.0266, 17, 6, (547-555), (2020).

Xu, Yu, PhD1; Wang, Limin, PhD2; He, Jiang, MD, PhD3. Prevalence and control of diabetes in chinese adults. *J. Am. Med. Assoc.*, 2014; 311(2): 200-201. Doi:10,1001/jama.2013. 283143)

Yu, Zhaoquan, Jian Hao, Baoguo Shi, Dispositional envy inhibits prosocial behavior in adolescents with high self-esteem, *Personality and Individual Differences*, 10.1016/j.paid.2017.10.022, 122, (127-133), (2018).

Zilboorg, Gregory. *A history of medical psychology*. New York: W. W. Norton and Co., 1941.

Zipf, G. K. *Human behavior and the principle of least effort.* Cambridge, MA: Addison Wesley, 1949.

Zerubavel, E. *The elephant in the room: Silence and denial in everyday life.* Oxford: Oxford U. Press, 2006.

Index

D

E

www.ingramcontent.com/pod-product-compliance
Lightning Source LLC
LaVergne TN
LVHW020414220926
848484LV00018B/2566/J
* 9 7 8 1 6 8 0 5 3 3 7 4 3 *